Banned in the Media

BANNED
IN THE MEDIA

A Reference Guide to
Censorship in the Press,
Motion Pictures, Broadcasting,
and the Internet

Herbert N. Foerstel

Greenwood Press
Westport, Connecticut • London

Library of Congress Cataloging-in-Publication Data

Foerstel, Herbert N.
  Banned in the media : a reference guide to censorship in the
press, motion pictures, broadcasting, and the internet / Herbert N.
Foerstel.
     p. cm.
  Includes bibliographical references (p.   ) and index.
  ISBN 0–313–30245–6 (alk. paper)
     1. Mass media—Censorship—United States. I. Title.
P96.C42U654 1998
363.3'1'0973—DC21   97–43931

British Library Cataloguing in Publication Data is available.

Library of Congress Catalog Card Number: 97–43931
ISBN: 0–313–30245–6

First published in 1998

Greenwood Press, 88 Post Road West, Westport, CT 06881
An imprint of Greenwood Publishing Group, Inc.

Printed in the United States of America

(∞)™

The paper used in this book complies with the
Permanent Paper Standard issued by the National
Information Standards Organization (Z39.48–1984).

10 9 8 7 6 5 4 3 2 1

Copyright Acknowledgments

The author and the publisher gratefully acknowledge permission for use of the
following material:

Excerpts from interviews conducted by Herbert N. Foerstel with Jerry Berman,
Walter Cronkite, Paul Jarrico, Howard Morland, Daniel Schorr and Peter Y. Sussman. Used by permission of interviewees.

Contents

Introduction

The 1996 Oxford Modern English Dictionary defines the "media" as "the main means of mass communication (esp. newspapers and broadcasting)." The 1995 Cambridge Paperback Encyclopedia (David Crystal, ed., 2d ed., 1995) says "media" is "a collective term for television, radio, cinema, and the press." This book will use these standard definitions, with one modification: the inclusion of the Internet, the newest and most controversial form of mass communication.

There is little doubt that the media have overwhelmed books as the preferred source of information and entertainment worldwide, and the United States is both the primary producer and the primary consumer of the media product. A recent study conducted by the U.S. Census Bureau and the New York communications investment house, Veronis Suhler, produced some startling figures. The media business has become one of the twelve largest industries in the United States. Profits are high; operating margins range from 5.4 percent for the emerging interactive digital media to more than 16 percent for broadcasters. Several of the big newspapers do even better. The expectation is that the growth rate of newspaper revenues will double between 1995 and the year 2000, and the other media will do almost as well.[1]

More interesting is the data indicating the stranglehold that the media have on the American public. The ordinary American spends 3,400 hours a year consuming the media output. That represents almost 40 percent of our lives, more time than we spend sleeping and far more time than we spend working. Radio and television represent

80 percent of our media consumption. Our reading occupies about an hour a day, half of it for newspapers. By the year 2000, according to the study, we will be reading even less, watching television even more, and spending more time on the Internet.[2]

Little wonder, then, that we hear so much about the power of the media and its influence on everything from morality to politics. The current problem is not the growing media power, but the narrowing corporate cabal that wields it. In 1983 Ben Bagdikian, then journalism dean at the University of California, Berkeley, published *The Media Monopoly*, which revealed that at least half of all media business was controlled by just fifty corporations. By 1987, when his second edition appeared, he reported that just twenty-nine corporations exercised that power, and by the time of his fourth edition in 1992, that number had shrunk to twenty. Bagdikian noted a similar evolution in newspapers and magazines. Of the 1,700 daily newspapers in this country, 98 percent were local monopolies and most of their combined circulation was controlled by fewer than fifteen corporations. Among magazines, Time, Inc., alone was responsible for 40 percent of industry revenues.[3]

Bagdikian wrote,

> [A] shrinking number of large media corporations now regard monopoly, oligopoly, and historic levels of profit as not only normal, but as their earned right. In the process, the usual democratic expectations for the media—diversity of ownership and ideas—have disappeared as the goal of official policy, and worse, as a daily experience of a generation of American viewers and readers. . . . It's no way to maintain a lively marketplace of ideas, which is to say it is no way to maintain a democracy.[4]

Bagdikian's trailblazing research and widely praised 1987 edition of *The Media Monopoly* were virtually ignored by the media. His explanation of why the major media had failed to discuss the disadvantages of media consolidation was simple: editors were not interested in these problems because they were all in the newspaper consolidation business themselves.

Indeed, the media's failure to address the most significant problem in its industry caused that very issue to be declared the "most censored news story of 1987" by the prestigious Project Censored. Every year since 1977, Project Censored, based at Sonoma State University, has published its list of the news issues or "stories" that have been most heavily suppressed during the previous year. The judges who selected the media monopoly story as the "most censored" during 1987 included John Kenneth Galbraith, Bill Moyers, and Judith Krug. Communications professor Carl Jensen, originator of Project Censored, said the judges selected the media monopoly story because it was the root cause for underreporting generally. "We have fewer sources, fewer outlets and more control by fewer people," said Jensen.[5]

The problem of media monopolies has worsened in recent years, but it continues to be ignored by the media. Project Censored's latest edition, *Censored 1997: The News That Didn't Make the News*, featured an article, "Free the Media," that literally mapped out the four giant corporations that control the major television news divisions: the National Broadcasting Company (NBC), the American Broadcasting Company (ABC), the Columbia Broadcasting System (CBS) and the Cable News Network (CNN). Author Mark Miller notes that two of the four holding corporations are defense contractors (both involved in nuclear production), and the other two purvey entertainment. Miller concludes that we are thus the subjects of a "national entertainment state," in which the news and much of our amusement are provided by the two most powerful industries in the United States.

Miller presents an elaborate chart that maps the tentacles of General Electric, Time Warner, Disney/Cap Cities and Westinghouse, the four media giants. He says a glance at each chart reveals why, say, Tom Brokaw might have difficulty covering stories critical of nuclear power, or ABC News will no longer be likely to do an exposé of Disney's policies, or, indeed, why none of the media is willing to touch the biggest story of them all—the media monopoly itself.

Miller says such maps "suggest the true causes of those enormous ills that now dismay so many Americans: the universal sleaze and 'dumbing down,' the flood tide of corporate propaganda, the terminal inanity of U.S. politics." He warns that "the same gigantic players that control the elder media are planning shortly to absorb the Internet, which could be transformed from a thriving common wilderness into an immeasurable de facto cyberpark for corporate interests, with all the dissident voices exiled to sites known only to the activists." Only a new, broad-based antitrust movement can save the media, according to Miller.[6]

The media have always been the captive of religion and politics, scorned and manipulated by both in ways beyond anything suffered by book publishers. A recent example of the former is the boycott launched by Baptists against the Walt Disney Company. On June 18, 1997, the Southern Baptist Convention in Dallas, Texas overwhelmingly approved a resolution urging the denomination's 15.7 million members to boycott all presentations and products bearing the Disney name and everything produced by the vast Disney conglomerate that includes Miramax Films, ABC television, ESPN, E! and Disney cable channels and Hyperion Books. The primary objection expressed by the Baptists was Disney's support for homosexuals, as represented by ABC's sitcom "Ellen," whose star is an admitted lesbian and Disney's willingness to grant health benefits to the partners of homosexual employees.

The Baptists admit that the effectiveness of the boycott may not be immediately evident, but Ted Baehr, chairman of the Christian Film and Television Commission, said, "The Crusades were not a high point in public relations for the church, but they give people a feeling of accomplishment, and this boycott may do the same for many Americans."[7]

Banned in the U.S.A. (1994) examined censorship in book publishing, but only in the context of schools and libraries. This book may be regarded as a sequel to *Banned in the U.S.A.*, but there are significant differences. *Banned in the Media* examines censorship in six formats—newspapers, magazines, radio, television, motion pictures and the Internet—in a wide variety of contexts. Whereas individual books can be plucked from school classrooms or library shelves by nervous school or library officials, much of the media product is ephemeral, and its censorship is wielded with a broader brush.

An important distinction between my methodologies for analyzing books and the media is the manner in which incidents of censorship are tallied and compared. The number of times a particular book title is banned from school curricula or removed from library shelves can be tallied and a list of the most banned books can be assembled, but much of the media does not admit to such particularization. The wide and disparate variety of media formats make it impossible to analyze statistically and rank incidents across the entire media. Frequently, it is even difficult to isolate and identify the origin of media censorship.

Serial publications, particularly magazines, are uniquely vulnerable to newsstand or convenience store boycotts. They also suffer censorship of individual articles or issues. Motion pictures, like books, have been banned in ways that allow statistical analysis, but the monolithic control of the Motion Picture Distributors Association has a homogenizing effect that masks the censorship of particular titles.

Within the broadcast media, the Federal Communications Commission has specified what "indecent" words may not be spoken on the air. Because most radio shows today are unscripted, censorship of "offensive" expression comes by way of punishment after the fact. Even then, the punishment is usually applied to the radio station, not to the individual program or performer. Television, a notoriously conservative medium, censors itself in the production process, preventing the very creation of controversial material.

The Internet is the most democratic and participatory of all the media, and it is therefore the most difficult to censor. There have been, of course, a number of incidents on university campuses where sexually oriented electronic bulletin boards or newsgroups were dropped from the campus computer systems because administrators feared liability under local obscenity laws. Similarly, some public libraries have removed certain Internet sites from their computers out of concern that they were inappropriate for children. But the electronic forums in question have no physical location, and current media law is unclear on whether institutional providers are liable for material that they do not author, publish or select. We can describe such Internet censorship incidents, but, at the moment, trying to isolate, tally and compare them is like trying to nail jello to the wall.

The unique characteristics of the six media forms examined in *Banned in the Media* suggest that their histories be treated separately. The first chapter is therefore divided into six major sections, one for each medium. The social and technological origins of newspapers, magazines, motion pictures, radio, television and the Internet are examined and the unique aspects of their censorship are documented. What emerges is a tiered structure of First Amendment protection for the media, with the print media receiving the highest level, the broadcast media the lowest, and the Internet carving out a niche of its own.

Chapter 2 examines prominent media censorship incidents from American history, including at least one for each of the media formats. Chapter 3 provides a chronological analysis of landmark U.S. Supreme Court cases and legal precedent relating to the media. Chapter 4 presents interviews with major figures from all the media, which reveal their experiences with and responses to censorship. The book concludes with a survey of censorship in the student press during the

1990s, examined in the context of the 1988 *Hazelwood v. Kuhlmeyer* U.S. Supreme Court decision that gave public school officials greater power to control student publications.

NOTES

1. Richard Harwood, "40 Percent of Our Lives," *Washington Post*, November 30, 1996, A19.
2. Ibid.
3. Ben Bagdikian, *The Media Monopoly*, 4th ed. (Boston: Beacon Press, 1992), ix, xxvii.
4. Craig McLaughlin, "Project Censored: Censored Stories and Media Monopoly," *San Francisco Bay Guardian*, June 8–15, 1988, 1–3.
5. Ibid.
6. Mark Crispin Miller, "Free the Media," in *Censored 1997: The News That Didn't Make the News*, ed. Peter Phillips (New York: Seven Stories Press, 1997), 187–93.
7. "Baptists Vote to Boycott Disney Fare," *Washington Post*, June 19, 1997, A8.

Banned in the Media

One

A Brief History of
Media Censorship

NEWSPAPERS

In the beginning was the word. The good word. Then there was the
written word. The book. The good book. And then the bad books. The
world came to accept the inevitable, that Gutenberg's Bible would be
followed by cheap novels telling tawdry tales of lust and violence. But
then came the print media—newspapers, magazines and pamphlets—
presenting revolutionary politics, real-life scandals and scathing satire
of public figures, naming names in sensational revelations of crime
and corruption that left even the highest officials soiled and sullied.
That was too much.

   Almost from its inception, the press was the adversary of government
and therefore the most politically dangerous form of communication.
It was for this very reason that the Founding Fathers felt the need to
provide the press with extraordinary constitutional protection. "The
publishing business is, in short, the only organized private business
that is given explicit constitutional protection," said former Supreme
Court Justice Potter Stewart. "The primary purpose of the constitutional guarantee of a free press was . . . to create a fourth institution
outside the government as an additional check on the three official
branches."[1]

   Journalist Alan Barth has stated the issue even more emphatically:
"The men who established the American Republic sought censorship
of government by the press rather than censorship of the press by the

government. This concept of the press was expressed by Americans even before they became a nation. The first Continental Congress referred to liberty of the press as a means 'whereby oppressive officers are shamed or intimidated into more honorable or just modes of conducting affairs.' "[2]

Nonetheless, the American press has been the target of censorship from its inception. Whereas the history of book censorship has consisted primarily of the suppression of naughty stories, press censorship has consisted primarily of the suppression of embarrassing truth. The press, the mother of all media, has been particularly vulnerable to governmental power when it steps on official toes or reveals state "secrets."

The reluctance of the government to suffer private criticism has a long history in English common law, the basis for much of American jurisprudence. The British tradition of censoring speech and press to preserve governmental power and dignity stems from the 1275 enactment of *De Scandalis Magnatum,* which initially imposed penalties for any false talk about the king and later covered such expression about any government officials. The law punished what was called "seditious words," because they contributed to public disorder and lawlessness. In the sixteenth and seventeenth centuries the law against defamation of the government, called "seditious libel," was formalized and used to exercise almost complete control over printing. Because truthful attacks on the government could be even more socially disruptive than false ones, the common law did not recognize the truth of a statement as a defense against seditious libel. Indeed, since the common law regarded any disruptive criticism of the government or its officials as libelous, the truth of a libelous statement was considered an "aggravation" of the injury.

The principles of libel law that eventually dominated English and early colonial common law were clearly stated in 1605 in *De Libellis Famosis.* "If it [libel] be against a private man it deserves a severe punishment . . . : if it be against a magistrate, or other public person, it is a greater offence; for it concerns not only the breach of the peace, but also the scandal of government."

The chief justice of Massachusetts in 1768 expressed the prevailing view in colonial America: "Every Man who prints, prints at his Peril; as every Man speaks, speaks at his Peril. . . . To suffer the licentious Abuse of Government is the most likely Way to destroy its Freedom."[3]

The most notorious example of governmental use of the libel laws to control the press in colonial America was the trial of John Peter Zenger, publisher of the *New York Weekly Journal* (see Chapter 2). Zenger was charged with libel after his paper criticized the powerful governor of New York. At the trial, the argument for the defense was that the truth cannot be libelous. When the justices rejected this argument, the defense successfully argued that a jury, not the judges, should determine the law and the facts in such cases. A jury subsequently returned a verdict of not guilty, setting an informal legal precedent and influencing the form of press freedom eventually embodied in the new nation's constitution.

Nonetheless, within a decade after freedom of the press had been stipulated in the U.S. Constitution, President John Quincy Adams approved the Alien and Sedition Acts of 1798, intended to silence newspaper criticism of public officials. The Sedition Act precipitated America's first constitutional and political crisis by specifying criminal penalties for anyone who produced any "scandalous" writing against the government of the United States. Many newspaper editors became martyrs to the new laws and the crime of seditious libel. The first victim was Mathew Lyon of the Vermont *Journal*, who was prosecuted, fined and sentenced to four months in jail for charging President Adams with corruption. The government's treatment of Lyon aroused Anthony Haswell, editor of the Vermont *Gazette*, to denounce such action in his paper, for which he himself was prosecuted. Lyon was denied the right to use the truth of his assertions as a defense—the very right that had been won by Peter Zenger sixty-four years earlier.

There were many other prosecutions of newspaper editors, most of which were successful because United States marshals, appointees of the president, selected juries that were favorable to President Adams and the Federalist party. Despite the fact that the Sedition Act was repealed in 1799, federal prosecutions against newspapers and individuals for seditious libel continued on the basis of common law. The prosecutions were used by the Federalists in Congress to turn public opinion against the Jeffersonian Republicans.

When Thomas Jefferson became president, he pardoned those who had been convicted under the act, insisting that the "law [was] a nullity as absolute and as palpable as if Congress had ordered us to fall down and worship a golden image."[4] Despite his eloquence in defending Republican newspapers from prosecution on seditious libel, Jefferson was not above recommending prosecution of Federalist editors for the same crime. He wrote to Governor McKean of Pennsylvania:

The federalists have failed in destroying the freedom of the press by their gag-law, seem to have attacked it in the opposite form, that is by pushing its licentiousness & its lying to such a degree of prostitution as to deprive it of all credit. . . . And I have therefore long thought that a few prosecutions of the most prominent offenders would have a wholesome effect in restoring the integrity of the presses. Not a general prosecution, for that would look like persecution: but a selected one. . . . If the same thing be done in some other of the states it will place the whole band more on their guard.[5]

Indeed, in *People v. Croswell* (1803), the Republicans prosecuted a New York Federalist editor for seditious libel against President Jefferson. Jefferson explained his seeming ambiguity on freedom of the press by claiming, "While we deny that Congress have a right to control the freedom of the press, we have ever asserted the right of the states, and their exclusive right to do so."[6]

Not until 1812, in *United States v. Hudson and Goodwin*, another prosecution for libel against the president, did the Supreme Court rule that there was no federal common law of crimes, including the crime of seditious libel. Nonetheless, by the end of the nineteenth century, the political doctrines of socialism, anarchism and syndicalism were considered a sufficient threat to the established order to cause a resumption of legislation and executive action against seditious libel.

In 1903 President Teddy Roosevelt actually sought criminal punishment of Joseph Pulitzer's New York *World* and the Indianapolis *News* for editorials charging corruption in the acquisition of the Panama Canal. Roosevelt attempted to have the critical editors transported to Washington in the hope of an easier prosecution than could be anticipated in Indianapolis and New York where the criticisms had been published, but eventually an Indiana judge, one of Roosevelt's own appointees, refused his sponsor's demand.

The rabid xenophobia and jingoism of World War I marked a period of great vulnerability for freedom of the press. A series of Supreme Court cases, including *Schenck v. United States, Frohwerk v. United States,* and *Abrams v. United States,* all decided in 1919, upheld the punishment of defendants for antigovernment political expression in leaflets or newspapers (see Chapter 3). By the end of World War I, thirty-two states had enacted laws against criminal syndicalism or sedition. More than 1,900 individuals were prosecuted for seditious libel and more than 100 newspapers, pamphlets or other periodicals were subjected to judicial and administrative penalties.

Under the Espionage Act of 1917, prosecutions were conducted against dissident or subversive speech, and the major newspapers were quickly intimidated into self-censorship. The act imposed criminal liability on anyone who, during wartime, made or communicated "false reports or false statements with the intent to interfere with the operations or success of the military or naval forces of the United States or to promote the success of its enemies" or to "willfully obstruct the recruiting or enlistment service of the United States."[7]

World War II marked the beginning of the modern era of press censorship, characterized primarily by government secrecy. Previously, newspapers had been punished, even closed, for publishing what the state or federal government regarded as hostile, unpatriotic or embarrassing information. By the time of World War II, the concept of seditious libel was no longer a legitimate legal doctrine, and the government increasingly had to rely on a kind of "supply-side censorship," that is, the withholding of government information from the press.

Newspapers, unlike the other media, rely almost exclusively on the "daily news," and in the era of big government this made them dependent on the willingness of federal officials to allow the press access to government information. World War II and the Cold War that followed it introduced an unprecedented national security apparatus that gave the federal government virtually unlimited power to cloak itself in secrecy. The new mechanisms of censorship not only were unprecedented during wartime, but were destined to be maintained in war and peace thereafter.

In 1941, shortly after Japan's attack on Pearl Harbor, the secretary of the navy requested the press to stop publishing military-related information without specific naval authorization. Both the U.S. Army and the U.S. Navy soon implemented press controls, and the director of the Federal Bureau of Investigation (FBI), J. Edgar Hoover, was given temporary censorship authority over all news and telecommunications traffic in and out of the United States. On December 18, 1941, President Franklin Roosevelt created a new Office of Censorship, which erected "voluntary" guidelines for domestic news censorship.

The Office of War Information (OWI) was created in June 1942 to function as America's propaganda agency and liaison between the government and the press. The OWI insisted that the press always picture the war effort in a positive light, but the government's failure to release accurate and timely information caused constant friction with the press.

It was the Office of Censorship, however, that most directly controlled the American press. Its censorship code was voluntary only in the sense that it was to be implemented by the nation's editors and reporters under guidelines created, monitored and administered by the Office of Censorship. It monitored all military-related information, but was concerned particularly with atomic information. In 1943 a directive was sent to 2,000 daily newspapers and 1,000 weeklies stating that nothing should be printed or broadcast about atomic energy, atomic fission, atom splitting, radioactive materials, cyclotrons and a wide range of chemical elements. The media dutifully placed a cap on atomic stories, but the Office of Censorship constantly reprimanded newspaper editors for their lack of restraint.

Even fiction was censored. A typical incident occurred on April 14, 1945, when the "Superman" comic strip published in most daily newspapers showed the Man of Steel in a university physics lab, where an evil professor told him, "The strange object before you is the cyclotron—popularly known as an 'atom smasher.' Are you still prepared to face this test, Mr. Superman?" When the Man of Steel accepted the professor's challenge, the assembled guests shouted in horror, "No, Superman, wait! Even you can't do it!"[8]

The Office of Censorship complained to the syndicate that distributed the comic strip, and the Superman plot was promptly rewritten to eliminate any future reference to atom smashing.

On August 15, 1945, the day after the Japanese surrender, the Office of Censorship was closed. The hot war was over, but the imminent Cold War not only would retain much of the wartime structure of information control, but also would build a massive new umbrella of secrecy around government information. As the government increasingly withheld information from the press and the public, it also manipulated what was released. During the 1950s, this process became known as "news management."

In 1955 the Associated Press Managing Editors Association adopted a resolution condemning "government secrecy that is withholding from American citizens facts about their Government that they are entitled to know." In deploring the Eisenhower administration's "news management," the resolution concluded, "Whatever it is called, it is objectionable in a free society which hitherto has not had to look to Government for its approval or advice before distributing facts and information of a nonclassified nature."[9]

In April 1955 Eisenhower's Defense Secretary Charles Wilson issued a directive to defense contractors, asking them to curtail their public information activities. Wilson said that henceforth, in order for an item to be cleared for publication, it not only had to meet security requirements, but must also make a "constructive contribution" to the Defense Department's efforts.

Wilson's new information chief, R. Karl Honaman, soon added fuel to the fire when he said that military officials should decide whether information was "useful, valuable, or interesting" before providing it to reporters. When reporters protested this new restraint on news, Honaman suggested that editors should voluntarily refrain from publishing information that might be helpful to the Russians. J. R. Wiggins of the *Washington Post* asserted, "The newspapers will not join in a conspiracy with this or any other administration to withhold from the American people nonclassified information. Honaman is asking them in effect to assume a censorship and suppression role which the Government itself is unwilling to undertake."[10]

In 1958 John B. Oakes, a member of the *New York Times* editorial board, wrote, "I believe most newspapermen would agree that during the past few years news has been censored at the source in various departments of government with increasing effectiveness. A kind of paper curtain has been set up by a multitude of government press agents."[11]

When President John F. Kennedy took office in 1961, many in the press anticipated a loosening of federal press controls; however, they were soon disappointed. On April 27, 1961, President Kennedy told the American Newspaper Publishers Association that the Cold War required the press to exercise voluntary censorship to prevent disclosure of information that might help our enemies. Kennedy acknowledged that such control of the news had customarily been restricted to wartime, but he noted that "in time of 'clear and present danger,' the courts have held that even the privileged rights of the First Amendment must yield to the public's need for national security." Kennedy concluded, "If the press is awaiting a declaration of war before it imposes the self-discipline of combat conditions, then I can only say that no war ever posed a greater threat to our security. . . . Every newspaper now asks itself with respect to every story: 'Is it news?' All I ask is that you add the question: 'Is it in the interest of national security?' ''[12]

The *New York Post* asked who was to define "the interest of national security." Would not some argue that national security would be damaged by any newspaper reports exposing economic and social injustice in the United States?

The *New York Herald Tribune* rejected Kennedy's call for news control by stating, "There is no need for further restrictive machinery. In days of peril especially the country needs more facts, not fewer. . . . In the long run, competent, thorough, and aggressive news reporting is the uncompromising servant of the national interest—even though it may be momentarily embarrassing to the Government."[13]

The *St. Louis Post Dispatch* took a similar position. "President Kennedy suggested the press submit itself to a system of voluntary censorship under Government direction, as has been customary in shooting wars. This, we believe, would undermine the essential mission of the press, which is to inform, interpret, and criticize."[14]

Even the *Christian Century* felt the need for a moral analysis of President Kennedy's request.

Assume for the moment that the press were prepared to attempt the self-censorship the President asks. . . . [I]f a way could be found to lay down the official line, how could the board of censors enforce voluntary compliance with its will? By definition, the project is impossible. . . . We had better lay hold with both hands of those principles which are consistent with "a free and open society." They require us to tell the truth, to espouse and act for freedom, to leave no doubt that the morality which is identified with responsibility to God is of a different order from the morality whose highest authority is that of the absolutist State. We ought to follow this line even if we were sure it would lead to our destruction.[15]

Kennedy had been explicit in declaring that the Cold War required the same press controls as those imposed during combat. Given the fact that America's involvement in the Vietnam War was begun covertly during the Kennedy administration, the president may have felt justified in such extravagant rhetoric. Ironically, the Vietnam War may have been the best-covered war in the history of the American press. Because the military did not control civilian transportation in South Vietnam, reporters were free to fly into and around the country. When a reporter's story was censored, he or she could simply board a plane out of Vietnam and file the story outside of military jurisdiction, where the only possible punishment was the loss of the reporter's Department of Defense (DOD) press accreditation.

Very few breaches of military security were caused by news reporting in Vietnam, but the stories brought a candid picture of war to an already disenchanted public. General William Westmoreland went so far as to claim that this was the first war in history lost in the columns of the *New York Times*. The Pentagon's subsequent determination that this would never happen again was seen during America's brief 1983 invasion of the tiny island of Grenada, during which the press was kept in total isolation. President Ronald Reagan was so impressed by the effectiveness of these press controls that he ordered the Pentagon to extend and formalize them in 1984, creating the Department of Defense Media Pool, a system requiring all reporters to function in escorted groups.

The Reagan administration was the most secretive presidency in modern history. Reagan's Executive Order 12356 dramatically reversed the previous inclination toward openness and extended the government's censorship power to all information that is "owned by, produced by, produced for, or is under the control of the United States Government." E.O. 12356 told information classifiers that "if there is a reasonable doubt about the need to classify information, it shall be safeguarded as if it were classified . . . and if there is a reasonable doubt about the appropriate level of classification it shall be safeguarded at the higher level of classification."[16]

Reagan sought to deny information to the press and public by gutting the Freedom of Information Act (FOIA) and exempting the Central Intelligence Agency (CIA) and the FBI from it entirely. The FOIA, signed into law in 1966 and amended in 1974 and 1986, required federal agencies to make information available to the public upon request, unless the information fell within nine statutory exemptions. Reagan also imposed a lifetime secrecy system on government officials, requiring them, for the rest of their lives, to submit all publications or public statements related to national security for pre-clearance.

When Reagan's vice president, George Bush, succeeded him as president in 1989, he maintained all of Reagan's executive secrecy and press controls. The DOD media pool system was again imposed during the 1989 invasion of Panama. The press-pool plane was held up in order to keep the press out of Panama City when the U.S. troops arrived, and when reporters were finally allowed into the capital, military escorts kept them from observing combat areas.

The full power of this new system of military press control was seen several years later in Operation Desert Storm in the Persian Gulf. In the Gulf War, direct access to troops was limited to small groups of reporters, always accompanied by official military escorts. These segregated press pools would then be expected to pass their news on to the full contingent of reporters. In addition to strict DOD restrictions on the kinds of information that could be reported, there was a review process by which military officials examined stories prior to release. For the first time in memory, Americans back home saw messages such as "Cleared by U.S. Military" on news stories.

In January 1991, a group of newspapers, magazines, radio stations and individual journalists brought suit in federal court challenging the press controls imposed during the Gulf War. The suit sought an injunction against hindering press coverage of U.S. combat forces or prohibiting the press from areas where U.S. troops were deployed unless legitimate security grounds could be demonstrated. Before the judge could consider the merits of the case, the Gulf War had ended and the case was dismissed.

Just two years later, during the Pentagon's planning for an invasion of Haiti, it became clear that the Pentagon's press controls were still alive and well. Reporters in Haiti were to be restricted to their hotels until military commanders gave them permission to cover the fighting. As it turned out, the invasion was canceled and the press controls were never imposed, but the *New York Times* commented, "It shows that the news-management policies that took root in the Reagan-Bush years and reached their full propagandistic flower during Operation Desert Storm are still in place at the Pentagon."[17]

The heavy-handed censorship of reporting on America's prison system has much in common with military censorship. For example, Policy Statement 1220.1A of the Federal Bureau of Prisons states, "Press reporters will not be permitted to interview individual inmates. This rule shall apply even where the inmate requests or seeks an interview." The Supreme Court has upheld this regulation, ruling that a prison is not a forum or public place and that the First Amendment does not therefore guarantee the press a constitutional right of access to prisons or inmates.

The secrecy surrounding prison life is also maintained from within prisons, through a regulation that prevents inmates from acting as reporters, publishing under a byline, or receiving compensation for any communication with the news media.

Peter Sussman, president of the northern California chapter of the Society of Professional Journalists, recently wrote,

> This "inmate reporter" regulation was drafted originally in the 1970s to control the writings of imprisoned anti-war activists and other "extremely anti-establishment" inmates, to use the words of the man who headed the Federal Bureau of Prisons at the time. In other words, it was a politically motivated regulation designed to control the content of free-world newspaper articles originating in prisons. . . . That federal prison regulation is still in effect, intimidating other prisoners who might recklessly consider writing down their views and submitting them to a newspaper or magazine.[18]

Sussman says such regulations are "directed less at managing the prisons than managing what we on the outside can read, see and hear from inside the joint. It is a classic violation of the First Amendment, a principle that was devised to assure our ability to learn about and talk freely about public officials and institutions."[19]

MAGAZINES

The significance of magazines, sometimes called "periodicals" because they are published serially, is often underestimated among contemporary media. Magazines had their origin in seventeenth-century Europe, when notices of new books were inserted in newspapers. Soon the notices were accompanied by critical reviews, leading to the rapid growth of literary journals. The first periodicals were not published in the United States until the early 1740s, by which time books and newspapers had already become established necessities. Because magazines developed as a kind of hybrid between books and newspapers, they shared the censorship patterns of both. The object of many American magazines at the turn of the twentieth century was social reform, and their attacks on the evils of big business and government, called "muckraking" by Theodore Roosevelt, were vulnerable to the same charges of seditious libel that had hounded newspapers. On the other hand, magazines frequently published serial versions of controversial books and suffered the same forms of censorship as the books themselves.

James Joyce's novel *Ulysses*, a twentieth-century classic, is best known as the book that was banned as obscene by the U.S. Treasury Department and then rescued in 1934 by a landmark Supreme Court case. Yet few remember that the first censorship of *Ulysses* came in 1918 when early installments appeared in the magazine *The Little Review.* Those issues were promptly burned by the Post Office Department. Not until four years later were five hundred imported copies of the complete book burned.

One of the earliest and most active censors of magazines and literature was Anthony Comstock, who in 1873 organized the New York Society for the Suppression of Vice. Comstock was the moving force behind the passage of the federal obscenity statute, also known as the Comstock Act, which established federal authority to prohibit objectionable material from being carried in the U.S. mail. This power to declare literature "unmailable" was a particular threat to magazines, which were increasingly dependent on mail subscriptions and second-class mail privileges. Comstock had himself appointed as a special agent of the Post Office, which allowed him to carry a gun as he pursued pornographers nationwide. Through the use of his "vice-squads," as they were called, Comstock arrested more than 3,500 people, although relatively few were found guilty in court.

Comstock's work later inspired the creation of the Boston-based New England Watch and Ward Society, which carried on the same kind of heavy-handed censorship. In 1925 the *American Mercury* published a hostile article about the Reverend J. Frank Chase, secretary of the Watch and Ward Society. The following year, Chase retaliated by banning the April issue of the magazine, which contained an article about a prostitute. The *Mercury*'s editor, H. L. Mencken, precipitated a famous court case by personally selling a copy of the April issue to Chase, who immediately had Mencken arrested. In court, Mencken secured an injunction restricting the activities of the Watch and Ward Society, but the indignant Reverend Chase succeeded in getting the Post Office to ban the April issue of the *American Mercury* from the mails (see Chapter 2).

In 1938 another powerful censorship organization, the National Office for Decent Literature (NODL), was created by the Catholic Bishops of the United States to organize a "systematic campaign in all dioceses of the United States against the publication or sale of lewd magazine and brochure literature." The NODL's activities included (1) the arousal of public opinion against "objectionable" magazines, comic books and paper-bound books; (2) support for the enforcement of existing laws and the passage of new legislation to suppress such literature; (3) preparation of monthly lists of magazines, comics and paper-bound books disapproved of by the organization; and (4) visits to newsstands and stores to secure removal of blacklisted literature.

Within less than a year after NODL's creation, many magazine publishers, willing to do almost anything to keep their magazines off the blacklist, began to ask for interviews with NODL's national committee. News dealers were similarly intimidated. Those who cooperated with the local "committees" of NODL were authorized to display the following monthly notice: "This store has satisfactorily complied with the request of the Committee to remove all publications listed as 'OBJECTIONABLE' by the National Organization of Decent Literature from its racks during the above month."[20]

The NODL had an extensive and effective system for reviewing and rating magazines and comic books, the magazines of choice for children. Comic books were reviewed every six months by a committee made up of 150 mothers. Magazines were reviewed once a year by the same committee of mothers, but with a slightly different procedure. One mother would read the magazines, mark the passages she found objectionable according to the NODL code, judge the acceptability of the entire magazine and send it along to the NODL office. Here five other reviewers would examine the marked passages to confirm the judgement of the original reviewer. If, at this point, all six reviewers agreed that the magazine was unacceptable, it would be placed on the objectionable list.

The NODL code for magazines prohibited:

1. Glorifying crime or the criminal

2. Describing in detail ways in which to commit criminal acts

3. Holding lawful authority in disrespect

4. Exploiting horror, cruelty or violence

5. Portraying sex facts offensively

6. Featuring indecent, lewd or offensive photographs or illustrations

7. Carrying advertising that is offensive in content or might lead to physical or moral harm

8. Using blasphemous, profane or obscene speech indiscriminately and repeatedly

9. Holding up to ridicule any national, religious or racial group.

The NODL's lists were frequently used for purposes of boycott. Even more disturbing, the lists were used as guides by police officials and army commanders who would prohibit the sale of "objectionable" titles. In response to such practices, the American Civil Liberties Union (ACLU) issued its 1957 "Statement on Censorship Activity by Private Organizations and the National Organization for Decent Literature," in which it objected to the use of the NODL's materials by police and military officials or by privately organized boycotts. The ACLU claimed that the NODL was imposing its values upon the entire society when it allowed its lists to be so used. The ACLU statement was signed by a number of prominent writers, critics and editors, including Arthur Miller, Reinhold Niebuhr, Katherine Anne Porter and Eleanor Roosevelt.

The ACLU's concern was increased when other censorship organizations emerged in the NODL's image. For example, a Chicago-based group called the Citizens' Committee for Better Juvenile Literature was organized along the lines of the NODL, but with particular focus on comic books. The Citizen's Committee had been created in a meeting called by the Chicago Police Department's Censor Bureau in February 1954.

The chairman of the Citizen's Committee, Mrs. Robert Johlic, had previously worked for the Council of Catholic Women, where she had directed parishwide "decency crusades" in cooperation with the NODL. Her interest in fighting the evil effects of comic books was in part influenced by the appointment in 1954 of the Senate Subcommittee to Investigate Juvenile Delinquency. Press reports of the hearing on comic books carried sensational testimony about their threat to American youth.

The most influential leader of the anti–comic book movement was New York psychiatrist Frederick Wertham, whose 1954 book *Seduction of the Innocent* inspired a south-side Chicago newspaper, the *Southtown Economist*, to begin an anti–comic book campaign. Among the items featured in the *Economist*'s campaign were coverage of a comic book–burning rally sponsored by a community police captain, a children's crusade which sponsored petitions calling for federal legislation to ban comic books, an anti–comic book resolution adopted by the National Council of Juvenile Court Judges, a report of the state attorney's support for the campaign and his promise to investigate comics, and a statement by the local Retail Druggists Association urging its members to refuse to accept "objectionable" literature in their stores.

The *Economist*'s campaign energized the Citizen's Committee for Better Juvenile Literature, which announced its intention to work actively to eliminate from publication and circulation any literature detrimental to, or having no beneficial value for, the intellectual, social, cultural or spiritual development of children and youth.

The Citizen's Committee followed the reviewing techniques of the NODL, using volunteer reviewers to judge comics and popular magazines according to established criteria. Its "code of objectionability" required screening of advertisements for sex, gambling and weapons; the story plot for horror, illicit love or lust, gambling and gruesome crime; the moral tone for religious or racial bias and glorification of crime; the vocabulary for blasphemy, obscenity and slang; and the illustrations for indecency, horror and gruesome appearance.[21]

The NODL reached its high point in the 1950s and 1960s and declined rapidly thereafter, when broad-based conservative Protestant organizations replaced Catholic leadership and assumed effective national control of censorship. Though the NODL no longer exists as a formal organization, its philosophy lives on in a number of current groups, such as Citizens for Decency through Law. This organization, founded in 1957 as Citizens for Decent Literature, today monitors not only newsstands, but bookstores, theaters and television as well. Its publication, the *National Decency Reporter*, has been used as a guide for blacklisted materials.

Attempts to suppress magazine literature persists to this day. Some of these efforts have been undertaken by private organizations, some by the government. Conservative groups have had mixed success in organizing consumer boycotts and advertising campaigns against convenience stores to force them to remove magazines like *Playboy* from their racks.

Of the current censorship groups, the American Family Association (AFA) has been particularly aggressive in boycotting magazine sales at newsstands and bookstores. A typical incident occurred in 1988 when representatives from the AFA visited a Michigan bookstore and demanded that several magazine titles be removed from the shelves or they would notify the police. The owners' refusal to submit to these demands provoked a boycott, which was debated in the local newspapers for months to come. The bookstore owners, James and Mary

Dana, then founded an anticensorship organization, the Great Lakes Booksellers Association, which played a key role in defeating a package of twelve censorship bills put before the state legislature by the AFA.

Magazine stores and newsstands continue to be vulnerable to private and official pressure. In late 1996, Kristina Hjelsand, the manager of a newsstand in Bellingham, Washington, was confronted with a demand that she remove a magazine from sale. When pressure mounted, she and the store owner, Ira Stohl, wrapped the remaining copies of the magazine in a six-foot chain and posted a sign on them stating: "WHILE WE SYMPATHIZE WITH INDIVIDUALS WHO TAKE OFFENSE AT A PARTICULAR ARTICLE OR IMAGE, WE FEEL THAT REMOVING THIS MAGAZINE SETS A DANGEROUS PRECEDENT THAT TRULY THREATENS OUR ABILITY TO EXIST AS A STORE AS WELL AS THE FIRST AMENDMENT RIGHTS OF ALL."

The county prosecutor threatened Hjelsand and Stohl with prosecution for distributing obscenity unless they agreed to stop selling the magazine or "anything like it" in the future. When Stohl responded that he could not read all 5,000 magazines in his store to make sure that no one would be offended, he and the manager were charged and threatened with a five-year jail sentence and a $10,000 fine. The National Coalition Against Censorship (NCAC) organized protests against the arrests and circulated a petition that was signed by more than 15 percent of the town urging the prosecutor to drop the charges. The petition was ignored.[22]

After a year's delay, Hjelsand and Stohl were found not guilty. They countersued Whatcom County for prior restraint and retaliatory prosecution, and in 1997 a district court in Seattle awarded them $1.3 million in damages. The court found that the county had violated Hjelsand and Stohl's First Amendment rights, had caused emotional suffering and had damaged their business.

The federal government has had more difficulty in censoring magazines than have private organizations. For example, in 1986, the federal district court in Washington, D.C., held that it was unconstitutional for the Library of Congress, acting in apparent acquiescence to the wishes of Congress, to cease producing copies of *Playboy* magazine in braille. In *American Council of the Blind v. Boorstin*, the court found that the library had eliminated *Playboy* from its braille program solely because of the magazine's sexual orientation. Such an action, said the court, was "viewpoint discrimination" and therefore unconstitutional. The government argued that the blind have no special right to a federal subsidy, such as the braille program, but the court concluded that once such a subsidy is conferred, "the government cannot deny it on a basis that impinges on freedom of speech."[23]

A more overt federal attempt to suppress sexually oriented magazines came in 1996, when Congress passed the Military Honor and Decency Act, which banned the sale or rental of sexually explicit magazines or videos on military bases. A judge initially prevented the law from going into effect, pending resolution of a constitutional challenge brought against the law by a magazine publisher and other media distributors. In federal district court in New York, lawyers representing the Pentagon argued that the sale of sexually explicit materials threatened the military's interest in promoting ethical and moral behavior. U.S. District Judge Shira Scheindlin, however, said that "if Congress wishes to restrict the sale or rental of expressive materials on military property, it must do so in a constitutionally acceptable manner."

Scheindlin ruled that the law proscribing "patently offensive" materials unconstitutionally singled out certain kinds of speech. "If there is a bedrock principle underlying the First Amendment," asserted Scheindlin, "it is that the government may not prohibit the expression of an idea simply because society finds the idea itself offensive or disagreeable."[24]

MOTION PICTURES

Among the media technologies, only the venerable printing press predates the motion picture projector. In 1894 Thomas Edison marketed his Kinetoscope, a peep-show machine that used a continuous roll of film. The following year, the French brothers Auguste and Louis Lumière developed a machine that projected film, and in December 1895 they held their first screening for a paying audience. The cinema was born.

For the next twenty years the United States and France competed for dominance of the motion picture industry, but when World War I crippled French film production, Hollywood assumed an international leadership that it has never relinquished.

The first American appearance of censorship in the new medium came in 1909, when a committee of the Association of Exhibitors in New York petitioned the local civic bodies to assist them in dealing with complaints that films were violent or vulgar. An unofficial board of censorship was established in New York, with control vested in a governing board of civic bodies. Though this board initially had local authority only, it soon evolved into the National Board of Censorship.

Movie producers were assessed a review fee, initially set at fifty cents per thousand-foot reel, to cover the board's expenses. A group of committees met in the various studios in New York to pass judgment upon films before they had been released. Because virtually all American motion picture manufacturers cooperated with the board, the censorship was indeed national in scope, and any manufacturer who failed to cooperate with the board was isolated.

The board's initial censorship guidelines were:

1. To prohibit obscenity
2. To prohibit vulgarity deemed offensive or bordering on obscenity
3. To prohibit details of crimes that might be imitated
4. To prohibit morbid scenes of crime
5. To prohibit unnecessary or prolonged brutality, vulgarity, violence or crime
6. To prohibit blasphemy
7. To prohibit libelous action and films related to criminal cases pending in the courts, and to forbid the exploitation of unworthy reputations
8. To forbid scenes or films which, because of elements frequently very subtle, tend to deteriorate the basic moralities or necessary social standards.

Numerous local organizations and boards, in cooperation with the National Board of Censorship, brought official and unofficial pressure to bear on movie exhibitors to comply with the board's standards. In 1913 the board examined 7,000 reels, 53 of which were totally condemned and 400 of which required some change. By June 1914, 98 percent of the films exhibited in the United States were being inspected by the board.

In other states, binding controls or prohibitions were soon imposed. In 1911 Pennsylvania enacted a movie censorship law, and Ohio and Kansas passed similar laws two years later. In 1916 a New York State censorship bill was passed, and only a veto by the governor prevented its implementation.

In 1916 the National Board of Censorship changed its name to the National Board of Review, claiming its purpose was to improve public taste through film selection rather than overt censorship of films. In 1918 the National Association of the Motion Picture Industry voted for self-censorship, adopting a code of standards which specified subjects and situations unacceptable for motion pictures. Among these were illicit love affairs, nakedness, and exotic dances. The association also announced that films would not be sold to exhibitors who showed disapproved films.[25]

In 1921 the National Association of the Motion Picture Industry announced the adoption of "a definite and concrete plan which will insure against the production of questionable films and will prevent also the exploitation of pictures in a manner offensive to good taste." The association, which included 90 percent of the nation's producers, specified that it would not produce

> exaggerated sex plays, white slavery, commercialized vice, themes that make virtue odious and vice attractive, plays that would make drunkenness, gambling, drugs, or other vices attractive; themes that tend to weaken the authority of the law; stories that might offend any person's religious beliefs; and stories and scenes which may instruct the morally feeble in methods of committing crime or by cumulative processes emphasize crime and the commission of crime.

The association also agreed to assist local authorities in prosecuting anyone "who shall produce, distribute or exhibit any obscene, salacious, or immoral motion picture in violation of the law."[26]

In its continuing search for public respect and political support, the motion picture industry decided to create a central authority, a "film czar." On January 18, 1922, Will Hays, then postmaster general of the United States, was named head of the film industry, at a reported salary of between $100,000 and $150,000. Hays promptly told the *New York Times* that "the way to prevent censorship of the movies is to make movies that will not stir any demand for censorship."[27] Toward this end, Hays called on the movie producers to toe the line. The first indication that this would be a tough line came after producer Adolph Zukor announced the release of three films by Fatty Arbuckle, a star of slapstick comedy. Because Arbuckle had just been acquitted of manslaughter charges in a sensational court case, Hays issued a ban on all Arbuckle films. The films were never shown.

Hays took his first major administrative action in 1922, when he established a new organization called the Motion Picture Producers and Distributors of America (MPPDA). Commonly known as the Hays Office, the new organization, representing 80 percent of all producers, dedicated itself to "maintaining the highest possible moral and artistic standards in motion picture production."[28]

In 1930 the Hays Office, now formally named the Motion Picture Association, introduced a new Motion Picture Code, which included prohibitions on the presentations of illegal drug traffic, the use of liquor (except as required by the plot), miscegenation, and profane or vulgar expressions, including Hell, damn, Gawd and S.O.B. A production code administrator had the authority to fine members of the association who violated the code's provisions.

In 1934 the newly formed Roman Catholic Legion of Decency offered national support for the Hays Office code. The legion had its own motion-picture rating system, which used four categories: A-1, morally unobjectionable for general patronage; A-2, morally unobjectionable for adults; B, morally objectionable in part for all; and C, condemned. A seldom used fifth category, for films that were not considered morally offensive, required the legion's explanation to protect the uninformed from drawing false conclusions. The movie *Martin Luther* received this rating.

During this same period, the legion adopted a lengthy pledge which began: "I wish to join the Legion of Decency, which condemns vile and unwholesome moving pictures. I unite with all who protest against them as a grave menace to youth, to home life, to country and religion." The pledge itemized the evils in such films, and concluded, "Considering these evils, I hereby promise to remain away from all motion pictures except those which do not offend decency and Christian morality." The Legion of Decency pledge was subsequently revised, but the emphasis remained on boycotting objectionable films and uniting with all who protested against them.[29]

When the United States entered World War II in 1941, the liberal causes supported by Hollywood radicals were popular, and Hollywood leftists, who wrote or directed most of the patriotic war films of this period, sounded the call for a common fight against fascism. Even after the war, left-wing writers were in demand to produce scripts addressing America's social problems, including racism and corruption. Paul Jarrico, a prominent film writer of that time, recalls the period after World War II as "very exciting in terms of the quality of the films made and the fact that films were tackling subjects that had been taboo."[30]

Nevertheless, a political backlash was brewing. Producer Edward

Dmytryk recalled that the "old line Hollywood people, the conservatives," were afraid that the young people were going to take over and bring with them their liberal social and political values. Dmytryk stated that the studios subscribed to conservative Hollywood columnist Hedda Hopper's view that movies that examined America's social problems served the Communist cause. "They followed Hedda's advice," said Dmytryk, " 'If you want to send a message, use Western Union.' "[31]

One group of Hollywood conservatives invited the House Un-American Activities Committee (HUAC), established in 1934, to investigate Communist infiltration of the film industry. The committee, which historically had used smear tactics, guilt by association, and a variety of extralegal tactics in an effort to destroy the progressive political structure in America, heard testimony from anticommunist film personalities for five days in October 1947. Film star Robert Taylor testified that there was a Communist influence in the writing of scripts, and he named actors and writers who, he thought, were "disruptive." Other conservative film stars did the same, often simply airing personal grudges or union disputes. The committee transformed these names into a list of traitors.

In a chilling warning of things to come, powerful Hollywood producer Louis B. Mayer urged the committee to produce legislation to get the leftists out of the motion-picture industry. As it turned out, legislation was unnecessary, because a new political force, blacklisting, was emerging as an ominous method to control the workforce in Hollywood and censor its products. Under political pressure from conservatives in Congress and the business community, the Hollywood studios began to fire any writers, directors or performers whose names appeared on "undesirable" lists prepared by anticommunist organizations.

The nation had entered what came to be known as the McCarthy Era, a period dominated by such right-wing demagogues as Senator Joseph McCarthy (R-Wis.). McCarthy's subcommittee would later conduct a series of frightening hearings and investigations of supposed Communists in government, but it was the House Un-American Activities Committee that first turned an intimidating spotlight onto America's entertainment industry. The HUAC subpoenaed nineteen Hollywood figures who were opposed to the hearings. Actress Marsha Hunt, one of the "uncooperative" witnesses brought before the committee, recently recalled the sense of disbelief with which she and the others viewed the committee's tactics. "I was watching disgraceful behavior in those hearings. People weren't allowed to finish their statements. They were shouted at. . . . It was ugly and a little frightening.''[32]

Of the nineteen "unfriendly" witnesses subpoenaed, only eleven were called to testify; the last witness was Bertold Brecht, the famous German author of the *Two Penny Opera*. Brecht returned to Europe as soon as his testimony was concluded. The ten other unfriendly witnesses (Alvah Bessie, Herbert Biberman, Lester Cole, Edward Dmytryk, Ring Lardner, Jr., John Howard Lawson, Albert Maltz, Samuel Ornitz, Adrian Scott and Dalton Trumbo), who were all cited for contempt of Congress, came to be known as the Hollywood Ten.

After the hearings had concluded, a group of Hollywood liberals bought time on ABC radio. Among the stars who spoke was Humphrey Bogart, who described the unprecedented behavior in the committee room. "We saw police take citizens from the stand like criminals, after they had been refused the right to defend themselves," said Bogart. He described the committee chairman's gavel "cutting off the words of free Americans." Bogart said the sound of that gavel rang across America, striking against the First Amendment to the Constitution.[33]

Shortly after the conclusion of the HUAC hearings, intimidated studio heads met in New York. Eric Johnston, president of the Motion Picture Association of America, read a statement promising to discharge the Hollywood Ten. The statement concluded by promising not to reemploy any of the ten until such time as they were acquitted or had "purged" themselves of contempt and declared under oath that they were not communists.[34]

The Hollywood Ten were now blacklisted, as were the eight unfriendly witnesses who had not testified. But this was only the beginning. The process of rooting out all leftists in Hollywood was now under way as part of the nationwide Red Scare that attacked radicals and progressives in all walks of life. The story of the Hollywood blacklists has been told many times (see interview with Paul Jarrico in Chapter 4), and it may suffice to say that it took a generation before the American film industry could recover from its devastating effects.

The immediate effects of the blacklisting and the pervasive fear that McCarthyism planted in Hollywood was a self-censorship that produced vapid pictures and a paucity of talent. It is no coincidence that the golden age of Hollywood came to an end during the McCarthy Era. Films with social content were seen as a "red flag" by anticommunist politicians, and they soon disappeared from Hollywood. Foreign films, unencumbered with American political censorship, began to recapture the interest of the American public.

The American film industry suffered from other problems as well. Until 1950 almost all theaters were owned by the producers. Only their films were widely shown, and close cooperation between the producers, the Code Administration and the American Legion ensured a well-controlled content. Then, in 1950, this censorship system was shaken by a Supreme Court ruling in *United States v. Paramount Pictures* that ownership of theaters by motion-picture producers was a violation of antitrust laws. The Supreme Court decision quickly spawned independent theaters whose owners were more willing to show films produced outside the studio system, whether or not the films had the approval of the Code Administration or the American Legion. Cold War politics still prevented a candid examination of major social and political issues, but controversial films like *The Moon Is Blue*, which contained sexually suggestive dialogue, and *The Man with the Golden Arm*, which addressed the sensitive issue of drug addiction, were shown widely and were well received by the public, despite being denied the code's seal of approval.

In *Joseph Burstyn, Inc. v. Wilson* (1952) the Supreme Court further undercut the system of film censorship. The Italian film *The Miracle* had been attacked by the Catholic Church as sacrilege. *The Miracle*, based on an original story by Federico Fellini, tells the tale of a peasant woman who, under the influence of wine and religious emotion, permits a stranger, whom she takes to be Saint Joseph, to seduce her. She subsequently bears a child whom she regards as immaculately conceived. Francis Cardinal Spellman condemned the film as "a vile and harmful picture," "a despicable affront to every Christian" and "a vicious insult to Italian womanhood." In a statement intended to go beyond the Catholic community, Spellman summoned "all people with a sense of decency to refrain from seeing it and supporting the venal purveyors of such pictures."[35]

The film was subsequently banned in New York City and New York State. The bans were challenged in court, and in *Joseph Burstyn, Inc. v. Wilson* the Supreme Court ruled that motion pictures were entitled to the guarantees of freedom of speech and press (see Chapter 3). In particular, the Court ruled that a movie cannot be banned on the charge of sacrilege, and the ban on *The Miracle* was lifted.

When Geoff Shurlock was appointed director of the Production

Code Administration in 1954, he concluded that unless the association dealt more flexibly with motion-picture producers, the code would soon be discarded as an irrelevancy. He oversaw an amendment to the code that removed taboos on miscegenation, liquor, and some profane words, but independent producers said it was not enough. Several producers, led by Samuel Goldwyn, demanded that the Motion Picture Code be revised, causing one author of the code to insist that this would be "tantamount to calling for a revision of the Ten Commandments." Nevertheless, a new code was published in December 1956. It began by stating three principles:

1. No picture shall be produced which will lower the moral standards of those who see it. Hence the sympathy of the audience shall never be thrown to the side of crime, wrong-doing, evil or sin.

2. Correct standards of life, subject only to the requirements of drama and entertainment, shall be presented.

3. Law—divine, natural or human—shall not be ridiculed, nor shall sympathy be created for its violation.[36]

Controversial subjects like drug addiction, prostitution and childbirth could now be treated "within the careful limits of good taste," but prohibitions were added on blasphemy, mercy killing, double entendre, physical violence, and insults to races, religions and nationalities. Mention of the word "abortion" was specifically forbidden, as was any "inference" of sexual perversion. Ministers of religion were never to be portrayed as comic characters or villains because "the attitude taken toward them may easily become the attitude taken toward religion in general."[37]

The ACLU described the new code as harsher than the old one, and many film companies responded by creating subsidiaries that were exempt from the rules imposed on members of the Motion Picture Association. Through such subsidiaries, the studios were able to distribute pictures that could not acquire the seal. In addition, most foreign-film importers bypassed the Production Code Administration.[38]

When a series of Supreme Court cases during the 1960s suggested that carefully crafted state laws could constitutionally prevent minors from attending certain movies, Jack Valenti, president of the Motion Picture Association of America (MPAA), quickly generated a system of classifying movies according to appropriate age groups. Valenti's prompt response may have preempted state legislation that would have imposed even more heavy-handed classification.

The new ratings system began on November 1, 1968, and the men who once enforced the production code now assumed responsibility for the new Code and Rating Administration. The ratings were nominally voluntary, with relatively flexible guidelines. The "G" rating was for general audiences of all ages. The "M" rating was for adults and mature young people. (Within a few years the "M" rating was changed to "PG," meaning Parental Guidance.) Movies rated "R" were not to be viewed by persons under sixteen years of age, unless accompanied by a parent or adult. The "X" rating meant that under no circumstances was a person under sixteen (later raised to seventeen) to be admitted to the theater. Such pictures were denied a seal.

Directors frequently found themselves carefully walking the thin line between "R" and "X" or "PG" and "R." Aaron Stern, director of the Code and Rating Administration, told movie producers that they were allowed to show love scenes, "but as soon as you start to unbutton or unzip you must cut. Afterward, you can show the two in bed, clothed. Anything else and you are going out of the PG rating."[39]

In the 1980s, the MPAA created a new rating, "PG-13," that was to include movies between "PG" and "R." Still, many in the film industry regarded the continuing pressure to produce films to fit a given rating as tantamount to censorship. In 1990 New York Supreme Court Justice Charles Ramos wrote an opinion describing the rating system as "censorship from within the industry rather than imposed from without, but censorship nonetheless." Justice Ramos concluded, "The rating of X is a stigma that relegates the film to limited advertising, distribution and income."[40]

In 1990 the MPAA replaced the "X" rating with a new "NC-17" rating, but it was a change in name only, intended to remove the taint of "X." Among other things, the advertising ban on X-rated films, imposed by major newspapers and television stations, was to be lifted for "NC-17" films; however, some video rental companies refused to buy "NC-17" movies and some theater chains refused to show them.

There remain many critics of the current rating system. The ACLU calls it "arbitrary MPAA censorship," but the current chairman of the Ratings Administration Board, Richard Mosk, insists that it is far more desirable than government-controlled censor boards. Mosk also defends the MPAA's long-standing policy of keeping the names of all members of the ratings board secret, claiming that an anonymous board enhances the integrity of the system.

RADIO

Late in the nineteenth century, Heinrich Hertz's discovery of electromagnetic waves led many prominent scientists to experiment with these "radio" waves. In 1894 Italian Guglielmo Marconi built a radio transmitter and receiver, and by the end of 1895 he had sent signals 1.2 miles across his family estate. When the Italian government refused to support his work, he moved to England where he installed a primitive commercial radio service in 1898.

American scientists soon assumed a prominent role in radio communications. Reginald Fessenden first transmitted the human voice by radio in December 1900, using a spark transmitter and a fifty-foot antenna to transmit speech to a station one mile away. Six years later Fessenden made what is generally regarded as the world's first high-quality radio broadcast, sending voice and music to ship-and-shore stations within fifteen miles of his transmitter. Lee DeForest subsequently gained publicity for radio by broadcasting from the Eiffel Tower in Paris in 1908 and from the Metropolitan Opera House in New York City in 1910.

Radio broadcasting to private homes originated in the work of amateurs like hobbyist Frank Conrad, a Westinghouse engineer who broadcast from his garage in 1919. The Westinghouse company quickly realized the commercial possibilities in broadcasting and provided Conrad with a large transmitter, a station at the Westinghouse plant in Pittsburgh, and regular broadcast schedules. Radio station KDKA in Pittsburgh was born, and it broadcast the election returns on November 2, 1920. The Radio Corporation of America (RCA) joined the rush to broadcasting and hired David Sarnoff for its New York station WJY, which broadcast the Dempsey-Carpentier fight on July 2, 1921. By the end of 1924 there were 583 radio stations on the air and an estimated three million receiving sets in use.

From the beginning, First Amendment protection for broadcasting had a unique fragility, deriving in part from the power of the state to "license" those who would communicate through the broadcast medium. If the government attempted to license newspapers, book publishers or even motion-picture producers, such action would immediately be regarded as prior restraint, the most presumptively uncon-stitutional form of information control. The authority of the Federal Communications Commission (FCC) to license and control commu-nication on the airwaves has traditionally been justified by the concept of "spectrum scarcity," the notion that because there are a limited number of frequencies available in the broadcast spectrum, the state must allocate them in the public interest.

Perhaps because of the constant threat of FCC action against con-troversial programming, there quickly developed a frontier mentality at local radio stations, which exercised arbitrary vigilante censorship. During the 1920s, political censorship was particularly common on ra-dio. For example, in April 1927, during a speech broadcast by Victor Berger, a Socialist congressman and former mayor of Milwaukee, the engineer at station WJZ carried the microphone off the speaker's plat-form. Later that year, a pacifist speech on New York's WGL was simi-larly cut off in mid-broadcast.

WGL's action was applauded by the American Legion, and when the station subsequently refused to broadcast the pacifist play *Spread Eagle*, by George Sprague Brooks, the broadcasting company's president, Louis Landes, explained, "This action has been decided upon after due consideration of criticism made by veteran organizations, and as this company consists mainly of veterans of the World War it will under no circumstances broadcast anything that has not the full endorsement of veteran and patriotic organizations."[41]

By 1930 broadcasters had taken it upon themselves to ensure that all programming was inoffensive. Every possible un-American ingredi-ent, from bolshevism to atheism to sex, was censored. The mere mention of sex, even in the driest, most academic discussion, was for-bidden. In October 1930, CBS cut a sentence from a speech on the research of prominent population expert Robert Malthus because it referred to "the strength of the sex impulse." In explaining their ac-tion, CBS said simply, "We are not permitted to mention sex over the radio."[42]

In the early 1930s, when the Prohibition Amendment to the Con-stitution banned the sale of alcoholic beverages, discussion of Prohi-bition was itself prohibited on virtually every radio station. Among the antiprohibition speakers barred from radio were ex-Senator James Wadsworth and Mrs. Charles Sabin, a prominent opponent of Prohi-bition and chairman of the Women's Organization for National Pro-hibition Reform. Mrs. Sabin complained, "This looks very much like the beginning of the end of free speech in this country." Another speaker, Hudson Maxim, was left talking into a dead microphone when his remarks turned to Prohibition.[43]

The broadcast networks themselves were aggressive censors. In 1935 CBS published its own guidelines for children's programs, listing "themes and dramatic treatment which are not to be permitted in broadcasts for children." The themes included "exalting criminals; cruelty, greed and selfishness; programs that arouse harmful nervous reactions in children; conceit, smugness or unwarranted sense of superiority over others; recklessness and abandon; unfair exploitation of others for personal gain; dishonesty and deceit."[44]

NBC issued its "Program Policies" in 1938, which included such broad statements as, "Controversial subjects are not good material for commercial programs and their introduction must be avoided." There were also eight specific "Requirements" for all broadcasters, including the reverent use of the Deity's name and the elimination of off-color songs or jokes. NBC also specified "program procedures" that required all spoken lines and commercial announcements to be submitted to network officials at least forty-eight hours in advance of broadcast. NBC reserved the right to reject any program or announcement if it did not meet the specified requirements or was "incompatible with the public interest."[45]

Lurking behind intimidated broadcasters was the threat of the Federal Radio Commission, later named the Federal Communications Commission. The Radio Act of 1927 had prohibited direct censorship of radio programs by the commission, but it authorized indirect censorship through the withholding of licenses for stations that it felt were not functioning "in the public interest."

In 1935 Henry Bellows, a former member of the Federal Radio Commission, candidly characterized the commission's actions in closing radio stations.

[T]he fact remains that these broadcasters were punished by the equivalent of decapitation, not because they were convicted violators of the law, but because the Commission did not approve of their programs. I do not say that this is wrong. . . . What I do say is that it constitutes censorship, and a very effective censorship, at that. . . . [E]very broadcaster in the country lives in abject fear of what the Commission may do.[46]

In September 1937, the FCC threatened to revoke the license of WTCN in Minneapolis because it broadcast Eugene O'Neill's play *Beyond the Horizon*. The citation was issued on the basis of a single listener complaint, the authenticity of which was never verified. A torrent of editorial criticism forced the FCC to set aside its action at its next meeting and to reconsider the imposition of "temporary" license renewals for ten other stations that had carried O'Neill's play.

After the O'Neill fiasco, the *New York News* editorialized:

> The reason given by the FCC for this ruling was that three expressions in the O'Neill play—"damn," "hell," and "for God's sake," are "obscene and indecent." . . . It may well be that whoever can control a nation's radio facilities in the future will control the nation. If we want a totalitarian United States, one way to bring it nearer fast is for us to take these censorship rulings of the FCC without protest.[47]

In December 1937, an appearance by movie star Mae West on NBC radio's Chase and Sanborn program caused another uproar. Certain lines in her dialogue with master of ceremonies Don Ameche and with ventriloquist dummy Charlie McCarthy were considered sexually suggestive by some; 400 letters of protest were sent to the commission and several speeches were made in Congress. *The Evangelist* magazine described the show as "a skit that defied even the most elementary sense of decency. . . . The thing was unbearably vulgar, besides being an insolent caricature of religion and the Bible." The editorial concluded, "No firm can afford to insult or incense prospective patrons of its products. The National Broadcasting Company also shares the responsibility. It holds a public trust in its right to broadcast. . . . The whole affair warrants a thorough investigation by the Federal Communications Commission. . . . The offense was too glaring to be permitted to pass without severe condemnation."[48]

A public reprimand was promptly issued by the FCC, and a broadcast apology from the sponsors followed. Mae West was barred from any further network programs.

The FCC soon began issuing aggressive warnings against controversial programming. FCC Chairman Frank McNinch attempted to calm the increasing fears of the radio industry when he spoke to the National Association of Broadcasters in February 1938. "Why have the jitters about censorship?" he said blandly.

You know as well as the members of the Commission what is fair, what is vulgar, what is decent, what is profane, what will probably give offense. It is your duty in the first instance to guard against them. It is the Commission's duty in the last instance to determine fairly and equitably and reasonably whether you have lived up to the high duty that is yours. . . . If something has been broadcast that is contrary to the public interest, is vulgar, indecent, profane, violative of any rules of fair play ordinarily recognized, or that might be reasonably anticipated to give offense, I conceive it to be the duty of the Commission to do something about it.[49]

Broadcasters were even more frightened after hearing the McNinch speech than they had been before. An editorial in *Collier's* magazine declared:

Listener censorship is all the censorship the radio needs. It's so easy to turn the dial and find a different tune. . . . And we think chairman McNinch of the Communications Commission had better begin confining himself strictly to regulation of technical radio details, and drop the motions he has been making recently toward government radio censorship. . . . Like the press, the radio can be free, or it can be a slave, but it can't be both.[50]

In spite of editorial criticism, the FCC continued its aggressive censorship of radio programming, and broadcasters became increasingly timid. *Variety* described it as follows: "Censorship in radio now more or less runs itself. The policy, somewhat along the lines of an honor system, makes a censor of everybody in the studio, from actors to control room engineers. Nobody has been taught what to avoid or bar and the material washing is left to personal discretion."[51]

Occasional attempts were made to challenge the FCC's authority in court, but in 1943 the Supreme Court upheld the constitutionality of federal regulation of broadcasting.

After World War II, the beginning of the Cold War brought about a shameful period of political censorship of radio and television, controlled behind the scenes through the process of "blacklisting." The broadcast industry began denying work to any performer listed in right-wing publications monitoring radio and television. The practice of blacklisting reached its height during the McCarthy Era, when hundreds of performers were fired on the basis of rumor and innuendo (see "Television" in this chapter).

More recently, radio has increasingly been censored for its "indecent" programming, and the FCC has cited the unique social characteristics of the medium as justification for restraint on speech. The FCC applied the concept of indecency in 1970, when it fined a Philadelphia radio station for broadcasting an interview with Grateful Dead star Jerry Garcia in which he used words denoting excrement and sexual intercourse. Rather than attempting to define indecency, the FCC claimed to be using the Supreme Court's "Roth Test" for obscenity. That standard, established by the Court in *Roth v. United States* (1957), said that a publication was obscene if, considered as a whole, its predominant appeal is to prurient interest. The FCC subsequently fined a Chicago station for a program that discussed female sexual habits.

In 1978 the FCC explicitly identified what it considered to be indecent language in a case precipitated by a single complaint lodged with the FCC against a New York radio station, Pacifica, for the broadcast of a twelve-minute monologue, "Filthy Words," from an album by humorist George Carlin. The offended listener demanded that speech such as Carlin's be prohibited from the airwaves. The FCC subsequently ruled that the program had been "indecent" and defined indecency to include language that describes sexual or excretory activities or organs. Pacifica appealed the FCC's ruling, which was then overturned by the U.S. Court of Appeals. The FCC appealed the decision to the Supreme Court, and in *Federal Communications Commission v. Pacifica Foundation* (1978), the Court held that the Carlin broadcast was indecent and should not be heard by children. The FCC was therefore free to apply its indecency restriction narrowly to the repetitive use of Carlin's seven dirty words during daytime hours (see Chapter 3).

During the 1980s the FCC significantly increased the frequency and scope of its regulation of indecent programming. On April 29, 1987, the FCC released its Indecency Policy Reconsideration Order, allowing "indecent" programs to be aired only between midnight and 6 A.M. In its order, the FCC also reaffirmed its previous decisions against three radio shows: the Howard Stern morning talk show, a broadcast play about AIDS and homosexuality, and the broadcast of a "vulgar" song. The order was appealed by a group of petitioners, including Action for Children's Television, as well as commercial networks, associations of broadcasters and journalists and various public interest groups. The petitioners argued that the FCC's definition of indecency was unconstitutionally vague and overbroad, and that the new hours during which indecent broadcasting was banned would effectively prohibit adult access to material protected by the First Amendment.

In *Action for Children's Television v. FCC* (1988), the appeals court found that the restriction of such programming to the hours from midnight to 6 A.M. was unreasonable. Despite the court's decision, Congress passed the Helms Amendment, which became law on October 1, 1988, requiring the FCC to promulgate regulations to enforce a twenty-four-hour-a-day ban on indecent broadcasting. Again, seventeen media and citizen groups, led by Action for Children's Television, appealed the twenty-four-hour ban. The D.C. Circuit Court of Appeals struck down the twenty-four-hour ban as an unconstitutional abridgement of speech, causing the FCC to propose a new 6 A.M. to 10 P.M. ban, which was eventually approved by an appeals court. FCC Chairman Reed Hundt stated that the decision vindicated the FCC's indecency policy and provided a legal foundation for enforced children's programming and the "V-chip," a microchip allowing categories of television programming to be screened out by parents.

TELEVISION

Television, the most popular and influential communications medium in the world, was first explored by a German scientist, Paul Gottlieb Nipkow, who in 1883 invented an electrical scanning device that could break down an image into tiny pictorial elements. In 1925 an American inventor, Charles Francis Jenkins, used elaborations on Nipkow's device to broadcast silhouette pictures from his lab in Washington, D.C. Ernest F. W. Alexanderson, who worked at the General Electric laboratories, began daily television tests on an experimental station in 1928, and in 1931 RCA conducted similar tests in New York. At that time, David Sarnoff, president of RCA, made the safe prediction that television would become as much a part of our lives as radio.

As president of the National Broadcasting Company (NBC), a subsidiary of RCA, Sarnoff announced in 1935 that the company would invest $1 million for program demonstrations, and in 1939 NBC began a regular television service. Opening ceremonies were held at the New York World's Fair, at which time President Franklin Roosevelt became the first president to be televised.

The FCC authorized commercial television beginning on July 1, 1941, with the first station, WNBT in New York City, offering fifteen hours of programming each week. World War II slowed the advance of commercial television, but by 1950 television had entered what is today regarded as its golden era.

According to David Halberstam, "[T]he moment of the greatest profit in the history of merchandising was coinciding with two other events: first, the arrival of the McCarthy era and the height of the Cold War, and second, the coming of national television."[52] Almost overnight, television came to dominate the media. Its ability to entertain was matched only by its ability to market products in a booming economy.

As one might expect, any medium that emerges simultaneously with the Cold War and McCarthyism will be a captive of right-wing politics.

By the late forties there was already growing political pressure on broadcasting. What was to become known as McCarthyism had already surfaced in the networks in terms of blacklisting—political pressure against the network and sponsors not to use certain actors and writers who had been tainted by earlier left-wing activities. CBS, which had at one period been considered the most liberal of the networks, quickly became the most sensitive to these organized pressures from the right, and acquiesced more readily than its competitors. It was a time of great cowardice, and many talented people were kept off the air.[53]

Halberstam noted that it was not just the right wing that worried broadcasters; it was the government as well. "All of this produced a desire among network executives not to do anything that might offend either the government or Madison Avenue," said Halberstam. "And very subtly and unconsciously there was a compensating narrowing in scope, in adventurousness on the part of the network, in terms of what could, would be said."[54]

Halberstam described a "cleansing of the airwaves" that extended to the news departments, where even the reigning star of television news, Edward R. Murrow, "found himself expending more and more energy in trying to protect members of his staff who were being attacked and red-baited by the right." Complaining of "the increasing timidity of his own profession and his own company," Murrow said he did not think he would be allowed to continue broadcasting much longer unless he used more and more anticommunism in his commentaries.[55]

At least one network, the Columbia Broadcasting System (CBS), required loyalty oaths that pledged employees to anticommunism. Every network had a vice president in charge of programs who used a "little black book" to screen employees. Fred W. Friendly, president of the News Department at CBS during this period, recalls, "By the early fifties the central nervous system of the vast broadcast industry was so conditioned that it responded to self-appointed policemen and black-lists as though they were part of the constitutional process." Friendly remembered one event at CBS that he felt represented all the noxious atmosphere of the period. "Murrow and I never believed in back-ground or mood music for documentaries," he explained, "but we did want to commission an original composition for the opening and clos-ing titles and credits of our broadcasts. . . . When the vice-president [in charge of programs] asked me what composer we had in mind, I handed him the names of three well-known modern composers. . . . He glanced at the top name and asked, 'Is he in the book?' " Thinking that he meant the phone book, Friendly answered, "I don't know, but I'm sure 'Music Clearance' has his number." The vice president re-sponded, "I know, but is he in the book?" He then pulled open a drawer of his desk and said, "This is the book we live by."[56]

It was a pamphlet titled "Red Channels," a blacklisting service run by a right-wing organization. Fortunately, recalled Friendly, the "book," did not contain the name of his first choice for a composer, but the other two composers were listed, which is to say, blacklisted.

"Red Channels" and its companion piece, "Counterattack," had indeed become the bible for broadcast companies, sponsors and ad-vertising agencies, among others, in determining who could be hired on television or radio. Friendly called these publications "a catalogue of quarter-truths, gossip, and confessions of ex-Communists and other informers of questionable credentials."[57]

One actor/informer, Leif Erickson, wrote in one of his columns for the conservative publication *Spotlight*,

> Now that TV is dominating the entertainment scene, the actor be-comes a guest in the American home. . . . But if he gave aid and comfort to the communists at any time in his past and still refuses to fight the Reds, he has no place on the TV screen, in the movies or on the stage. Let's forget the communist-inspired squeals about "blacklisting." No loyal producer or director has any business hiring an actor who for ten years fronted for subversion and still refuses to tell the truth or to fight the Reds. If this type of actor doesn't know

the score by now, let him starve to death and please omit the flowers.[58]

Fred Friendly recalls that the sponsors had "their own little dark books" which they used to control hiring. "When I was at NBC in 1949, the sponsor, an oil company, dictated a blacklist of its own which NBC accepted. The list of objectionable guests included Norman Thomas, Al Capp, Oscar Levant, Henry Morgan and several prominent senators and congressmen."[59]

The large advertising agencies also maintained their own lists. Mark Goodson, the biggest television producer in the 1950s, recalls that there were "lists on top of lists," and the networks, ad agencies and sponsors exchanged blacklisting information on a regular basis. Any performer, writer, musician, producer or director who appeared on one list immediately found himself on another list.

Goodson's first major television production, *What's My Line?* included poet Louis Untermeyer as a celebrity panelist. No sooner had Goodson booked Untermeyer than CBS and the sponsor began to receive letters of protest saying that Untermeyer was listed in "Red Channels." Apparently, he had permitted his name to be affiliated with the Joint Anti-Fascist Refugee Committee and had been a sponsor of the 1948 May Day parade. Goodson and Untermeyer were summoned to the office of Ralph Cohn, the principal CBS attorney at the time, where Cohn admonished Untermeyer for being naive about the communist threat.

Untermeyer was promptly fired. Indeed, he was the last of the blacklisted performers to even be informed of the reason for their being fired. Goodson has described his feeling of helplessness and embarrassment at this strange trial that "permitted no witnesses, no cross-examination, and where the prosecutor was also the judge."[60]

Before booking a panelist or guest on *What's My Line?*, the name had to be checked against a variety of lists, including "Red Channels." If the name was on any list, the performer would simply be told that he was "not cleared." Among the performers rejected in this way were Leonard Bernstein, Judy Holliday, Harry Belafonte, Abe Burrows, Gypsy Rose Lee, Jack Gilford, Uta Hagen and Hazel Scott. Producers like Goodson were told that under no circumstances were they to let performers know that they were being blacklisted.

Goodson was forced to follow the same procedure with his 1952 show, *I've Got a Secret.* When panelist Henry Morgan was named in

"Red Channels" because of his estranged wife's politics, the sponsor, R. J. Reynolds Tobacco, said they would cancel unless Morgan was dumped. When Goodson protested that the charges against Morgan were nonsensical, he was told that Camel cigarettes wasn't interested in the truth of the charges against Morgan. They were in the business of selling tobacco, and hostile mail made them edgy.[61]

A subsequent Goodson show, *It's News to Me*, produced an even more absurd incident. Goodson received a call from the ad agency, Young and Rubicam, requesting that he drop one of the panelists, English actress Anna Lee. Goodson told the caller that Anna Lee had never been on any list, and he asked for an explanation. The caller said that such matters were never discussed and told Goodson that he should find a pretext to fire her.

Goodson went to Young and Rubicam and met with the executives. He told them that Anna Lee was about as leftist as Herbert Hoover and that the charges against her were absurd. One of the executives admitted that, after a little more checking, they discovered there was another woman named Anna Lee who sometimes wrote for the Communist newspaper *Daily World*.

A relieved Goodson said he was glad that the matter had been resolved, but to his surprise the executive said that they were going to have to drop Anna Lee anyway. They had already begun to receive negative mail, and they could not risk associating the sponsor with protests, warranted or not.

Goodson was furious. He told the executives that they could cancel the show if they wanted to, but he was not going to fire Anna Lee simply because she had the same name as someone else. When he got back to his office, there was a message for him from a longtime friend at the agency warning him not to lose his temper again in front of influential people. The message said that after Goodson stormed out of the office, the executives asked, 'Is he a pinko?' "

Years later, Goodson recalled the "dark terror of the television blacklisting days" and admitted that most of those who had been caught in the middle of the storm had developed fuzzy memories—perhaps deliberately. "We dig into our consciences to examine the part we played in that shameful era," said Goodson. "Like the French after the liberation, we all claim to have been part of the resistance. . . . I can't help the feeling that if I had shown more courage, if I'd stood up earlier, if more of us had been willing to take the heat, we might have brought that disgraceful era to a more rapid close."[62]

Television's early history of blacklisting has left it with a legacy of timidity and conservatism. In 1993 award-winning television writer Barbara Hall wrote, "To fight the issue of censorship in television is already an absurd project. It is currently the most censored art form in existence. Every week our scripts are scrutinized by a faceless contingent of people who tell us when we've crossed the line. Even so, you won't hear a lot of TV writers railing against Broadcast Standards because we have long ago accepted the obligations of the industry to censor itself."[63]

Because of its conservative tradition, television has had nothing comparable to radio's high-profile rows with the FCC over indecent programming, but there is one area in which television has stretched the limits of acceptable programming: violence. In 1989 Senator Paul Simon (D-Ill.) attracted strong support for his Television Violence Act, an attempt to get the major television networks to "voluntarily" meet and reform their propensity toward violence. To Simon's chagrin, Senator Jesse Helms (R-N.C.) tacked on a "sex and drugs" rider expanding the scope of the bill into broader First Amendment territory. Simon's bill eventually regained its focus on violence and garnered enough bipartisan support to pass.

In December 1990, President George Bush signed the Television Violence Act, granting the television networks, cable operators and independent stations three years of immunity from antitrust regulations to allow them to establish voluntary guidelines for television violence. Many in the industry feared that the standards would leave the networks open to First Amendment lawsuits. Network officials recalled a 1976 lawsuit by Hollywood guilds that led a federal judge to remove television's so-called "family viewing policy," which established sex-and-violence guidelines for programs between 7 P.M. and 9 P.M. The court rejected the broadcasters' claim that they had adopted the policy "voluntarily," saying it had been foisted upon them by the FCC.

Nonetheless, by the end of 1992 the three major television networks had announced a joint plan for limiting violent programming. Still, political pressure continued to build for more direct controls on television violence. In 1993 Attorney General Janet Reno warned the television industry to clean up its act or legislative action would be "imperative." Representative Edward Markey (D-Mass.) introduced a bill requiring new television sets to come equipped with a V-chip enabling parents to block violent programming. Representative John Bryant (D-Tex.) offered a bill under which television stations could lose their licenses and face heavy fines for violating the bill's antiviolence standards. Bryant's bill, regarded by many as unconstitutional, failed, but Markey's V-chip bill was eventually passed as part of the 1996 Telecommunications Bill.

Markey's bill not only required all television sets to contain a computer chip allowing parents to block objectionable programming, but required the development of a ratings system to guide parents in the use of the chip. If the industry did not produce a ratings system acceptable to the FCC within one year, a politically appointed commission would establish rules for rating violence and other objectionable content. Thus the door was left open for controls that went far beyond violent programming.

Just a few weeks after the V-chip legislation was passed, the frightened television industry announced the outline of their own ratings system. The heads of ABC, CBS, NBC and Fox, along with such cable magnates as Ted Turner and Michael Ovitz, met with President Bill Clinton to promise a ratings system similar to that used by the Motion Picture Association of America. Although the V-chip got its name from the original desire to reduce television violence, it must rely on an associated ratings system to make judgements about program content. According to Brandon Tartikoff, former head of programming at NBC and now chairman of New World Entertainment,

> It may not be Hitler going into Poland, but it's still an invasion. Once you're inviting two things to happen: censorship, and the government getting into a business it has no business being in. Where is it going to end? Next, we'll have the S-chip for sexuality, the R-chip for religious beliefs that are controversial, and PIC-chip for politically incorrect material.[64]

On December 18, 1996, representatives of the four leading television networks, station owners, cable officials and Hollywood producers voted unanimously to adopt a six-category rating system for television. The first four categories were "TV-G," recommended for general audiences; "TV-PG," parental guidance suggested; "TV-14," parents of children under fourteen strongly cautioned; and "TV-M," mature audiences only. The other two rating categories, to be applied only to children's shows, were "TV-Y," suitable for all children, and "TV-Y7," recommended for children seven and older.

These codes were to be used by the television networks and syndicators to assign ratings to their own shows. On January 1, 1997, the codes began appearing in the upper left-hand corner of the screen at the beginning of most network and cable entertainment shows.

"I'm seriously concerned about the effect on creativity," said Jeffrey Cole, director of UCLA's Center for Communication Policy. "If there's controversy over a show's rating and you happen to be a big advertiser, you'll just as soon take your advertising to a show where there's no controversy."[65]

The political pressure on television soon worsened, as demands emerged for an even more intrusive rating system, one based directly on the content of programming rather than on the recommended age of viewers. Congressional demagogues threatened to impose their own controls on television programming if the industry did not accept voluntary content-based ratings. Prominent television critic Tom Shales described "crazed" Commerce Committee hearings chaired by Senator John McCain (R-Ariz.), which "turned into the proverbial feeding frenzy." When Senator Ernest Hollings (D-S.C.) introduced a bill that would restrict violent television programming to late-night hours, it passed the Commerce Committee by a vote of nineteen to one, with the support of Senate Majority Leader Trent Lott (R-Miss.). Senator Dan Coats (R-Ind.) wrote a bill to forbid the FCC from renewing a station's license unless it provided detailed information about sex and violence in its programs.

According to the *Washington Post*, Congress was "threatening the television industry with government censorship: bills to regulate program content and to yank broadcast licenses unless stations provide detailed information and establish a new ratings system that satisfies some ill-defined but government determined standards."[66]

In June 1997, in return for a congressional promise to withdraw all punitive legislation under consideration, several broadcast and cable networks agreed to consider adding the rating symbols "S" for sex, "V" for violence, and "L" for language to their existing age-based ratings. Representative Markey, who had authored the V-chip bill in the House and a later bill to require labeling on violent programming, said that the television industry's willingness to discuss additional ratings was the result of "irresistible political forces."[67]

Opponents of the proposed ratings pointed out that accepting a deal with Congress would only encourage politicians to demand more censorship. "We are not inclined to make yet another deal that no one in [Congress] feels obligated to live up to," said one broadcaster, referring to past promises to leave television alone if it accepted the V-chip and age-based ratings. "At some point we're going to have to say enough is enough, . . . we'll see you in court."[68]

For most of the television industry, enough was not yet enough. On July 9, 1997, television programmers agreed to a new content-based rating system that would be added on to the existing system. Effective on October 1, 1997, cable and broadcast networks agreed to add "S," "V" and "L" to their ratings, along with still another symbol, "D" for suggestive dialogue. There was more. The symbol "FV" was to be used with children's shows that contained "fantasy violence," such as might be found in cartoons.

There was only one significant defector from the agreement reached between Congress and the television industry. NBC, the top-rated network, said it would not support the content-based ratings but would instead use its own advisories, similar to the "viewer discretion" warning that it shows before some programs. "While we believe that more information is useful to parents, NBC is concerned that the ultimate aim of the current system's critics is to dictate programming content. NBC has consistently stated that, as a matter of principle, there is no place for government involvement in what people watch on television. Viewers, not politicians or special interest groups, should regulate the remote control."[69]

NBC also expressed doubt that Congress would honor its promised moritorium on legislation affecting television programming. Senator McCain, who chairs the Commerce Committee, revealed a letter signed by nine senators that promised "several years" of government forbearance on legislation affecting "television ratings, program content or scheduling." The fact that McCain said these assurances would not extend to NBC or other networks that did not accept the new rating system cast some doubt on their "voluntary" nature. "This was voluntary in that we did not dictate the terms of the agreement, and yes, we expect everyone to comply with it," said McCain. "Yes, there has been the threat of legislation, but the end result, we think, is something that American families will be very happy with."[70]

But even the networks that accepted the new system expressed fear that content-based ratings would scare off advertisers and make shows easy targets for boycotts by interest groups. Hollywood's three leading creative guilds, the Writers Guild of America, the Screen Actors Guild and the Directors Guild of America, threatened to sue to block implementation of the new system if it affected producers' decisions about what is aired.

"A content-based system is just another word for censorship," said Dick Wolf, a prominent television producer. "There is no way that anybody can rationalize a system that essentially decides what adults can watch." Wolf pointed out that FCC Chairman Reed Hunt had admitted a year earlier that the purpose for the new rating system was to ensure that certain shows would end up with labels that would be "advertiser unfriendly" and would therefore be canceled. "That's economic censorship," said Wolf.[71]

Eric Mink, television critic for the *New York Daily News*, explained that the new rating system would allow special-interest groups to target television shows. The interest groups could then tell advertisers not to advertise on any shows that have "V" or "L" or "S" ratings. According to Mink, most of the television industry, except for NBC, the number-one network, agreed to cut a deal with Congress.

"We have a lot of other issues on the table with regard to Congress and the FCC," said Mink, "issues of spectrum allocation, digital conversion, analog channels . . . things in which billions of dollars are at stake. And I think the industry mistakenly believes that by cutting this deal they can get some slack on that side too."[72]

Though the broadcast networks have been the major players in these deals and compromises, the cable industry has quietly capitulated as well. Their timidity has been surprising, since cable television has not been subject historically to federal regulation on the basis of spectrum scarcity. Indeed, cable television has a more recent and much milder history of federal control than broadcast television.

In *Turner Broadcasting System v. Federal Communications Commission* (1994), the Supreme Court ruled that cable television was entitled to virtually the same constitutional guarantees of free speech as newspapers and magazines. Nonetheless, in January 1994, the cable industry responded to congressional criticism of violent television programming by submitting an eleven-point plan for a voluntary rating system and an outside monitor for violent content. Following the lead of broadcast television, the cable rating system would work in consort with the V-chip.

Cable television has also come under federal pressure to curb its sexually explicit programming. In early 1996, in *Denver Area Educational Telecommunications Consortium, Inc. v. Federal Communications Commission,* the Supreme Court heard arguments concerning the constitutionality of the 1992 indecency restrictions sponsored by Senator Helms. On June 28, 1996, the Supreme Court struck down two sections of the law, concluding that they were "not tailored to achieve the basic, legitimate objective of protecting children from exposure to patently offensive material."[73]

On the other hand, in 1997, the Supreme Court upheld a law that requires cable operators to scramble the signals of certain sexually explicit programs (see Chapter 3).

INTERNET

Telecommunications, the transmission of information by wire, radio, optic or infrared media, has been subject to its share of secrecy, censorship and surveillance from its inception, but the emergence of the Internet signaled a telecommunications revolution that seemed to be free from the traditional forms of information control. The Internet is a system of linked computer networks, worldwide in scope, that greatly extends the reach of each participating system. Initially established by the U.S. Department of Defense in the early 1970s, the Internet became a public fixture when thousands of corporate computer systems and commercial service providers joined the network. By the mid-1990s, the Internet was serving over twenty million users through two million host computers, and one million new users were being added each month.

As the most recent of the media technologies, the Internet has the potential to combine all previous media in a personal, interactive form that could be virtually free from state or corporate censorship. It offers the promise of a truly democratic form of information exchange by combining the immediacy of telephone, the intimacy of mail, the graphics of television, and the social interaction of a community bulletin board. But new forms of restraint on Internet communication have emerged, particularly with respect to what are called computer bulletin board systems (BBSs).

At the heart of the BBS is a central computer, set up and operated by the system operator (sysop). Users link their computers to the central computer, allowing them to communicate with other users, access databases, obtain software or perform a wide variety of other activities. The constitutional protection for these BBSs is still murky because it depends on whether the law regards the sysop as comparable to (1) a newspaper publisher or editor, (2) a secondary publisher, such as a library or bookstore, (3) the broadcast media, (4) a common carrier, such as the telephone, or (5) a private real property owner.

The ambiguity surrounding a sysop's liability for a user's action lies behind much of the self-censorship on the Internet. If a sysop has knowledge of a user's actions and control over those actions, there is a greater likelihood of liability. Currently, there is a wide variety of levels of control over, and responsibility for, users' messages. Prodigy, one of the early commercial providers of Internet services, claims to be responsible for its users' messages, and therefore it claims the rights of a print publisher selectively to print or reject those messages. Toward that end, Prodigy has, in the past, prescreened all messages to ensure that they are suitable for every family member.

In 1990 Prodigy drew nationwide attention when it imposed content restrictions on the messages that could be posted on its electronic bulletin board. Prodigy claimed that it was curtailing public postings about suicide, crime, sex or pregnancy, but Jerry Berman of the ACLU and Marc Rotenberg of Computer Professionals for Social Responsibility pointed out, in the *New York Times*, that controls were also imposed on messages considered contrary to Prodigy's corporate interests. For example, when some of Prodigy's subscribers posted public complaints on the Prodigy bulletin board about a proposed rate increase, Prodigy announced that public messages about Prodigy's fee policy could no longer be posted. When subscribers turned to the private electronic mail (e-mail) service to communicate their complaints, Prodigy responded by canceling the protesters' memberships without notice, and it imposed a general ban on e-mail communications with merchants.[74]

Prodigy claimed that it was not a common carrier required to carry all messages, and that there were other electronic forums available to satisfy the free speech needs of its canceled or curtailed subscribers, but there was wide concern that the emerging electronic networks would soon be carved up among private providers with no common carrier obligations to free speech.

Berman and Rotenberg concluded, "Prodigy's dispute with its subscribers shows why, to protect First Amendment rights in the electronic age, we need to press Congress to establish the infrastructure for an accessible public forum and electronic mail service operating under common carrier principles."[75]

After attorney Laurence Tribe relied on the First Amendment to argue a case successfully that allowed Bell Atlantic Corporation to offer video programming over its phone lines, many concluded that the telecommunications companies would be afforded the same free speech opportunities and protections as newspapers. Comparable court rulings gave other "Baby Bells" similar freedoms, and these rulings offered the possibility that the First Amendment, not antitrust laws or FCC rulings, would become the preeminent industrial policy of the Information Age.

In the meantime, however, recurring censorship incidents on the Internet suggested otherwise. A husband and wife in Tennessee were convicted of distributing pornography via their members-only computer bulletin board. A postal inspector had joined the Internet bulletin board under a false name in order to bring charges against the couple for transmitting obscenity through interstate phone lines.

Colleges and universities have been particularly vulnerable to Internet censorship. In California, two female junior college students sued for sexual harassment and successfully silenced an on-line campus discussion group. A University of Michigan student was indicted on federal criminal charges that he had used an Internet discussion group to threaten a fellow student. When Carnegie Mellon University banned all sexually oriented on-line discussion groups, it precipitated a nationwide debate on "cyberporn," in part because of the university's recognized leadership in computer technology, but also because the fear of institutional liability for Internet content was the basis for the university's willingness to censor (see Chapter 2).

Officials at other universities began wondering whether they could be found in violation of state obscenity laws by simply providing access to the Internet. "At this point, we don't have a policy that explicitly covers this type of thing," said Joseph Bennett, Purdue University's vice president for university relations. "Obviously it's something that's a really new phenomenon. We're looking at the situation that happened at Carnegie Mellon and seeing if we need to take any action."[76]

Bennett acknowledged that there was offensive material on the Internet, but he said, "It appears it would be extremely difficult to enforce a policy to try to restrict the access of our staff and students to many types of user groups."[77]

The electronic news groups in question are just one small part of the Internet, but they address thousands of topics, including sex. These electronic forums have no physical location. Messages are simply bounced around the Internet, and users can read them at their own access points. "That's why institutions are nervous," said Professor Fred Cate at the Indiana University School of Law. "If an outraged citizen or police agency decides to bring charges . . . they're going to bring them against the institutionalized provider."[78]

Despite the growing concern of campus officials about Internet liability, Cate believes that criminal charges would be unsuccessful. "All we're doing is providing access to a broad array of resources," he said. "The university isn't writing these stories or posting these images. A public university, like IU, is bound by the First Amendment and is not permitted to restrict speech . . . just because they find it distasteful."[79]

Nonetheless, administrators at Indiana University–Purdue University at Indianapolis, (IUPUI) decided to rule the entire category of alternative news groups off limits, unless a faculty member requests that a specific one be included.

Like motion pictures and television, the Internet is currently forced to endure the indignity of a classification system imposed on its content. An organization called the Recreational Software Advisory Council (RSAC) has developed a rating system for web sites. Stephen Balkam, RSAC's executive director, offered the usual defense of ratings, claiming that they would preempt federal censorship. "What we've tried to do is walk a fine line and a balance between being pro-free speech, which we definitely are, but also pro-parental choice."[80]

The RSAC approach is appealing to web site operators because it is voluntary and allows them to rate their own sites. It relies on a special protocol, the Platform for Internet Content Selection (PICS), developed at the Massachusetts Institute of Technology (MIT). Each web site operator fills out a questionnaire to determine the nature of the site material and its consequent rating. One of the questions, for example, asks, "Does your content portray any passionate kissing, clothed sexual touching, non-explicit sexual touching, explicit or non-explicit sexual acts, or sex crimes?"[81]

The questionnaire is graded by a computer which calculates the rating in four categories: nudity, sexual activity, harsh language and violence. The site operator is then sent a tag containing the rating, and the tag is added to the top of the site's home page, where it is visible only to browsing or screening software. The Internet Explorer browser automatically recognizes the tags, and Netscape Navigator, the most popular browser has added the tags to its latest version. By using such browsers, parents can block any site with an unacceptable rating, or a site with no rating at all.[82]

Despite these attempts to enable parental control, demands for federal censorship have persisted. In 1995 Senator James Exon (D-Neb.) introduced a bill regulating electronic communications, amending an existing law against harassment, obscenity or threats made by telephone and changing the word "telephone" to "telecommunications devices." The Exon bill extended criminal liability to anyone who makes available any "comment, request, suggestion, proposal, image or other communication" that is found by a court to be "obscene, lewd, lascivious, filthy or indecent." The penalties under Exon's Communications Decency Act (CDA) of 1995 included fines of up to $100,000 and two years in jail, and it applied even to privately exchanged messages between adults.

A coalition of public interest groups, including the American Library Association (ALA) and the Electronic Frontier Foundation, submitted a joint letter to Senator Exon expressing concern that the bill posed a significant threat to freedom of speech and the free flow of information in cyberspace. It also raised questions about the right of government to control content on communications networks.

An electronic petition against the bill, which appeared on the Internet's World Wide Web, generated 56,000 signatures in two weeks. The text accompanying the on-line petition said,

> The more people sign the petition, the more the government will get the message to back off the online community. We've been doing fine without censorship until now—let's show them we don't plan on allowing them to start now. If you value your freedoms—from your right to publicly post a message on a worldwide forum to your right to receive private email without the government censoring it— you need to take action NOW.[83]

Senator Patrick Leahy (D-Vt.) urged an alternative approach. "Empowering parents to manage—with technology under their control— what the kids access over the Internet is far preferable to bills . . . that would criminalize users or deputize information-service providers as smut police," said Leahy. "[G]overnment regulation of the content of all computer and telephone communications, even private communications, in violation of the First Amendment is not the answer—it is merely a knee-jerk response."[84]

Two members of the House of Representatives introduced the Internet Freedom and Family Empowerment Act whose purpose was to encourage the on-line industry to police itself. The sponsors of the House bill, Representatives Christopher Cox (R-Calif.) and Ron Wyden (D-Ore.), rejected the Senate bill, saying they hoped instead to spur technologies that would help companies, parents and schools to block out objectionable material from the Internet. Their legislation would also ensure that on-line companies could screen out obscene material without being held liable for every message transmitted over their systems.

In a surprise development, House Speaker Newt Gingrich (R-Ga.) condemned the Communications Decency Act as a clear violation of free speech and the rights of adults to communicate with each other. Senator Exon responded by characterizing Gingrich as out of touch, and support for the CDA continued to grow.

While the political battle over cyberspace was proceeding, *Time* magazine's July 3, 1995, issue featured a sensationalized cover story, "Cyberporn," showing a terrified child and a headline, "A new study shows how pervasive and wild it really is." The study touted by *Time*, which had been conducted by an undergraduate student at Carnegie Mellon University, was later shown to be seriously flawed and possibly fraudulent. For example, the Carnegie Mellon study said 83.5 percent of Internet content was pornographic, when in fact the most common measure was 0.5 percent. Nonetheless, the *Time* article concluded that kids should stay off the Internet.

Encouraged by such media hysteria, the Exon bill, known as the CDA, easily passed through committee and on to the full Senate. President Clinton issued a go-slow request to the Senate, saying there were important First Amendment issues that needed to be addressed before the legislation was rushed through, but in June 1995 the CDA passed the full Senate by an overwhelming vote of eighty-four to sixteen. Many in the media expressed concern that the bill represented sweeping censorship, which, even if overturned by the courts on First Amendment grounds, could create paralysis, and perhaps permanent damage, to a uniquely promising technology.

The House then passed its version of the CDA by a vote of 420 to 4. Despite the considerable improvement over the Senate bill, the House bill nonetheless included an amendment that would make it a crime to use offensive terms about "sexual or excretory activities or organs" in computer communications with someone who is believed to be under eighteen years of age. Like the earlier Senate bill, the House bill provided prison sentences and heavy fines for anyone who "knowingly" transmits obscene or indecent material to minors or to public areas of the Internet where minors might see it.

A discouraged Representative Wyden said, "This idea of a federal Internet-censorship army would make the Keystone Kops look like crackerjack crime fighters. Our view is that the private sector is in the best position to guard the portals of cyberspace and to protect our children."[85]

When the House and Senate bills were combined by congressional conferees, the hard-line provisions of the original Exon bill were retained. Ralph Reed, director of the Christian Coalition, was delighted with the heavy new restrictions, for which he had lobbied heavily. Barry Steinhardt of the ACLU declared, "Congress is making it ever more clear that we will have to turn to the courts to uphold free speech in the promising new medium of cyberspace." A spokesman for Prodigy complained that the new decency standard was ill-defined and unenforceable. "It's going to wind up in the courts and be there for years," he warned.[86]

According to the *Washington Post*, the language negotiated by the House and Senate conferees "combines some of the worst of a broad array of misguided restrictions on speech, none of them likely to protect children." Noting that the new provisions would make the Internet more tightly restricted than print, radio or even television, the *Post* concluded, "The conferees should dump this disasterous legislation entirely and give the public—and Congress—more time to learn what this medium is about."[87]

Shortly before the vote was taken on the telecommunications bill containing the CDA, an international Internet incident arose that dramatized the danger of applying local community standards of decency to global cyberspace. CompuServe Inc., a major on-line provider, announced that it was blocking access to 200 "newsgroups" on the Internet in response to complaints by German authorities. The German authorities identified 200 newsgroups which they said contained indecent material. Prodigy contended that there was a real possibility of arrest if they did not comply with German demands, so they banned the newsgroups to all Americans as well.[88]

Suddenly the borderless quality of the Internet appeared to be an international liability, not the great strength that had been claimed. Internet users were dismayed at CompuServe's willingness to censor massively on the basis of charges that had never been formally filed, much less proved in court. Among the items CompuServe chose to hide from its users were serious discussions about human rights, marriage, and the Internet censorship being planned by Congress.[89]

On February 1, 1996, Congress passed the Telecommunications Act of 1996, including the Communications Decency Act, which imposed heavy criminal penalties for Internet indecency. In addition to the decency provision, the bill made it a crime, punishable by up to five years in jail and a maximum fine of $250,000, to transmit or receive electronically any information about ways to obtain or perform an abortion. This cyberspace gag rule was a resurrection of the 123-year-old Comstock Act, which was used eighty years ago to arrest Margaret Sanger for distributing leaflets on birth control (see "magazines" in this chapter).

When President Clinton signed the Telecommunications Act, the CDA became law, but there was widespread concern in Congress that the law would never withstand constitutional scrutiny by the courts. Senator Leahy said, "I am concerned this legislation places restrictions on the Internet that will come back and haunt us." He warned that quoting from literary classics on-line could result in criminal prosecution. "Imagine if the Whitney Museum . . . were dragged into court for permitting representations of Michelangelo's David to be looked at by kids."[90]

An on-line publication, *American Reporter*, announced that it would publish an article intentionally laced with "indecent" language, and would sue immediately after publication. "We want to move promptly to have this statute set aside as unconstitutional," said Randall Boe, attorney for the *American Reporter*. "The longer it's in place, the greater the harm to the Internet and to the First Amendment."[91]

Several public service organizations, including the ACLU and the Electronic Frontier Foundation, brought suit, challenging the constitutionality of the CDA. On February 15, *ACLU v. Reno* was heard by U.S. District Judge Ronald Buckwalter, who blocked government enforcement of the Internet decency provision. As provided in the telecommunications bill, a three-judge panel was to rule on the challenge to the indecency provision, after which the matter could be appealed directly to the Supreme Court.

The Clinton administration defended the indecency provision, claiming that it applied only to communications to minors, though the Justice Department had earlier written to Senator Leahy warning that the provision would "impose criminal sanctions on the transmission of constitutionally protected speech" and "threaten important First Amendment and privacy rights."[92]

On February 26, 1996, another group of organizations brought suit against the CDA, this time under the umbrella of the ALA. The suit, which included the major on-line companies as well as the trade and professional associations of newspaper publishers, editors and reporters, was combined with the ACLU suit. On June 12, 1996, the three-judge panel addressing *ACLU v. Reno* declared that the Internet restrictions in the CDA violated the First Amendment. Government lawyers promptly appealed the decision to the Supreme Court.

June 26, 1997, the Supreme Court struck down the CDA as an unconstitutional abridgement of the freedom of speech. Writing for the Court, Justice John Paul Stevens stated,

> The record demonstrates that the growth of the Internet has been and continues to be phenomenal. As a matter of constitutional tradition, in the absence of evidence to the contrary, we presume that governmental regulation of the content of speech is more likely to interfere with the free exchange of ideas than to encourage it. The interest in encouraging freedom of expression in a democratic society outweighs any theoretical but unproven benefit of censorship.[93]

The press was generally enthusiastic about the Court's decision. According to the *Washington Post*, the Internet "has been freed to grow and develop as buoyantly in the future as it has up till now—freed, that is, from the threatened constraints of the so-called decency law, which if upheld would have constituted the most serious and potentially hobbling limitation that a U.S. court has sought to impose on the Internet in its short lifetime."[94]

Congressional supporters of the CDA vowed to redouble their efforts to produce a bill that would survive scrutiny. "A judicial elite is undermining democratic attempts to address pressing social problems," said Senator Coats, a sponsor of the CDA. "The Supreme Court is purposely disarming the Congress in the most important conflicts of our time."[95]

President Clinton was disappointed with the Court's opinion, but not surprised by it. He and his top advisers knew from the beginning that the legislation was on shaky constitutional grounds. In a statement issued by the White House after the CDA was struck down, the president said he would bring together industry executives and groups representing parents, teachers and librarians to seek a solution to the problem of on-line pornography. "We can and must develop a solution for the Internet that is as powerful for the computer as the V-chip will be for the television and that protects children in ways that are consistent with America's free speech values," President Clinton said. "With the right technology and rating systems, we can help insure that our children don't end up in the red-light districts of cyberspace."[96]

On July 1, 1997, President Clinton announced his "Framework for Global Electronic Commerce," calling for a minimally regulated, secure and duty-free environment for Internet information flow and electronic commerce. Financial leaders, such as Robert Hormats, the vice chairman of the investment firm Goldman, Sachs (International), believes that this new initiative will become one of Clinton's fundamental foreign policy legacies.

> The Internet erodes government control over information. It joins the printing press, radio, television and the fax in the pantheon of technologies of freedom. Of these it is the most dispersed globally and the least controllable. It promotes freedom from government as the most influential source and arbiter of information. It gives citizens access to entertainment or material that governments or private citizens might find offensive. . . . By promoting freer global flows of information, ideas and business, the Internet can become the most prominent symbol of the post–Cold War era.[97]

Despite the intense involvement of Congress and the President in the development of the Internet, state and local officials may be playing a more pivotal role. The struggles of public libraries to deal with political pressures to restrict Internet access are a good example. In early 1997, Boston Mayor, Thomas Menino ordered local public libraries to install "filtering" software on library terminals, blacking out Internet sites that had sexual content. When library officials protested the order as a violation of patrons' First Amendment rights, a compromise was reached that installed the filters only on computer terminals used by children.

Texas and Ohio are among several states considering legislation to require all libraries to install filtering software on Internet terminals. Currently, Ohio's Cuyahoga County libraries require children under

18 years of age to get written permission from their parents before using the Internet. Public libraries in Maryland and northern Virginia are debating whether to restrict access to the Internet. "We can't really pull the plug on something because we don't appreciate the subject matter," said John Newell, president of the Board of Trustees of the Anne Arundel libraries in Maryland. "We have to respect peoples' rights to access what they want to access."[98]

Judith Krug, director of the American Library Association's Office for Intellectual Freedom, was even stronger in opposing restrictions on Internet access. "It's nobody's business what you read in the library but yours," she said. "It's nobody's business what you access on the Internet but yours. The library is not a government-paid baby-sitting service. Our role is to provide ideas and information."[99]

But the pressure to control Internet access continues to build. In October 1997, officials in Fairfax County, Virginia proposed letting librarians bar children younger than 13 from using the Internet in public libraries. Charles Fegan, a member of the Fairfax County Library Board of Trustees and the plan's author, said, "I don't believe in censorship at all, and this is not censorship. We don't live in an Ozzie-and-Harriet kind of world any more."[100]

In November 1997, Fairfax County officials rejected Fegan's plan, concluding that parents, not librarians, should be responsible for monitoring the library habits of their children.

Even as local institutions seek negotiated solutions to the Internet controversy, Internet providers are moving toward a more arbitrary and centralized response. In December 1997, several of the largest technology and media companies, fearing federal regulation, embraced a wide-ranging set of "voluntary" actions to prevent children from accessing adult-oriented material on the Internet. The on-line industry announced plans to use television ads and school-based programs to tout screening software and to warn of the danger of allowing children to search the Internet without supervision. Some of the companies, including America Online and Walt Disney Co., said they would release their own tools to screen the Internet. The on-line firms also promised to assist law enforcement personnel investigating crimes against children.

A coalition of free-speech and privacy-rights organizations expressed concern that in attempting to protect children from a small amount of allegedly harmful material, the industry proposals would deny them access to the vast majority of useful and educational material.

NOTES

1. Potter Stewart, "Or of the Press," *Hastings Law Journal* 26 (January 1975): 631.

2. Alan Barth, "Freedom and the Press," *Progressive*, June 1962, 29.

3. David M. O'Brien, *The Public's Right to Know: The Supreme Court and the First Amendment* (New York: Praeger, 1981), 30–33.

4. Ibid., 49–50.

5. Ibid.

6. Ibid.

7. Ibid., 70.

8. "Superman," *Washington Post*, April 14, 1945, B7.

9. "Editors Condemn Federal Secrecy," *New York Times*, November 19, 1955, 10.

10. "Censorship at the Pentagon," *Time*, July 4, 1955, 62.

11. John B. Oakes, "The Paper Curtain of Washington," *Nieman Reports*, October 1958, 3.

12. "President Urges Limits by Press," *New York Times*, April 28, 1961, 14.

13. "Press Is Divided on Kennedy Talk," *New York Times*, April 30, 1961, 68.

14. Ibid.

15. "News and National Interest," *Christian Century*, May 17, 1961, 612.

16. Herbert N. Foerstel, *Secret Science: Federal Control of American Science and Technology* (Westport, Conn.: Praeger, 1993), 21–22.

17. "Military Censorship Lives," *New York Times*, September 21, 1994, A22.

18. Peter Sussman, "Crimes of Silence," in Peter Phillips, *Censored 1997: The News That Didn't Make the News* (New York: Seven Stories Press), 201–2.

19. Ibid, 206.

20. Leon Hurwitz, *Historical Dictionary of Censorship in the United States* (Westport, Conn.: Greenwood Press, 1985), 272.

21. "The Citizen's Committee and Comic-Book Control: A Study of Extragovernmental Restraint," *Law and Contemporary Problems* xx, no. 4 (Autumn 1995): 621.

22. Leanne Katz, National Coalition Against Censorship, *Press Release*, September 1996, 1–2.

23. Rodney Smolla, *Free Speech in an Open Society* (New York: Knopf, 1992), 184.

24. "Military Base Ban on Sales of Explicit Materials Rejected," *Washington Post*, January 23, 1997, A15.

25. "The Morals of the Movies," *Outlook*, June 20, 1914, 387–88.

26. "Agree to Clean Up Motion Pictures," *New York Times*, March 7, 1921, 7.

27. "Will H. Hays Signs to Direct Movies," *New York Times*, January 19, 1922, 17.

28. Harold C. Gardiner, *Catholic Viewpoint on Censorship* (Garden City, N.Y.: Image Books, 1961), 92.

29. Ibid.

30. *Blacklist: Hollywood on Trial,* documentary film written and directed by Christopher Koch for American Movie Classics (AMC) (1995) televised on November 24, 1997.

31. Ibid.

32. Ibid.

33. Ibid.

34. Ibid.

35. Hurwitz, *Historical Dictionary of Censorship,* 248.

36. Leonard J. Leff, *The Dame in the Kimono* (New York: Grove Weidenfeld, 1990), 233.

37. Ibid.

38. Ibid.

39. Robert Radnitz, "It's Time to Eliminate the Present Movie Rating System," *Los Angeles Times,* July 30, 1990, F5.

40. Ibid.

41. Vita Lauter and Joseph H. Friend, "Radio and the Censors," *Forum,* December 1931, 359–66.

42. Ibid.

43. Ibid.

44. *New Policies,* Columbia Broadcasting System, May 15, 1935.

45. Henry A. Bellows, "Is Radio Censored?" *Harpers,* November 1935, 697–709.

46. Ibid.

47. *NAB News Review,* October 19, 1938, 1.

48. "Tainting the Air," *Evangelist,* December 17, 1937, 4.

49. Frank McNinch, "McNinch Speaks before NAB Convention," *Broadcasting,* February 15, 1938, 15.

50. "We Needn't Be Spoon-Fed," *Collier's,* February 25, 1939, 66.

51. James Rorty, *Order on the Air,* John Day Pamphlets, no. 44 (New York), 11.

52. David Halberstam, *The Powers That Be* (New York: Knopf, 1979), 138.

53. Ibid., 137.

54. Ibid., 138.

55. Ibid., 137.

56. Fred W. Friendly, *Due to Circumstances Beyond Our Control . . .* (New York: Vintage Books, 1967), 23–24.

57. Ibid., 15.

58. Leif Erickson, "A Time for Honesty," *Spotlight,* August 1955, 1.

59. Friendly, *Due to Circumstances Beyond Our Control,* 15.

60. Mark Goodson, "If I'd Stood Up Earlier," *New York Times Magazine*, January 13, 1991, 22.

61. Ibid.

62. Ibid., 22, 43.

63. Barbara Hall, "Death by Prime Time," *LA Weekly*, September 9, 1993, 1.

64. Tom Shales, "Chip of Fools," *Washington Post*, March 10, 1996, G5.

65. "A Blurry View of TV," *Washington Post*, June 9, 1997, A18.

66. Ibid.

67. Ibid.

68. "Networks Split over Ratings," *Washington Post*, June 3, 1997, A1.

69. "TV Ratings Agreement Reached," *Washington Post*, July 10, 1997, A1.

70. Ibid.

71. *News Hour with Jim Lehrer*, Public Broadcasting System, July 9, 1997.

72. Ibid.

73. *Denver Area Educational Telecommunications Consortium, Inc. v. Federal Communications Commission*, 116 Sup. Ct. 2374 (1996).

74. "Free Speech in an Electronic Age," *New York Times*, January 6, 1991, sec. 3, 13.

75. Ibid.

76. George McClaren, "Colleges Begin to Limit Access to Pornography on Computer Systems," *Indianapolis Star*, January 1, 1995, D1.

77. Ibid., D5.

78. Ibid.

79. Ibid.

80. Hiawatha Bray, "Rated: P for Preemptive,"*Boston Globe*, July 25, 1996, E4.

81. Ibid.

82. Ibid.

83. Nat Hentoff, "The Senate's Cybercensors," *Washington Post*, July 1, 1995, A27.

84. Ibid.

85. "Internet Users Relieved by House Measure's Provisions on Indecent Material," *Chronicle of Higher Education*, August 18, 1995, A20.

86. "Congress Nearing Passage of Rules Curbing On-Line Smut," *Washington Post*, December 7, 1995, A1.

87. "Internet Mess: Return to Sender," *Washington Post*, December 15, 1995, A24.

88. "Worldwide Net, Worldwide Trouble," *Washington Post*, January 1, 1996, A20.

89. Ibid.

90. *ACLU Spotlight*, Spring 1996, 3.

91. Ibid.

92. "Judge Blocks On-Line Smut Law Enforcement," *Washington Post*, February 16, 1996, B1.

93. *American Civil Liberties Union v. Reno* (1997), in *United States Law Week*, 65 LW 4715, at 4730.

94. "Yes, the Net Is Speech," *Washington Post*, June 27, 1997, A24.

95. "Clinton Readies New Approach on Smut," *New York Times*, June 27, 1997, A21.

96. Ibid.

97. Robert D. Hormats, "Foreign Policy by Internet," *Washington Post*, July 29, 1997, A15.

98. "Libraries Urged to Nip Internet in the Buff," *Washington Post*, April 21, 1997, B1.

99. Ibid.

100. "Should Children Be Kept Offline?" *Washington Post*, October 15, 1997, B1.

Two

Prominent Examples of Media Censorship

THE TRIAL OF JOHN PETER ZENGER, 1735

The most important episode of media censorship in early American history was the case of John Peter Zenger, publisher of New York City's *Weekly Journal*, who was prosecuted in 1735 for printing criticism of a British colonial governor. In those days, New York City had a population of about 10,000, of whom 1,700 were black slaves. There were less than 2,000 houses in the city, and residents could shoot quail just east of Broadway. Virtually the only business being transacted was the importing of supplies for the colonies.

New York, like the other colonies, had a popular assembly, but the governor had the power to convene and dissolve the assembly at his pleasure and had an absolute veto over its acts. Governor William Cosby, who served from 1732 to 1736, exercised his authority in an arbitrary and despotic fashion, generating political unrest bordering on revolution. During the first few years of Cosby's administration, New York's only newspaper, the *New York Weekly Gazette*, served as a mouthpiece for his party, the Court party. Founded by William Bradford in 1725, the *Gazette* was the first newspaper published in all the colonies and carried considerable political influence.

Unable to find critical discussion of the Cosby administration in the *Gazette*, New York's citizenry gathered at their favorite meeting places, the Black Horse Tavern and the marketplace, to exchange information and express their dissatisfaction. The popular antagonism toward

Cosby gave rise to an organized opposition to the governor's influence. Cosby's political troubles came to a head in 1733, when he dismissed Chief Justice Lewis Morris from the Supreme Court of New York. Morris was not only New York's foremost politician, but one of its wealthiest citizens, and he quickly molded the opposition movement into a party dedicated to the defeat of the governor.

Morris and his son were elected to the local assembly in November 1733 despite the ruthless efforts of Cosby's sheriff to defeat them. In October 1734, all but one of a slate of Morrisite candidates were elected to the Common Council of New York. Late in 1734, the Morrises and their allies launched a newspaper, the *New York Weekly Journal,* in an effort to counter the *Gazette* and arouse popular opposition to the governor. The *Journal,* America's first party newspaper, quickly developed into a powerful weapon against the governor. It was printed and published at the shop of John Peter Zenger, a German immigrant who had served as an apprentice to William Bradford, publisher of the *Gazette.* The guiding genius behind the *Journal* was James Alexander, an attorney who had represented opponents of Cosby and who would later defend Zenger against Cosby's charge of libel.

Each issue of the *Journal* contained essays on political theory, freedom of the press, and, of course, strident criticism of Cosby. Such essays were usually presented in the form of unsigned letters to the editor. The pro-Cosby *Gazette,* on the other hand, printed essays defending the established order and condemning the *Journal*'s alleged radical politics and irresponsible attacks on the reputation of government officials. Cosby charged that his opponents were seeking to lead the weak and unwary into tumult, sedition and disturbance of the peace, endangering all order and government. He complained to the Board of Trade that Alexander and his party were supporting a press that had begun "to swarm with the most virulent libels" and that Morris's "open and implacable malice against me has appeared weekly in false and scandalous libels printed in Zenger's *Journal.*"[1]

In its second and third issues, the *Journal* printed a manifesto on freedom of the press which claimed that a critical press was necessary to protect the citizenry against the arbitrary power of corrupt officials who were beyond the reach of the law. "[F]or if such an overgrown criminal, or an impudent monster in iniquity, cannot immediately be come at by ordinary justice, let him yet receive the lash of satire, let the glaring truths of his ill administration, if possible, awaken his conscience, rouse his fear, by his actions odious to all honest minds."[2]

The manifesto concluded, "The loss of liberty in general would soon follow the suppression of the liberty of the press; for it is an essential branch of liberty, so perhaps it is the best preservative of the whole. Even a restraint of the press would have a fatal influence. No nation ancient or modern ever lost the liberty of freely speaking, writing or publishing their sentiments, but forthwith lost their liberty in general and became slaves."[3]

In colonial New York, like eighteenth-century England, the major restraint on freedom of the press was the law of libel. According to the law of "seditious libel," any published statement, whether true or false, which contained written criticism of public men for their conduct or of the laws or institutions of the country was liable to prosecution. Indeed, the law of seditious libel was governed by the maxim, "The greater the truth, the greater the libel."[4]

Common law courts had jurisdiction over such prosecutions, and the judges reserved to themselves the power to decide whether words were libelous. Juries were also involved in the process, but only to establish whether the words actually referred to the people or institutions as charged. Only the judges could decide whether an author or publisher was guilty. In colonial New York, those charged with the crime frequently argued that juries were the proper judges of law as well as fact, but such arguments had not yet established respectable precedent.

Zenger's *Journal* frequently published articles favoring an expanded role for juries in libel prosecutions. One article, published on the very day of Zenger's trial, argued that when law and fact are inseparable, the jury must determine both. In particular, the *Journal* suggested that law and fact were inseparable in libel cases.

Zenger had only been publishing the *Journal* for two months when Cosby took action to silence it. He had newly appointed Chief Justice James DeLancey request indictments for seditious libel against Zenger. When the grand jurors refused to act, DeLancey brought the libels before the next grand jury. This time, the jurors were willing to identify two articles in the *Journal* as libelous, but they said they were unable to discover the identity of the author or publisher of the articles. Undaunted, Cosby managed to get the local council to request the assembly's concurrence in ordering the burning of copies of the *Journal* containing the offending articles. When the assembly refused to cooperate, Cosby and the council acted on their own. On November 2, 1734, the council declared that the specified issues of the *Journal* were seditious, that they should be burned, that the governor should offer a reward for the discovery of the authors and that Zenger, the printer, should be imprisoned.

On November 17, 1734, the sheriff imprisoned Zenger, charging him with printing and publishing seditious libels which tended to inflame the minds of the people against the government. The Morrisites came to Zenger's defense, knowing that if the press was silenced, their campaign against Cosby would be emasculated. In a crowded New York courtroom, Zenger's lawyers, James Alexander and William Smith, requested moderate bail for the poor printer, but Chief Justice DeLancey set bail at £400, an unprecedented amount in New York's legal history. Unable to raise bail, Zenger remained in jail until the end of his trial eight months later.

On January 28, 1735, Attorney General Richard Bradley made the charges against Zenger more specific by identifying the thirteenth and twenty-third issues of the *Journal* as libelous. The following charges were made against Zenger:

> Being a seditious person; and a frequent printer and publisher of false news and seditious libels, both wickedly and maliciously devising the administration of His Excellency William Cosby, Captain General and Governor in Chief, to traduce, scandalize, and vilify both His Excellency the Governor and the ministers and officers of the king, and to bring them into suspicion and the ill opinion of the subjects of the king residing within the Province.[5]

The defense responded by challenging the authority of two of the Supreme Court judges, Chief Justice DeLancey and Justice Frederick Philipse. DeLancey not only refused to consider the challenges, but disbarred Alexander and Smith for showing disrespect. Deprived of legal counsel, Zenger was forced to petition the court to appoint a new lawyer for him. DeLancey assigned the job to John Chambers, a competent attorney but a Cosby man. The Morrisites promptly sought to improve the defense team by engaging Andrew Hamilton of Philadelphia, a professional associate and friend of Alexander's and reputedly the best lawyer in America.

When Zenger's trial commenced on August 4, 1735, Chambers was still Zenger's counsel of record, but Hamilton dramatically rose to announce his participation. From that moment on he dominated the trial. It has been said that Hamilton conducted his defense according to "the law of the future," since the law of 1735 was clearly against him. Disregarding contemporary English practice, he argued that the court's law was out of date, that truth was a defense against the charge of libel and that the jury had a right to render a verdict where law and fact were intertwined.

The basis for Hamilton's defense of Zenger was his claim that citizens had a right to criticize their rulers. Arguing politics rather than law, Hamilton declared that the right to criticize the government derives from the assumption that the rulers of the state are merely guardians of the public good. He claimed that when political power threatens individual rights, the citizens need not obey their magistrates. In arguing that public criticism is the best safeguard against the misuse of political power, Hamilton contended that all free men had a right to speak publicly against official abuses of power.

The attorney general stated the case against Zenger with simplicity and confidence. Since Hamilton had admitted the printing and publishing of the offending articles, he said, "the Jury must find a Verdict for the King; for supposing they were true, the Law says that they are not the less libelous for that; nay indeed the Law says, their being true is an Aggravation of the Crime."[6]

Hamilton responded quickly, "You will have something more to do, before you make my Client a Libeller; for the Words themselves must be libellous, that is, false, scandalous, and seditious, or else we are not guilty."[7]

Hamilton then declared that, if the attorney general could prove Zenger's articles to be false, he would admit them to be scandalous, seditious and a libel. "So the Work seems now to be pretty much shortened," said Hamilton, "and Mr. Attorney has now only to prove the Words false, in order to make us Guilty."[8]

The chief justice immediately attempted to end that line of argument, saying that Hamilton was not allowed to enter the truth of a libel in evidence. Ignoring the chief justice's ruling on this matter, Hamilton then boldly questioned his authority to judge guilt or innocence in the case, something well established under current law. The chief justice was particularly disturbed when Hamilton proceeded to describe the failings of judges in past cases. Indeed, in his closing remarks, the chief justice addressed the jury as follows:

The great pains Mr. Hamilton has taken, to shew how little Regard Juries are to Pay to the Opinion of the Judges; and his insisting so much upon the Conduct of some Judges in Tryals of this kind; is done, no doubt, with a Design that you should take but very little Notice, of what I might say upon this Occasion. I shall therefore only observe to you that, as the Facts or Words in the Information are confessed: The only Thing that can come in Question before you is, whether the Words as set forth in the Information, make a Lybel. And that is a Matter of Law, . . . which you may leave to the Court.[9]

The jury ignored the chief justice, just as Hamilton had requested them to do. Because the law was against him, Hamilton had seen to it that Zenger was tried by the public, not by the law. At the end of a single day of arguments, it took the jury only a few minutes to return a verdict of not guilty. When the acquittal was announced by the jury foreman, the small courtroom erupted in cheers.

Though the Zenger verdict was not regarded as formal legal precedent, it established the power of juries to return general verdicts and to acquit men considered libelers by the judges. It thus rendered prosecutions for seditious libel uncertain at best.

The public in New York and throughout the colonies regarded the verdict as a great victory for freedom of the press and the right of the people to confront arbitrary political power, but the factional politics of New York was not significantly changed by the Zenger verdict. Within a year, Governor Cosby died, but Cosby's principal advisor, councilor George Clarke, was appointed to succeed him. James Alexander and William Smith were quietly reinstated to the bar, but the Morrisite opposition soon lost its prominence. Nevertheless, the effect of the trial transcended local politics, preparing the way for the revolutionary concepts of popular sovereignty and the people's right to know, which were eventually embodied in the U.S. Constitution.

In an effort to extend the influence of the sensational Zenger trial, Hamilton and Alexander decided to publish an account of the trial. In March 1736, Hamilton sent Alexander his notes, authorizing him to edit and correct them for publication. Titled *A Brief Narrative of the Case and Trial of John Peter Zenger, Printer of the New York Weekly Journal*, the book was circulated throughout the American colonies, as well as England. It was reprinted fifteen times before the end of the century and was used several times to support the defense of citizens charged with seditious libel.

In his 1963 introduction to *A Brief Narrative*, Stanley Nider Katz wrote,

Because of the insight it stimulated into the popular aspect of American political life, the Zenger case has always served as a useful symbol of the development of political freedom in America. Whenever the popular basis of politics has appeared to be threatened, Alexander's pamphlet has been recalled, and the unassuming and unheroic Zenger has come to symbolize the idea that personal freedom rests upon the individual's right to criticize his government. Thus the Zenger case, though it did not directly ensure freedom of the press, prefigured that revolution "in the hearts and minds of the people" which was to make an ideal of 1735 an American reality, and it has served repeatedly to remind Americans of the debt free men owe to free speech.[10]

H. L. MENCKEN AND THE HATRACK CASE, 1926

H. L. Mencken may have been the most prominent journalist, magazine publisher and social commentator of his time. He was a prolific author who was never more articulate and inspired than when battling American Puritanism. He had always despised Puritanism and the censorship that flowed from it, characterizing it as "the haunting fear that someone, somewhere, may be happy." He warned that whereas America's old Puritanism sought to wash away our own sins, the new Puritanism crusaded against the sins of others.[11]

In his 1917 article, "Puritanism as a Literary Force," Mencken described the old Puritan crusader Anthony Comstock and anticipated his own monumental battle with the new censors almost a decade later. He wrote,

> The new Puritanism is not ascetic, but militant. Its aim is not to lift up saints but to knock down sinners. Its supreme manifestation is the vice crusade, an armed pursuit of helpless outcasts by the whole military and naval forces of the Republic. Its supreme hero is Comstock himself, with his pious boast that the sinners he jailed during his astounding career . . . would have filled a train of sixty-one coaches, allowing sixty to the coach.

Mencken complained,

> I find that the Comstocks, near and far, are oftener in my mind's eye than my actual patrons. The thing I always have to decide about a manuscript offered for publication, before ever I give any thought to its artistic merit and suitability, is the question whether its publication will be permitted . . . whether some roving Methodist preacher,

self-commissioned to keep watch on letters, will read indecency into it. Not a week passes that I do not decline some sound and honest piece of work for no other reason.

Mencken described the fate of a magazine editor who did not accommodate the whims of the censors. "Any professional moralist could go before a police magistrate, get a warrant upon a simple affidavit, raid the office of the offending editor, seize all the magazines in sight, and keep them impounded until after the disposition of the case. Editors cannot afford to take this risk. Magazines are perishable goods. Even if, after a trial has been had, they are returned, they are utterly worthless save as waste paper."[12]

Indeed, less than a decade later, Mencken himself would endure such a fate. The "new Puritanism" of the 1920s found its center in Boston, where censorship was exercised through an organization called the New England Watch and Ward Society, whose secretary, Reverend Jason Franklin Chase, became its spokesman and supreme censor. Chase seldom had to go to court, because it was common knowledge that the Boston judges and jurors would give him whatever he wanted. He operated an effective censorship system from his office, which coordinated two self-censoring bodies, the Boston Booksellers' Committee and the Massachusetts Magazine Committee, which represented the wholesalers and chain retailers in the state. Whenever a book or magazine article offended Chase, he simply sent a letter to the appropriate committee which barred the sale of it.

The occasional newsdealer who was bold enough to defy Chase would receive a warrant and a stiff fine. Magazine publishers were helpless in the face of Chase's power because the newsdealers simply refused to handle their magazines. Throughout this process, Chase remained behind the scene, providing little evidence of his controlling hand.

During this period, Mencken was publishing a new magazine, the *American Mercury.* An upgraded version of Mencken's earlier *Smart Set,* it was a constant threat to the sensibilities of people like Reverend Chase. Mencken later wrote,

Since its first issue, in January, 1924, it had been decidedly out of favor with the Puritans of the country . . . and had devoted a great deal of its space to opposing and ridiculing them. Among its contributors had been some of the most conspicuous foes of the bluenose moral scheme. . . . There had been many demands in the religious press, and even in the newspapers, that it be suppressed, and at frequent intervals it had been barred from the news-stands of various communities. . . . Those were the palmy days of comstockery in the United States, and the professional comstocks recognized the magazine as an uncomfortable and perhaps even dangerous opponent.[13]

The *American Mercury* did not employ pontifical rhetoric to denounce the "wowsers," as Mencken derisively referred to the new Puritans. Instead, it used withering satire under which the wowsers writhed. The *Mercury* treated religion in general with satire and denigration, but by 1925 Mencken had narrowed his attacks to religious censorship, and thence to Reverend Chase himself. Mencken was aware of Chase's astonishing power in Boston, and in early 1925 he began to hunt for someone to write an article in the *Mercury* about it. He quickly discovered that Boston newspapermen were almost as completely intimidated by the Watch and Ward Society as the newsdealers. Mencken finally found a journalist for the Springfield *Union* who agreed to interview Chase and write an article describing his practices.

The resulting article was printed in the September 1925 issue. Titled "Keeping the Puritans Pure," it ridiculed Chase throughout as an "unctuous meddler." Chase was furious and threatened to have the *Mercury* banned not only in Massachusetts but nationwide. Mencken gleefully responded with an article titled "Boston Twilight," which blamed Chase for the city's declining fortunes.

In the April 1926 issue, Mencken published an article titled "The True Methodists," which spoke scornfully of Chase. The issue also contained an article titled "Hatrack," which told the story of a small-town prostitute who wanted to be treated as a fellow Christian. Chase promptly moved to ban the April issue from the newsstands. Following his usual procedure, he mailed a copy of the issue to his Magazine Committee along with the customary threat of legal action. He also issued a statement to the Boston papers, identifying "Hatrack" as a threat to New England morals. By making an issue of an article that did not attack himself or the Watch and Ward, Chase hoped to avoid the appearance of self-serving action.

Most of the Boston newsstands and wholesalers quickly complied with Chase's orders, although many retail newsdealers first attempted to sell out their small stock on hand. Most of them succeeded in doing so, but Felix Caragianes, a Greek with a stand in Harvard Square, was arrested.

Mencken decided that something would have to be done, "for if Chase were permitted to get away with this minor assault he would be encouraged to plan worse ones, and, what is more, other wowsers elsewhere would imitate him."[14] After consulting with his publisher, Alfred A. Knopf, Mencken contacted Arthur Garfield Hays, who had been one of the attorneys for the defense in the notorious Scopes trial held in July 1925. Hays, who had often represented the American Civil Liberties Union (ACLU) and had great experience in fighting censorship, proposed that he and Mencken go to Boston, where Mencken would publicly sell a copy of the April issue to Chase himself and defy Chase to arrest him. Hays warned Mencken that Chase would probably be able to choose his own judge and thus assure a conviction, but that there was a good chance of winning on appeal.

Mencken eagerly embraced the plan, which was announced to the press on April 3, 1926, and reported in the next morning's papers. When Mencken and Hays arrived at the appointed location for the sale, they found a huge crowd assembled, most of them Harvard undergraduates. Mencken carried three copies of the April issue under his arm, while Hays carried a bundle of fifty copies for general sale in case Chase failed to appear.

Soon the crowd became restive.

"Where's Chase?" they cried.

"Yes, where's Chase?" echoed Mencken.

"Here he is," shouted some people on the fringe of the crowd. "He can't get through."

"I'll get him here," said a tall policeman, and he parted the crowd for Chase.

When Chase approached Mencken, the hostile crowd shouted, "Is this a free country or not? Why did we fight the revolution?"[15]

Mencken later recalled, "Chase identified himself, I offered him a copy of the magazine, he handed me a silver half dollar, I bit it as if to make sure that it was good coin, and Chase said to [police officer] Patterson, 'I order this man's arrest.' "[16]

The *Baltimore Sun* described the event as follows:

Plainclothes city policemen and constables of the New England Watch and Ward Society, fought their way this afternoon to the center of a tightly packed throng of over 5,000 people assembled on

Boston Common. They plucked therefrom H. L. Mencken, of Baltimore, editor of the *American Mercury*, engaged at the moment in selling his magazine to citizens of Boston. The officers fought their way out again with their prisoner, one woman fainting in the process. They marched him down Tremont Street, four blocks to police headquarters, where he was later arraigned on a charge of "selling literature tending to corrupt the morals of the young." He was released in his personal surety of $1,000 to appear in Municipal Court tomorrow morning.[17]

Mencken spent more than an hour in police custody before he was formally arraigned. While waiting for the judge to appear, Mencken told the assembled reporters, "I courted arrest and I hope to establish a test case. . . . Our object is simply to end the system of predatory organizations by which they attack the innocent newsdealer. . . . The result of this is that the owner of the magazine gets an untried verdict that his publication is obscene. I allege that this is dishonest and malicious and I intend to use the law to settle the grievance."[18]

Chase publicly claimed that the "Hatrack" story was "bad, vile and raw. It should be suppressed. He's here to dare Boston and I have accepted his challenge."[19]

Mencken pleaded not guilty to both possession and sale of improper literature, and Judge William Sullivan thereupon signed the warrant and held Mencken for trial. After he was released on his own recognizance, he and Hays proceeded to draw up a bill of complaint to be filed in federal court in Boston, requesting an injunction to restrain Chase from further interference with the *American Mercury*'s business. The bill of complaint sought a permanent injunction against Chase and the society, accusing them of "substituting their own opinion for the law."[20]

Meanwhile, Mencken still had to appear in municipal court before a presumably unsympathetic judge. The courtroom was jammed with spectators, including many reporters, photographers and students from Harvard and Radcliffe. Mencken was given an ovation upon both his entrance and exit. The judge insisted that all testimony and argument be conducted sotto voce in a small corner of the room, because he considered the evidence to be unfit for the spectators' ears.

Chase's attorney, John W. Rorke, began by denouncing Mencken as a corrupter of youth and a flouter of decency. Hays then called Mencken to the stand, where he testified as to the usual contents of the magazine and some of its prominent contributors, including a bishop and a U.S. senator. Mencken said he had planned his arrest and had come to Boston for that purpose, but he denied that there was anything obscene or anything that would tend to corrupt morals in the "Hatrack" story. He said Chase and his followers could smell out immorality in any publication from the Bible on down.

Herbert Asbury, the author of "Hatrack," then testified that the events depicted in his story were substantially true and had occurred in his hometown. When asked by Rorke whether he considered his story to be obscene, Asbury, who came from a family of Methodist ministers and bishops, responded, "Obscenity can only be created in the mind of a person reading my story when that mind is already obscene and its possessor is perverted. My article was intended for pure-minded, thinking people, well and firmly grounded in their moral standards."[21]

The attorneys' arguments followed, with Hays maintaining that the constitutional guarantees of free speech and free press were being menaced by Chase's actions against legitimate publications. "This action is getting down to dangerous ground," said Hays, "not only in Boston, but through the United States. It is a case of the minority setting themselves up to dictate what the majority should read. . . . The fundamentals of American liberty are involved, and Mr. Mencken comes to the court as the bulwark of safety for that same liberty." Hayes then asked the court to dismiss the case against Mencken.[22]

Since Chase's case was based entirely on the article's content, Hays argued that the court could judge "Hatrack" only by reading it. Judge Parmenter announced that he would read the magazine and be ready with his decision the following morning.

Indeed, when the time came for the judge to announce his decision, he had a copy of the magazine on his desk. Judge Parmenter first addressed the question of whether the language used in the "Hatrack" article was obscene, indecent or impure. "This is plainly not the case and is not claimed to be so," said Parmenter. "I cannot imagine anyone reading the article and finding himself or herself attracted toward vice." Parmenter then addressed the question of whether the subject matter presented was indecent within the meaning of the statute. He said that the *American Mercury* appeared to be a magazine appealing to persons interested in the discussion of serious subjects, and he concluded, "The magazine is quite different from the cheaper publications one sees on the newsstands. I cannot believe that this article would be at all likely to have an injurious effect upon its readers."[23]

Mencken later recalled, "As he proceeded I was quite bewildered. I had assumed almost as a matter of course that he would declare me guilty and hold me for trial, and when he began disposing of Chase's contentions one by one I began to wonder what would be left to justify that verdict."[24]

In rendering his judgment, Judge Parmenter stated: "Viewing the matter, then, from every phase, including the language used, the nature of the article and its effect on the readers and the general makeup of the magazine and its distribution, I find that no offense has been committed and therefore dismiss the complaint."[25]

Newspaper reporters, many of whom represented papers friendly to Chase, swarmed around Mencken, who hinted that he might sue Chase and the Watch and Ward for damages. But first he attended a luncheon at Harvard University where he was honored by 2,000 students and several prominent faculty members. The huge hall of Harvard Union was packed when Mencken arrived, and he was greeted with a triumphal storm of noise. Professor Felix Frankfurter of the law school, later to become a famous Supreme Court justice, presided and introduced Mencken. "We assembled to condole with a martyr," said Frankfurter. "We did not hope to greet the martyr vindicated. . . . And so he dared to do what he did. After he had done it and while his fate was in the balance in the courts we wanted him to know that he was already acquitted by Harvard. His was the courage to resist brutality."[26]

Mencken spoke briefly.

> The reason we tackled this poor fool and his organization and ruined him was an effort to substitute the courts of law for back-alley assassination. . . . The worst thing that can happen to a country or a State is indolence regarding these sniffers. . . . They've been chased out of the Free State of Maryland years ago. They used to go sniffing and smelling down there just as they are doing here, but they were knocked off just as you can knock them off.[27]

Mencken returned to Baltimore and rejoiced in his victory. "The system that I attacked in Boston," he said,

> is vicious, dishonest and lawless. Its purpose is to wreak cruel and wanton injuries upon men without giving them a chance to defend

themselves. The so-called Watch and Ward Society, an organization
of fanatics led by a Methodist clergyman, is its sponsor and chief
agent. . . . Consider now the position of the publisher and editor of
the magazine. Their property has been attacked behind the door;
they have been deprived of any chance to defend themselves. . . . It
was to upset this system that I went to Boston. . . . I am asking that
Chase be restrained from threatening any news dealer who sells my
magazine until and if he has brought me into open court.[28]

Mencken added that the *Mercury* was asking for $50,000 in damages
for Chase's false accusations. "There is here no desire to ruin a misguided man, now brought to book," said Mencken. "There is only a
desire to force him to conduct his unpleasant business in a lawful manner and in accordance with common decency."[29]

But Chase had another trick up his sleeve. He had slipped down to
New York where he induced the postmaster there to prevail upon the
U.S. Post Office Department to bar the April issue of the *Mercury* from
the mails. Horace Donnelly, solicitor to the Post Office Department in
Washington, D.C., obliged Chase by declaring the April issue unmail-
able.

When asked to comment upon the Post Office's action, Chase said,
"I have been advised by my attorneys to say nothing pending the outcome of the Federal suit Mr. Mencken has filed against me." But Chase
added that "it is almost needless to say I am immensely pleased."
When asked if he now felt vindicated in his own attempts to ban the
Mercury from Boston, Chase answered, "Absolutely so. Coming from
such a source and on top of a temporary setback, what else could I
call it but a vindication?"[30]

Mencken described the action as purely gratuitous and malicious.
After all, the April issue had already gone through the mails after being
examined and approved by Post Office officials. Mencken feared that
the subsequent issue of the *Mercury* might be similarly treated. The
May issue, already being printed, contained an article titled "Sex and
the Co-Ed," which, though quite harmless, might be exploited by
Chase and Donnelly. If they were successful in barring the May issue
from the mails, it would result in the revocation of the *Mercury*'s
second-class mailing privileges on the ground that it had missed two
consecutive issues and was therefore not a "continuous publication."
This trick had been used successfully against various radical magazines
during the Red Scare following World War I. The loss of second-class
privileges was a death sentence for any magazine.

Mencken reluctantly decided to scrap the May issue, at considerable cost, and replace the doubtful article with one titled, "On Learning to Play the Cello." The already printed copies of the May issue were destroyed, and a revised issue was printed and bound at an additional cost of more than $8,000, almost as much as all of the other costs in the "Hatrack" case combined.

Having temporarily avoided further problems with the Post Office, Mencken and Hays went to federal district court in Boston to argue for an injunction and $50,000 in damages against Chase and the Watch and Ward Society. The complaint alleged that there was "venom and malice" behind Chase's actions which were threatening any book or magazine seller in connection with his business.[31]

The proceedings began with Chase and the society's lawyer, Edmund Whitman, asking Judge James Morton to dismiss the bill of complaint. Whitman claimed that since no actual harm had been done to the *Mercury* by Chase's actions, and no further actions were imminent, an injunction would be inappropriate. When Hays said he could not be certain that the society would not try to ban the May issue just as they had done in April, Whitman told Hays that if he would submit the May issue to the Watch and Ward Society, "we could tell you in ample time whether it is alright."[32]

Hays exploded, calling Whitman's statement "outrageous and presumptuous." He said he had no intention of submitting anything for approval. "Our tribunal is the bench, not the Watch and Ward Society," said Hays. "We want nothing from them at all, but that they be made to mind their own business."[33]

Reverend Chase was then called to the stand, where he was asked by Hays to describe his method of censorship. Chase said he approached the magazine distributor, gave him notice and threatened him with arrest.

Hays asked whether Chase's action was intended as "a bluff."

"A warning," said Chase.[34]

On April 14, Judge Morton announced his decision; he granted Mencken's injunction and sustained his full bill of complaint. Judge Morton explained,

Few dealers in any trade will buy goods after notice that they will be prosecuted if they resell them. . . . The defendants know this and trade upon it. They secure their influence, not by voluntary acquiescence in their opinions of the trade in question, but by the coercion and intimidation of that trade through the fear of prosecution if the defendants' views are disregarded. In my judgment this is clearly illegal. The defendants have the right of every citizen to come to the courts with complaints of crime. But they have no right to impose their opinions on the book and magazine trade by threats of prosecution if their views are not accepted.[35]

An injunction was then issued enjoining Chase and the Watch and Ward Society from interfering with the sale and distribution of any future issues of the *American Mercury* by organized threat and intimidation.

The battle, however, was far from over. On April 15, 1926, Mencken and Hays appeared before Post Office Solicitor Donnelly to resolve the question of the "mailability" of the *American Mercury*. Hays argued that since Judges Palmenter and Morton clearly had found "Hatrack" not to be obscene, there was no ground for barring it from the mails. Donnelly answered dryly that the Massachusetts obscenity statute and the Postal Act were not the same. Mencken then charged that the action of the Post Office had been set in motion by Chase, who was vengefully seeking to accomplish through administrative order what he could not do through the courts.

Donnelly denied being influenced by Chase. "I want to say that the actions of the Watch and Ward Society have no connection with this department," he said. As he called the hearing to an end, Donnelly left little doubt about his verdict when he said, "I will tell you frankly, Mr. Hays, that you have not convinced me this thing does not come within the statute."[36]

On April 23, Donnelly wrote to Hays announcing that "after further very careful consideration of the case, the department adheres to the original ruling that the April issue of the *American Mercury* is unmailable."[37]

On April 28, Hays filed suit in the federal district court in New York, asking for an injunction to prevent the implementation of Donnelly's ruling. The hearing, held before Judge Julian Mack on May 11, was brief. "What is all this about?" asked Judge Mack impatiently. "I am a subscriber to the *Mercury* myself. I have read 'Hatrack' and I must say that I have found nothing obscene in it. The article is not one to excite lust."[38]

Taken aback by the judge's firm rejection of his charges, the federal attorney suggested that another article in the April issue might be considered obscene. Judge Mack perused that article and, finding nothing offensive in it, dismissed the government's point again. Seeking once more to find something objectionable in the issue, the federal attorney pointed out an advertisement of a set of the works of Pierre de Bourdeille seigneur de Brantome, an early seventeenth-century author whose works included *Illustrious Dames of the Court of the Valois Kings.* The court quickly ruled that Brantome's works were classics and that such an advertisement was not covered by the statute in question. Judge Mack then concluded that inasmuch as there was clearly no violation of the law anywhere in the magazine, he was overruling the Postmaster General and rescinding the ban.

The government appealed, but it was not until May 1927 that the case was heard. During the intervening period, the two-pronged attack on the *Mercury* by Chase and Donnelly had cost the magazine a great deal of money. The *Mercury* was little more than two years old, and if it were characterized as a sensational and pornographic magazine, it might well be ruined. Mencken's personal position was also somewhat precarious. "I had accumulated, through my writings during the war and afterward, a large crop of bitter enemies, and some of them were extremely enterprising. They now had, thanks to the three wowsers, a good stick to beat me with, and they employed it with much industry."[39]

On November 3, 1926, news of Chase's death reached Mencken, who said it gave him no noticeable grief. Unfortunately, Chase's death actually heartened the other wowsers in the Watch and Ward Society, for now they could blame all their errors on him. Hays had already concluded that it would be difficult to prove damages against the Watch and Ward Society, and the case against them was subsequently dropped. Though the *Mercury* received no damages, the injunction granted to the magazine by Judge Morton remained in effect. The only legal matter left to be resolved was the government's appeal of the *Mercury*'s victory over the Post Office.

The sitting judges were Martin T. Manton, Learned Hand, and Thomas W. Swan. Hays's main argument was one that he had presented in the court below—that the Post Office had attacked the *Mercury* wantonly and without cause, *after* the April issue of the magazine had already gone through the mails. Unfortunately, this was precisely the fact that defeated the *Mercury* in the end, for the appeals court ruled that, in the absence of impending harm to the magazine, the lower court should have denied the request for a temporary injunction. The order was therefore reversed.

Mencken later wrote,

> This was the end of the "Hatrack" case. The injunction against the Watch and Ward Society that Judge Morton had given us in Boston was still good, and we never heard another word from the wowsers there so long as I was editor of the *American Mercury*, but the Post Office went unscathed for Donnelly's malicious and disingenuous attempt to injure us. To be sure, we were never troubled by him again, but the April issue was still barred from the mails, at least in theory. . . . To this day those who remember the case at all appear to believe that we won all along the line. Morally speaking, we undoubtedly did, but in the legal sense we were floored finally by three judges in high esteem as Liberals! It was an ending not without its ironies.[40]

But Mencken never doubted the correctness of his decision to challenge Reverend Chase in court. "The general success of our attack," wrote Mencken, "inspired many other persons to resist the fiats of wowserism, and for ten years following the *American Mercury* case there were frequent combats. Many of these flowed directly out of our own adventures. We had made the first really determined and pertinacious attack on the censorship of printing in Massachusetts, and other victims of it followed in our path."[41]

JOHN HENRY FAULK AND THE RADIO BLACKLIST, 1955

John Henry Faulk was born on August 21, 1913, in Austin, Texas. His father, a sharecropper unable to read or write until the age of seventeen, went on to become a prominent attorney and judge, known for his liberal politics and support of civil rights. Like his father, young John Henry took a passionate interest in social justice and constitutional rights. While on furlough from the army during Christmas of 1945, he was introduced by his friend Alan Lomax to a number of New York radio executives who were captivated by his down-home humor and storytelling skills. In April 1946, John Henry began broadcasting a weekly radio series on Columbia Broadcasting System (CBS) called *Johnny's Front Porch*.

In the early 1950s, John Henry's radio show climbed nearly to the top of the Nielsen ratings, and he began appearing on television shows as well. "I was choppin' in the tall cotton," recalled Faulk proudly. Nevertheless he was acutely aware of the chilling Cold War climate. "There was a vast uneasiness that ran throughout the whole land," he said.[42]

Cold War politics and McCarthyism were increasingly intimidating the entertainment industry, and John Henry's network (CBS) and his union, the American Federation of Radio Actors (AFRA), began to investigate the "loyalty" of its employees and members. In 1951 AFRA merged with the television actors' union to form the American Federation of Television and Radio Artists (AFTRA) and passed a resolution to expel any members who refused to answer questions from a congressional investigating committee. The practice of blacklisting uncooperative union members soon became a part of the broader witchhunt conducted by Senator Joseph P. McCarthy (R-Wis.) and the House Un-American Activities Committee (HUAC), and concerned members of AFTRA sought new leadership. Because of his service in the war and his lack of involvement in union politics, John Henry seemed like the perfect choice.

Faulk later recalled how he and some fellow entertainers got together to discuss the union's failure to confront blacklisting. "I got up and made a speech about how we weren't founded by cowards and shan't be saved by cowards. Gentlemen, I concluded, let's run in our own candidates and wipe them out. And we did."[43]

In the summer of 1955, Faulk organized a middle-of-the-road slate of AFTRA officers: newsman Charles Collingwood would run for president, comedian Orson Bean for first vice president, and John Henry Faulk for second vice president. During the campaign for the union elections, John Henry spoke forcefully against the practice of blacklisting. "I could no longer sit silently by and watch the results of these blacklisting operations," he said. "Their influence in the industry had to be fought."[44] In December 1955, a record number of AFTRA voters gave the "Middlers," as they were called, twenty-seven of the thirty-five seats on the board.

Shortly after the election victory, however, John Henry was accused of Communist activities by a right-wing organization called AWARE. "Since I had never done anything the AWARE people could feed on, I felt immune," said Faulk. "But now I found out that I had done the unpardonable. I had opposed them, and this was the standard that made me a subversive. It seemed strange and eerie. Here, men and women with whom I had never met or talked were out to destroy me and my family."[45]

AWARE had already used innuendo and guilt by association to destroy the careers of entertainers it regarded as soft on communism, and it claimed that John Henry's opposition to blacklisting was really part of a secret plan to protect Communists. John Henry described AWARE as follows: "It had as its stated purpose to combat the communist conspiracy in the communications industry. That presumes two things: that there *was* a communist conspiracy in the communications industry, and that AWARE was the proper and authorized group to combat it. I accepted neither one of those prescriptions."[46]

AWARE's tactics included publication of a list of persons who, perhaps twenty years earlier, had signed a petition, marched in a parade, or entertained before a group under circumstances that AWARE considered disloyal. The list was circulated to radio and television executives and sponsors, who responded by firing the persons listed. "They never called them in and asked, 'Is this true or false?' " recalled John Henry. "The networks didn't want to get involved." The people who were fired were never charged with any violation of the law in any way. They were simply entered on what came to be called the blacklist. "They became untouchables," according to John Henry. "It was a dread period because dear and fine friends of mine had their careers totally smashed and destroyed."[47]

One of AWARE's directors was Vincent Hartnett, whose frequently updated publication *Red Channels* listed names of entertainment industry figures with alleged ties to "Communist-front" organizations. Hartnett also served as a private consultant for advertising agencies, screening performers on the basis of their politics and patriotism. Advertising agencies that subscribed to Hartnett's service would not permit the hiring of a performer who received a bad rating from AWARE. Hartnett had an influential ally, Laurence Johnson, whose ownership of several supermarkets gave him influence over manufacturers who feared that their products would be boycotted from his stores if they sponsored blacklisted performers.

Johnson sent formal letters to supermarket owners and merchandisers asking, "Do you realize you are helping the communists? How? By pushing the products of certain manufacturers! Yes, manufacturers who employ those people in their radio and television advertising who have contributed to communism and communist-front activities."[48]

In February 1956, AWARE Bulletin 16 charged that Faulk had been listed as appearing at, sponsoring or sending greetings to seven Communist-front functions. The bulletin was sent to newspaper editors and columnists, radio and television stations, advertising agencies, sponsors, motion-picture studios, law enforcement agencies, veterans' organizations and Faulk's employer, Frank Stanton, president of CBS.

At that time, Faulk was earning $35,000, and with growing television popularity he had the prospect of earning much more. When asked if he was afraid of AWARE's attacks, he said, "I'm scared. Not of the people who put out that bulletin. I'm scared of what these lies can do to our lives and my career."[49]

Faulk knew that performers, announcers, writers and directors had been denied work because advertising agencies, sponsors or employers had seen their names on blacklists prepared by organizations like AWARE. Individuals were seldom confronted by formal charges. They were simply denied work because the charges alone made them controversial.

About ten days after AWARE's Bulletin 16 appeared, a CBS executive called Faulk in and told him that Laurence Johnson was in town talking to his sponsors. The executive told Faulk that several of the sponsors were dropping his show, and he warned, "It looks like you're a dead duck."[50]

The executive suggested that Faulk provide formal answers to AWARE's charges in the form of an affidavit, but Faulk said that would simply dignify the lies and admit that AWARE had the right to circulate them. Instead, Faulk submitted a sworn statement of his views to CBS, which circulated it to the advertising agencies. He then made a personal appointment with one of the largest agencies in the country, one that represented sponsors who were dropping him as the result of pressure from AWARE. Faulk told the agency representative that the charges against him were lies and that he intended to sue. The official agreed that the people attacking him were "vicious," but said that the political atmosphere in the country made it impossible to fight them. "It can't be done," the official said. "But don't get me wrong. We'd like to see these people removed from our business."[51]

Finding few people of courage within his profession, and none within the advertising industry, Faulk hired Louis Nizer's law firm to challenge the lies that AWARE was circulating about him. On June 18, 1956, Nizer filed suit against AWARE, Hartnett and Johnson, asking for $500,000 in compensatory damages plus punitive damages from each party. The legal complaint charged that AWARE had conspired with the advertising agencies and the networks to defame John Henry's reputation, destroy his livelihood and remove him from AFTRA.

Nizer warned Faulk that it would be a long and bitter fight, and that he would be placing his career on the line. Though Nizer asked for a relatively low retainer fee, Faulk was unable to cover it. A few days later, Edward R. Murrow, the reigning star of television news, called Faulk and offered to pay the remainder of his legal fees. When Faulk protested that he might never be able to repay the loan, Murrow said, "I'm not lending you the money Johnny. I'm investing it in our country."[52]

John Henry received wide public support for his suit, and when his ratings went up, many thought that he had beaten AWARE. However, the lawsuit had made him more controversial than ever. Soon, under pressure from powerful conservatives, more sponsors began to withdraw from his radio show and he was no longer hired for television appearances. Even some of the members of John Henry's middle-of-the-road AFTRA group began to lose their nerve. When influential columnist and Television host Ed Sullivan removed Orson Bean from a scheduled appearance on his show and CBS canceled his pilot series, Bean called John Henry and said that, in order to save his career, he would have to resign from the AFTRA slate. Shortly thereafter, Bean reappeared on Ed Sullivan's television show.

In a letter to friends, John Henry wrote,

> I am involved in about the biggest fracas that I have ever managed to get into. As you know, our side won last Fall in a bitter Union fight. The defeated side, a pack of McCarthyites, took in after us with a vengeance. They scared the hell out of the summer soldiers on our side, and scattered them like a covey of quail. . . . [T]he next thing I knew, I was standing there on the limb all by myself, like a half-feathered jay bird.[53]

AWARE made it clear to Faulk that, if he would name union members that he suspected of having Communist ties, things might go better for him. John Henry refused, characterizing AWARE as a bunch of blackmailers preying on entertainers and using patriotism as a smokescreen.

Faulk was under heavy pressure to drop his suit against AWARE. Both CBS and his manager expressed concern about his intention to go through with the suit, pointing out that his sponsors had come back and that if he would just forgive and forget, he would be safe. Faulk told them, "If AWARE Inc. gets off this time, they will do the same thing to somebody else next month and one month after that. The reason they have flourished so long is that nobody would ever wade into them and yank them out into the bright light of day for the public to look at in all their rusty gut ugliness. So I'm going through with it."[54]

Despite the network's nervousness, John Henry's ratings were still good, and in the summer of 1957 CBS assured him that his job was secure. Faulk took a brief vacation, and when he returned he was told that he had been fired. He was now on the blacklist, unable to earn a living.

The power of the blacklisters made him suddenly unemployable. AWARE used its close relationship with the HUAC to have him subpoenaed before the committee, and though the subpoena was eventually canceled, its issuance alone was publicized in such a way as to close all avenues of employment for John Henry. His savings were soon exhausted. Even his wife's longtime employment with an advertising firm was threatened by AWARE, and she eventually had to take a job as a waitress and saleswoman. At the end of 1959, heavily in debt and facing an eviction notice from his landlord, John Henry returned to his hometown, Austin, Texas, where he worked at odd jobs to eke out a living.

Meanwhile, preparations for the libel trial moved on slowly. In pretrial negotiations, Hartnett had suggested that he would recommend Faulk for employment if the libel action were dropped. Faulk told Nizer that he did not enjoy suffering, but that a trial was the only way to bring the facts about the blacklisters before the public.

Hartnett withdrew his offer to endorse Faulk and hired a new attorney, the notorious Roy Cohn, former counsel for Senator McCarthy's Investigations Subcommittee. Still, the case dragged on at an agonizing snail's pace, and the Faulks were forced to live from hand to mouth. In 1962 there were more than fifteen different motions, appeals and applications. Two judges died while matters were pending before them, forcing Nizer to reinstigate those proceedings.

In February 1962, a still unemployed but hopeful John Henry wrote to his friends about his difficulties while awaiting trial. "For the first time in my life I have experienced the feeling of having erstwhile friends turn their backs, and felt the cumulative effect of one turn down after another, week after week. It is not unlike Chinese water torture—a drop at a time on the forehead until dizziness sets in."[55]

Finally, in April 1962, John Henry's suit against AWARE was brought to trial in New York Supreme Court, where Nizer asked that the demand against the defendants be raised to $1,000,000. "It took five years to herd AWARE into the courtroom," said John Henry, "but we did it. Nizer had assembled the most astonishing library of wrong-doing on these people: the lives they'd smashed . . . how they had literally run the hiring practice of the radio and television industry."[56]

Justice Abraham Geller advised the court that labeling a person as a Communist sympathizer exposed him to hatred and contempt, and, if untrue, constituted libel. Faulk was the first witness, and he described the hardships he had endured as the result of AWARE's attacks on him. A number of prominent figures in the entertainment industry then described the way the blacklist worked.

David Susskind, a major television producer, testified that he had to submit thousands of names to the advertising agency representing his sponsors. The names were then checked with organizations like AWARE to determine their political acceptability. No one could work unless he or she was given clearance. Susskind testified that about one third of the names came back labeled "politically unreliable." No reason or justification was given. Even an eight-year-old actress was rejected as politically unreliable because her father was suspect. Susskind said he had been directed to fabricate an artistic reason for denying work to such people.[57]

Television star Garry Moore testified that a similar procedure was required when he hired performers for his show. Mark Goodson, producer of the popular television shows *What's My Line?* and *The Price Is Right*, testified that the innocence or guilt of those accused was never addressed during this process and the word blacklisting was never used. Goodson said a notation was simply made that the people were unacceptable, and it was understood that the reasons were political.

Thomas D. Murray, a senior account executive for a beverage company that had sponsored Faulk's radio show, testified that Laurence Johnson called him in March 1956 to complain that his company was using a Communist, John Henry Faulk, to advertise its product. Johnson told Murray that he'd better get in line or Johnson would remove the beverage displays in his stores.[58]

Justice Geller advised the jury that to avoid liability for Faulk's damages, the defendants would have to prove the truth of AWARE's Bulletin 16. Nizer then proceeded to quiz Hartnett about the bulletin's charges, and, line by line, he demonstrated that they were groundless.

Next came the process of establishing the level of damage caused to Faulk by AWARE's unsubstantiated charges. Nizer drew estimates from experts on what Faulk's income might have been if he had not been blacklisted. Garry Moore testified that if Faulk had remained on radio and television between 1956 and 1962, he could have earned anywhere between $200,000 and $1,000,000 per year.

On the morning of June 27, 1962, Nizer delivered his summation, saying that the issue in this case was whether private vigilantes could be allowed to take the law into their own hands. He stated that damages should be awarded in order to stop the blacklisting which was destroying people's lives. The following afternoon, the jury retired to deliberate. Less than five hours later, they returned and shocked the courtroom.

"We went back in and sat down," recalled John Henry. "The judge said, 'Mr. Foreman, have you reached a decision?' The foreman said, 'No, we want to ask a question in open court. May the jury give more than $2 million?' Well, Nizer looked as though somebody had caught him between the eyes with a ballpeen hammer."[59]

Justice Geller told the jury that they could fix whatever amount they believed was proper according to the degree of malice, intent or recklessness of the particular defendant. Seventy minutes later the jury returned its verdict, awarding Faulk $1,000,000 in compensatory damages against the three defendants and separate awards of $1,250,000 in punitive damages against both Hartnett and AWARE—a total of $3,500,000—the largest libel judgment in history, as of that time. As it turned out, John Henry saw very little of the record-breaking settlement because AWARE had insufficient money to pay more than a fraction of the judgement. Most of what John Henry received was used to cover legal fees and pay off the debts he had incurred in six years of unemployment. Even after his court victory, job offers were not forthcoming because the networks now regarded him as an embarrassing reminder of their shameful collaboration.

"I got something far more important than money," said John Henry. "I was being described by people whom I loved and respected as 'courageous and heroic.' I couldn't figure it out. These are two attributes that are quite absent from my personality . . . I was anxious to understand why a principled act was regarded as one of courage and heroism."[60]

Look magazine editorialized, "The John Henry Faulk story has a nightmarish quality. Yet it is sadly true." The editorial declared that the guilt for John Henry Faulk's ordeal, and the dozens of other tragedies that never came to public attention in the ugly days of McCarthyism and its aftermath, must be shared by all—magazines, newspapers, radio and television, advertising agencies and just plain citizens. "He who made no protest at the time has no license for smugness now," concluded *Look.* "Let us hope that we have learned our lesson well."[61]

In 1963 Faulk wrote *Fear on Trial,* a book about his ordeal and that of the many others who had been blacklisted for their lack of political orthodoxy. In 1965 John Henry returned to Austin, Texas, to start a new life. Twelve years later, his book was made into a television docudrama and broadcast on CBS. The movie led to renewed interest in John Henry as a performer, and he made regular appearances on the television show *Hee Haw* (1975–1980) and on National Public Radio. He also toured the country as a lecturer on First Amendment rights, often discussing the parallel between blacklisting and censorship. In January 1980 John Henry and his friends Eric Sevareid and Walter Cronkite formed the "First Amendment Congress," a national forum organized to protect free expression and the separation of church and state.

"My blacklisting wasn't about whether I was a subversive or wasn't a subversive," John Henry said. "It was about repression of our basic freedoms . . . a way of shutting off the dialogue in this country and destroying dissent." John Henry was emotional in opposing those who would deny our First Amendment freedom, but he always had fun caricaturing them. "I'm not against free speech," he paraphrased the right-wingers. "It's this damn *dissent* I'm trying to put a stop to."[62]

John Henry Faulk died on April 9, 1990, after a long and valiant battle against cancer. A few months later, author and columnist Molly Ivins wrote, "We miss John Henry Faulk awful bad. . . . It was more fun to go freedom-fightin' with that man than anyone else I ever knew."[63]

THE *PROGRESSIVE* TELLS THE H-BOMB SECRET, 1979

The Pentagon Papers case, *New York Times, Co. v. United States* (1971), is considered the premier legal judgement on the question of prior restraint against the media (see Chapters 3 and 4), but within a few years of the case the courts faced an even more sensational test of whether the press was free to publish classified information. This time the press was confronting the Atomic Energy Act of 1946, which defines the most secret category of government information, called "Restricted Data."

The Atomic Energy Act had introduced the concept of "born classified," the notion that virtually all nuclear information becomes classified the moment it is conceived, without the need for any government action to identify and mark it as classified. Under the Atomic Energy Act, all Restricted Data was considered classified from the moment it was conceived, whether in a government agency or in the mind of a private citizen. This broad category of information was defined as "all data concerning the manufacture or utilization of atomic weapons, the production of fissionable material, or the use of fissionable material in the production of power."[64]

In 1979 journalist Howard Morland trespassed on this strange territory with an article called "The H-Bomb Secret: How We Got It, Why We're Telling It." The article was scheduled to appear in the April 1979 issue of the *Progressive* magazine, but the government attempted to impose a prior restraint on its publication. Author Morland had no formal training in science and his only purpose was to criticize and expose a secrecy bureaucracy which maintained public ignorance about the nuclear weapons establishment. The oddity here was the government's claim that the advanced physics of nuclear fusion was revealed by a layman journalist who relied primarily on the *Encyclopedia Americana* and his freshman textbook from college. The government seemed less concerned with the actual information disclosed in Morland's article than with the appearance of a compromised security apparatus.

Erwin Knoll, who had been editor of the *Progressive* since 1973, was a renowned political progressive, who took pride in the fact that he was on President Nixon's Official Enemies List. In 1976, with the assistance of Sam Day, editor of the *Bulletin of the Atomic Scientists*, Knoll had published "The Doomsday Machine," a treatise on the nuclear peril, that led to the creation of Mobilization for Survival, a national antinuclear organization. In 1978 Sam Day joined the *Progressive* as managing editor and with a mandate from Knoll to make nuclear issues a major focus of the magazine. The stage was now set for a historic confrontation between a small magazine and the full power of the U.S. government. Shortly after Sam Day's arrival at the *Progressive*, he fulfilled an earlier commitment to debate Charles K. Gilbert, deputy administrator of the Department of Energy, on the issue of nuclear weapons. The debate was candid but amiable, and afterward Day asked Gilbert whether he might be allowed to tour the nation's nuclear factories. Gilbert agreed, and Day notified Knoll that there might be a story in this.

In preparing for his tour of the factories, Day was told about an antinuclear activist named Howard Morland, who had put together an informative slide show on nuclear weapons for the Mobilization for Survival. Day and Morland together hatched the idea for an article on the H-bomb. "I was impressed with the intensity of his interest in trying to figure out the dynamics of the nuclear-weapons program," Day said of Morland. "He felt you couldn't understand nuclear weapons until you understood how they were made. He had done all the reading he could and had put together some sketches. I was just fascinated. I said to myself: This is very important."[65]

Morland's article was submitted with the intention of stimulating public debate and understanding of the nuclear weapons industry while showing that the secrecy surrounding the bomb was a sham. Morland explained in his introduction that he had written his article without access to classified materials and that his purpose was to show that nuclear secrecy contributed to a political climate within which the nuclear establishment could conduct business without public scrutiny.

In the process of researching his article in the encyclopedia, magazine articles, textbooks and interviews, Morland realized that anyone could piece together a basic explanation of the workings of the hydrogen bomb. After Morland submitted a draft of his article to the *Progressive*, the editor sent it to several reviewers to check for accuracy. Without the magazine's knowledge or consent, one of the reviewers sent the article to the Department of Energy (DOE) for security screening. Secretary of Energy James Schlesinger took the article to Attorney General Griffin Bell, complaining that it could help foreign nations to build thermonuclear weapons.

Shortly before the deadline for the *Progressive*'s April 1979 issue, the DOE's general counsel called the magazine's editor, warning that unless he withdrew Morland's article, the government would prevent the publication of the entire issue. The DOE offered to rewrite the article to make it suitable for publication, but it would not identify the parts that it considered "secret." After consulting with the *Progressive*'s staff, the magazine's attorney notified the DOE that they intended to publish the article without changes.

On March 9, 1979, Federal Judge Robert Warren issued a temporary restraining order on publication of the article after accepting the government's claim that "national preservation and self-interest permit the retention and classification of government secrets"—but how could information taken from the *Encyclopedia Americana* and a freshman physics textbook be considered government secrets? Again, Judge Warren accepted the government's argument that "its national security interest also permits it to impress classification and censorship upon information originating in the public domain, if when drawn together, such information acquires the character of presenting immediate, direct and irreparable harm to the interests of the United States."[66]

Warren rejected the defendants' reliance on *New York Times v. United States*, declaring that the *Pentagon Papers*, unlike the Morland article, contained only historical material that did not represent an immediate threat to the national security. Warren added, "A final and most vital difference between these two cases is the fact that a specific statute is involved here. The Atomic Energy Act prohibits anyone from communicating, transmitting or disclosing any restricted data to any person 'with reason to believe such data will be utilized to injure the United States or to secure an advantage to any foreign nation.' "[67]

Though he had not bothered to read the article, Warren said he did not want to give the hydrogen bomb to foreign dictators like Idi Amin of Uganda. A few days later, he issued a preliminary injunction barring Morland and the *Progressive* from publishing or otherwise communicating any of the Restricted Data in the article. Warren admitted that his order would "constitute the first instance of prior restraint against a publication in this fashion in the history of this country," would "curtail defendants' First Amendment rights in a drastic and substantial fashion," and would "infringe upon our right to know and be informed as well." Nonetheless, he justified his injunction by declaring, "A mistake in ruling against the United States could pave the way for nuclear annihilation for us all."[68]

Most of the press and the scientific community saw the injunction for what it was. The *New York Times* editorialized, "What the Government really aims to protect is a system of secrecy, which it seeks now to extend to the thought and discussion of scientists and writers outside Government." *In These Times* commented, "The Government's attempt to prohibit publication by the *Progressive* of a story on 'The H-Bomb Secret' has less to do with anxiety over nuclear weapons proliferation than over the proliferation of legitimate information about the nuclear weapons industry among the American people."[69]

During Morland's trial, even the most trivial scientific statements were censored. Not only was the *Encyclopedia Americana* article on the hydrogen bomb treated as secret, but the affidavits by which it was introduced were secret and the court's opinion about these "secrets" was secret. The court insisted that Morland's undergraduate physics textbook be kept secret until he erased his underlining. Morland tried to explain, to no avail, that he had done the underlining as a freshman preparing for an exam.

The affidavits for the government were led by statements from the secretaries of state, defense, and energy, while *all* affidavits for the defense came from physicists, who were unanimous in stating that all the information in Morland's article was readily available from countless unclassified public sources.

In his written opinion imposing the preliminary injunction, Judge Warren predicted, "This case in its present posture will undoubtedly go to the Supreme Court because it does present so starkly the clash between freedom of the press and national security."[70]

Some members of the press feared the outcome of such a legal struggle and advised the *Progressive* to strike a deal that would allow government censors to rewrite the article, but the magazine's editors never doubted that they could win their case. Indeed, the government's position was soon undercut when an ACLU investigator found highly technical H-bomb reports, far more revealing than Morland's amateur article, on the open shelves of the public library at Los Alamos Scientific Laboratory. The government tried to claim that the reports must have been declassified by mistake, and the Department of Energy promptly classified them and closed the library. Many in the Justice Department wanted to drop the case at this point, but upon the advice of the intelligence agencies, Attorney General Griffin Bell concluded, "The public interest and the Atomic Energy Act require that we do our best."[71]

By the time the case reached the appeals court in Chicago, the government was claiming that "technical" information, unlike political expression, was not protected by the First Amendment. Such extreme arguments had the appearance of desperation, and the editors and publishers at the *Progressive* began to suspect that the government would try to drop the case, declare the issue "moot" and thus avoid a formal ruling that might invalidate the secrecy provisions of the Atomic Energy Act.

Indeed, the rationale for Judge Warren's injunction continued to unravel as other publications were discovered that contained the same information found in Morland's article. A "nuclear hobbyist" named Charles Hansen soon organized a nationwide "H-Bomb Design Contest," with the winning entry defined as the first design to be classified secret by the DOE. Hansen also wrote a lengthy letter to Senator Charles Percy (R-Ill.) in which he summarized the technical data from Morland's article and other sources. On September 16, 1979, Hansen's letter was published in a Madison, Wisconsin, newspaper. The next day the Justice Department announced that it would seek dismissal of its case against the *Progressive*, and the appeals court vacated Judge Warren's injunction. Morland's original article was then published without alteration in the November 1979 issue of the *Progressive*.

From the beginning, the attorneys for the *Progressive* had considered their case to be a strong one, which, if taken to the Supreme Court, would demonstrate that the secrecy provisions of the Atomic Energy Act were unconstitutional. After Judge Warren's injunction was vacated, the *Progressive* asked the court to open the records of the case to the public, since they had been censored throughout the trial. Unfortunately, the Justice Department immediately moved to declare the case "moot," maintaining the trial's secrecy and leaving no formal legal judgement on the constitutionality of the government's prior restraint against the *Progressive* or of the Atomic Energy Act upon which it acted.

Thus, *United States v. Progressive* produced a tainted victory. The press overcame a government-imposed prior restraint, just as it had in *New York Times v. United States*; however, because the case was legally considered moot, no precedent emerged to prevent similar acts of government control of the press.

WARNING: POLITICAL PROPAGANDA MAY BE DANGEROUS TO YOUR HEALTH, 1983

The willingness of motion-picture producers and distributors to impose labels and ratings on the content of their films is often attributed to the industry's fear of even heavier regulation by the federal government. Yet many moviegoers are unaware that the government already does just that to foreign films shown in this country.

Through the use of the Foreign Agents Registration Act of 1938 (FARA), the government has imposed a chilling system of labeling upon any foreign documentary films considered to be "political propaganda" by the Department of Justice. The original thrust of the FARA was against seditious or revolutionary expression, but by the time of the Reagan administration, the FARA was being applied arbitrarily against any political advocacy that contradicted administration policy.

In July 1982, the National Film Board of Canada (NFBC) submitted to the Department of Justice a list of the films it had distributed in the United States during the first half of 1982, as required by the FARA. The Department of Justice promptly requested review copies of five of those films, and on January 13, 1983, it ordered that three of the films be declared "political propaganda," thus invoking the FARA's other requirements.

One of the films, *If You Love This Planet*, subsequently won the Academy Award for Best Short Documentary of 1982. That film included brief footage from a World War II–era Defense Department movie starring Ronald Reagan, but it featured an antinuclear weapons speech by Dr. Helen Caldicott, a leader of the nuclear-freeze movement and President of Physicians for Social Responsibility. In a later interview, Caldicott said, "It was a routine speech I gave two years ago in New York. Perhaps it's the first time they've seen me give a speech."[72]

Columnist Mary McGrory suggested that it was not Caldicott's verbal opposition to nuclear weapons but her "call to action" that roused the ire of the Reagan administration. "She urges the people of Plattsburgh . . . to take their babies to Washington and plant them on the desks of hawks," wrote McGrory. " 'Set your naked toddlers loose in the Senate chamber,' she abjures them in her ringing Australian tones."[73]

Another of the targeted films, *Acid Rain: Requiem or Recovery*, had won the award of excellence from the American Society of Foresters as well as broad critical acclaim. It had already been circulated in the United States for nine months before the Justice Department decision was publicly announced, and environmental groups charged that the department's action was a deliberate attempt to retard public understanding of the problem of acid rain.

The third film was *Acid from Heaven*, another documentary on acid rain. Robert Rose, a Washington spokesman for the National Clean Air

Coalition, said, "The chilling effect is obvious. This is the criminal division of the Justice Department. The film police—I guess that's what you'd call them—and the effect will be to deny American voters one of the few opportunities to learn about acid rain and make an informed judgement." Rose charged that the decision to require a propaganda label on the acid rain films was politically motivated. "The Reagan administration has a conscious policy to retard public understanding of acid rain and the need to control acid rain," he said. "If this is a part of that policy, it goes to the heart of a fundamental American value—the right of the people to know about the issues that affect their lives."[74]

All three films had received critical praise and public attention, but the U.S. government was unwilling to allow them to be shown without a firm and official warning to the American moviegoer each time the films were shown. The Justice Department's letter to the NFBC insisted that the labels identifying the films as "political propaganda should be . . . placed at the beginning as a film (leader) and projected long enough to permit audiences to read it." The letter also said that the NFBC was required to provide the Department of Justice with the names of all major distributors of the films and a list of all specific groups and theaters that asked to show the film. [75]

Canadian Environment Minister John Roberts said, "It sounds like something you would expect from the Soviet Union, not the United States. This action is an extraordinary interference with freedom of speech"; William Litwack, head of distribution for NFBC, characterized it as "regrettable, insulting, and shameful."[76] The ACLU called the action "blatantly unconstitutional" and said it would bring suit on behalf of the distributors; and Mitchell Block, president of Direct Cinema Company, the sole distributor of *If You Love This Planet*, called the government's action "scary" and "chilling," adding, "I wish they had just called it pornography. Then we could distribute it in plain brown wrappers."[77]

Thomas DeCair, the principal spokesman for the Department of Justice, defended the action in a letter to selected members of Congress and the media. "Contrary to the uninformed hysteria which has developed in some quarters," wrote DeCair, "the Justice Department is not censoring any film in this country. Nor is it trying to curtail the dissemination of any movie. Nor does it seek to intimidate anyone who watches a movie." DeCair insisted that the department was doing something more analagous to "truth in packaging," and he pointed out that twenty-four other films had been classified as foreign political propaganda during the Reagan administration. Only films that sought to influence public opinion, said DeCair, were subject to the statute.[78]

After the Canadian government unsuccessfully requested a reversal of the Justice Department's decision, an NFBC spokesman complained of the chilling effect it would have on the film's distribution. The NFBC pointed out that it had felt the need to withdraw a 1974 film from U.S. distribution after the Nixon administration had classified it as political propaganda.

Editorial opinion in the American press was highly critical. The *New York Times* rejected the Justice Department's attempt to downplay the ruckus as routine and procedural. "All this is no 'procedural matter.' It's official action to debase the films," said the *Times*. "There is nothing surreptitious about the Canadian films and implying otherwise is a dumb affront. As Charles Wick, director of the U.S. Information Agency remarked, 'I don't think it's a credible decision.' "[79]

New York Times columnist Anthony Lewis wrote, "How H. L. Mencken would have loved the Justice Department's order that two Canadian films on acid rain and one on nuclear war be labeled foreign 'political propaganda.' The booboisie at work again, he would have said." Lewis concluded, "[T]here is more to the film affair than philistine ignorance. It reflects a general and dangerous characteristic of the Reagan Administration: a fear of open debate and information, a fear of freedom."[80]

Columnist Mary McGrory saw a clear political motive behind the Reagan administration's action against the films. "Justice Department wizards figured out that President Reagan's principal political problems are the scandal at the EPA and the nuclear freeze movement and reasoned from that that the thing to do was to keep quiet about them," wrote McGrory. "So they have said that it is un-American to be against nuclear war and acid rain. It's an odd message at this time, but Reagan is letting it stand."[81]

Congressional reaction was also negative. Senator Edward Kennedy (D-Mass.), after announcing that he would show the films to all his colleagues on the Judiciary Committee, declared, "It is one thing for the right wing to say 'Let Reagan be Reagan.' But it is a very different thing for them to say 'Let Reagan be Orwell.' " Kennedy said he wanted Attorney General William French Smith to appear before his committee "to explain this inexcusable action."[82]

Even fellow Republican Representative Jim Leach of Iowa urged

President Reagan "to reverse this childish decision without delay." Leach said, "It may be too extreme to label this minor league act of censorship a harbinger of McCarthyism, but it sends a chilling message to those Americans deeply concerned about environmental issues in general and about the ultimate environmental issue—the survival of the planet."[83]

On March 18, 1983, Representative Don Edwards (D-Calif.) convened hearings on the film controversy before his Subcommittee on Civil and Constitutional Rights. Edwards began by stating, "In this case, the subject of the films and the timing of the Department's decision raised serious questions about the motives of the administration and the use of the Foreign Agents Registration Act to chill debate on some of the most important political issues of this decade."[84]

Chairman Edwards asked Joseph Clarkson, chief of the Justice Department's Registration Unit, why he singled out the nuclear freeze and acid rain films. "It was . . . because we have an idea of what issues are important," answered Clarkson. "We know that nuclear disarmament is an issue. We know that acid rain is an issue and we selected the films based on their titles."[85]

Chairman Edwards noted that the Reagan administration had been "very political" in its treatment of the nuclear freeze movement. "The President has said there were KGB connections within that movement," remarked Edwards, "and the FBI jumped in and said, yes, the President is correct. Then this surfaces. So you can understand the political implications of it."[86]

D. Lowell Jensen of the Justice Department's Criminal Division insisted that when a film came before his unit, it was examined objectively "to see whether or not it comes within the statutory definition of political propaganda . . . not whether it has any implications in terms of the position taken or the Government that is making that statement."[87]

Chairman Edwards asked, "[D]o you really think that we ought to have a law that . . . would require films like this to be labeled and to file reports—isn't it paternalistic? . . . Don't you think that is a pretty chilling thing to have to require? If I were a timid distributor and I knew that my name was going to go to the Justice Department and be put on some list . . . I wouldn't accept the film from the Canadians." Mr. Jensen said he was unaware of such problems in connection with his department's action.[88]

Representative Robert Kastenmeier (D-Wis.), who had already introduced a bill to eliminate the government's authority to classify films and other materials as propaganda, said, "There must be thousands, tens of thousands of film titles deriving within the United States that must contravene American policy in many respects, and somehow we live with that. . . . We produce . . . thousands of domestic films which take on American policy of any administration . . . but under the First Amendment, we tolerate that. . . . I think the people in this country are able to make that judgement for themselves."[89]

The subcommittee also heard testimony from Susan Shaffer, staff counsel for the ACLU. Shaffer had served as counsel to the plaintiffs in *Block v. Smith*, which challenged the application of the FARA to the three Canadian films. She told the subcommittee that the government did not need to inform the American people of what is true and what is suspect about the books they read or the films they see. "The American public is perfectly well able to determine for itself what it believes and what it doesn't," said Shaffer, "and it isn't any more likely to be hoodwinked by acid rain films produced in Canada than by acid rain films produced in the United States."[90]

The ACLU was particularly concerned that, under the FARA, the government maintains the names of all groups or persons distributing or screening "propaganda" films and the dates and estimated attendance at any screening. "The Government will have at its disposal a list of all groups in the country who are distributing and exhibiting films dealing with issues such as nuclear disarmament which have been of great political concern to this administration," said Shaffer. "The groups which take a different political view of these issues than does the administration are particularly apt to be chilled by knowing that the Government is following their activities so closely."[91]

The House subcommittee hearing led to several unsuccessful legislative attempts during the 1980s to amend the FARA by narrowing the definitions of "foreign agent" and "propaganda." The furor over the Canadian films also led to several lawsuits that challenged the FARA and sought to prevent the Justice Department from enforcing the registration, labeling and reporting requirements of the act. In 1983 California State Senator Barry Keene asked the U.S. district court in Sacramento for a preliminary injunction against continuation of the act's labeling requirements, claiming that they prevented him from obtaining "the best information available on matters of public importance, as a prelude to free and open debate." The suit, *Keene v. Smith*, asserted that distributors, concerned about being labeled disseminators of foreign propaganda, would be discouraged from offering such films.

In September 1983, District Judge Raul Ramirez granted the preliminary injunction, stating, "This court harbors some doubt about the power of Congress to select a term which has a widely understood negative connotation and designate it as a term of art theoretically having no negative connotation." Judge Ramirez found that the labeling requirements effectively prevented unfettered distribution of films and abridged the free speech rights of distributors without protecting any significant public interest. Because the labeling process involves content-based evaluation of the films and threatens First Amendment rights, Ramirez concluded that there was sufficient grounds to enjoin the Justice Department from characterizing the films as "political propaganda."[92]

At about the same time, the ACLU filed a similar suit, *Block v. Smith*, in U.S. district court in Washington, D.C., arguing that the review and disclosure requirements of the act violated the First Amendment. The ACLU, representing the distributor of *If You Love This Planet* and five other plaintiffs, said a label telling the viewer that the government disagrees with the content of a film brands it as false and misleading and discourages people from seeing it. The district court rendered summary judgement for the government, and the case was appealed to the U.S. court of appeals in the District of Columbia as *Block v. Meese*. The case was argued before conservative Judge Antonin Scalia, soon to join the U.S. Supreme Court.

In an extraordinary opinion, Judge Scalia not only rejected the ACLU's First Amendment claims, but declared that any attempt to prohibit the imposition of the "political propaganda" label on films would be an inappropriate restraint on the *government*'s speech. "The short of the matter," said Scalia, "is that control of government expression (which would always seem to fall in the category of political expression, the most protected form of speech) is no more practicable, and no more appealing, than control of political expression by anyone else." Scalia showed little interest in the negative effect that the government's labeling would have on filmmakers. "If the first amendment considers speakers to be so timid, or important ideas to be so fragile, that they are overwhelmed by knowledge of government disagreement, then it is hard to understand why official government *action*, which speaks infinitely louder than words, does not constantly disrupt the first amendment 'marketplace,' " said Scalia. "It cannot be . . . that the only subjects off-limits to the government are those as to which there is less than a substantial unanimity among the people—thus permitting official positions on war heroism and motherhood, but excluding nuclear disarmament and acid rain."[93]

This same argument was used when the Supreme Court heard *Meese v. Keene*, the government's appeal of *Keene v. Smith*. Though the Court leaned on much of Scalia's argument, it did not come from Scalia himself, who, though now a justice on the Supreme Court, did not participate in the decision. The Court's opinion in *Meese v. Keene*, delivered by Justice Stevens, claimed that the labeling requirements of the FARA actually enhanced First Amendment values by telling the public more about the films than they would otherwise have known. "Ironically, it is the injunction entered by the District Court that withholds information from the public," wrote Stevens. "The suppressed information is the fact that the films fall within the category of materials that Congress has judged to be 'political propaganda.' "[94]

Though acknowledging that the viewing public might regard a film so labeled as "suspect," the Court concluded that this was not the intention of the statute. "As judges it is our duty to construe legislation as it is written, not as it might be read by a layman."[95]

Justice Blackmun's dissent, joined by Justices Brennan and Marshall, stated,

> The Court's decision rests upon its conclusion that the term "political propaganda" is neutral and without negative connotation. It reaches this conclusion by limiting its examination to the statutory definition of the term and by ignoring the realities of public reaction to the designation. But even given that confined view of its inquiry, it is difficult to understand how a statutory categorization which includes communication that "instigates . . . civil riot . . . or the overthrow of . . . government . . . by any means invoking the use of force or violence," can be regarded as wholly neutral.[96]

Blackmun concluded, "By ignoring the practical effects of the Act's classification scheme, the Court unfortunately permits Congress to accomplish by indirect means what it could not impose directly—a restriction of appellee's political speech."[97]

The Court's decision in *Keene* was widely criticized by legal scholars. An article published in the *Oregon Law Review* declared,

> [T]he central premise in *Keene* is untenable. Contrary to the Court's
> labored attempt to cleanse the Foreign Agents Registration Act by
> declaring the term "political propaganda" neutral, the legislative
> history of the Act, the present cultural climate, and the empirical
> evidence concerning the term "propaganda" all overwhelmingly ex-
> pose the label as a pejorative term selected to negatively influence
> viewers and perhaps dissuade them from viewing the film at all.[98]

Congress had been aware of the problems with the FARA for some
time. A 1977 Congressional Research Service report had recognized
that "to accomplish the removal of [the] stigma" in the act's labeling
requirements it would be necessary to change the statute's language.
It recommended changing the term "propaganda" to "promotional
material" in order to "eliminate pejorative connotations." Indeed, in
the aftermath of *Keene,* the Justice Department indicated its willingness
to replace "political propaganda" with "a more neutral term like political 'advocacy' or 'information.' "[99]

Recognizing congressional discomfort with the FARA and wishing to
avoid further public embarrassment, the Justice Department has, since
the *Keene* decision, applied the FARA selectively, with few applications
to the media. Perhaps because of the FARA's relative inactivity, Congress has yet to enact any of the recommended changes in the act. A
number of bills have been proposed, but all have languished in committee.

During the 1990s, legislators have instead attempted to broaden the
application of the statute to require former U.S. government officials,
who represent foreign governments, to register more promptly and
fully as "foreign agents." Thus, though the statute still contains the
seeds of First Amendment conflict, concerns about government insid-
ers representing foreign interests have, for the time being, led the
application of the FARA away from politically manipulated labeling of
foreign films. Nonetheless, the FARA, the product of legislatures facing
a world war, retains its pejorative language and sensibility.

Helen Caldicott, whose antinuclear speech in *If You Love This Planet*
caused the labeling of that film, recently recalled the flap.

> It happened just before my National Press Club address, so the spot-
> light inappropriately turned on me. It gave the issue a lot of noto-
> riety and may have even helped the film win an academy award. But
> the "propaganda" label definitely chilled distribution in the United

States. It was shown all over Canada, but rarely seen here. Unfortunately, that negative label is still attached to the movie, chilling the distribution enormously. What a terrible thing.[100]

THE TOBACCO WARS, 1994

Of all the media, television is the most conservative and corporate-controlled. The television industry's inclination toward quiet self-censorship has masked the frequent prior restraint of programming exercised by network executives to accommodate corporate power. A recent case in point was the shocking ability of the tobacco industry to control television news coverage.

Television's tobacco wars began to heat up in early 1994 when the American Broadcasting Company (ABC) television news show *Day One* aired investigative reports that accused the tobacco industry of manipulating nicotine in cigarettes to cause addiction. A whistleblower from within the industry appeared on camera, with face blacked out, to describe the practice of fortifying cigarettes with nicotine. Because the Federal Drug Administration (FDA) was conducting its own investigation to determine whether nicotine should be controlled like other drugs, the *Day One* story was an important revelation. It also provided ammunition to the growing number of lawyers who were seeking damages for tobacco-related health problems.

On March 24, 1994, tobacco giant Philip Morris launched a $10 billion libel suit against Capital Cities/ABC Inc. In a suit filed in Richmond, Virginia, Philip Morris charged ABC and two of its journalists with defamation for the February 28 and March 7 reports aired on *Day One*. The suit claimed, "Philip Morris does not in any way shape or form spike its cigarettes with nicotine. These allegations are not true and ABC knows that they are not true." An ABC News spokesman said the network was reviewing the lawsuit but that "ABC News stands by its reporting on this issue." The fact that Philip Morris chose to sue when the *Day One* reports had focused primarily on its chief rival, the R. J. Reynolds Tobacco Company, was somewhat ironic, but legal experts regarded the lawsuit as a shrewdly calculated public relations move designed to head off the prospect of FDA regulation of the entire industry.[101]

On April 14, 1994, just five weeks after the ABC-TV report, seven tobacco executives were summoned before a congressional subcommittee where they were asked about the *Day One* allegations. Like a disciplined chorus, the executives denied that nicotine was addictive and claimed that their companies had never spiked their cigarettes with nicotine.

As ABC prepared to fight the Philip Morris suit, the network's journalists acquired damning new information about the tobacco industry, including documents leaked from the archives of the tobacco giant, Brown and Williamson. When ABC reporters took this spectacular information to their in-house lawyers and proposed a new investigative report, however, they were told to scuttle the story.

New York Times reporter Philip Hilts was shocked: the Brown and Williamson documents could be the single most important pieces of paper on the issue of tobacco versus the public health. The documents included information from the company's internal files, including their views on nicotine addiction, the hazards of cigarettes and much more.

Crip Douglas, a lawyer and antitobacco activist who had been interviewed in the *Day One* report, told Daniel Schorr on Public television's *Frontline* that when the Brown and Williamson documents were brought to the attention of ABC's lawyers, they "freaked out." The lawyers seized not only the originals, but the copies of all the documents from the reporters. They even seized the reporters' hard drives from their computers, and they prohibited them from pursuing the story.[102]

On *Frontline*, veteran television reporter Daniel Schorr asked ABC News executive vice president Paul Friedman why he would not run what was potentially a major scoop on a matter of great importance to public health. Friedman responded testily that the journalists had consulted with ABC's lawyers and followed their advice.

Within a few months, the *New York Times* highlighted the distinction between newspaper and television journalism by publishing detailed stories based on some of the same Brown and Williamson documents that ABC-TV had suppressed. *Times* reporter Hilts said that his paper's lawyers had expressed few concerns. "They said almost nothing. The story was solid. . . . In fact, all the way along, the lawyers at the *Times* were very supportive. They wanted to see the stories in the paper."[103]

There were more tobacco revelations to come. On May 12, 1994, 4,000 pages of Brown and Williamson documents arrived unexpectedly at the office of Professor Stanton Glantz at the University of California in San Francisco. Glantz made this scientific treasure available to researchers through the university library until Brown and Williamson discovered them, claimed that they had been stolen and sued for their return. University lawyers responded as had the *Times* lawyers, saying the university was fulfilling its mission to bring truth to the people and to provide scholarly research. The lawyers promised to defend Glantz, and they did.

In California Superior Court, university attorney Chris Patty argued that because they were publishing the documents over the World Wide Web, the university was functioning like a newspaper and had the same protections afforded to newspapers and other media outlets. The California court agreed, and the university continued to scan the 4,000 pages of documents onto its World Wide Web site.

Paul Friedman of ABC News was asked why ABC did not take the position of the *New York Times* and the University of California—that publication of the documents was clearly protected by the First Amendment. Once more, he said ABC simply had gotten different advice from their lawyers, and they had accepted that advice.

Meanwhile, ABC was preparing a strong defense against the $10 billion libel suit filed over the original *Day One* report. They had scheduled Dr. C. Everett Koop, former U.S. surgeon general, as their leadoff witness. They even tested their case before two mock juries in Raleigh, North Carolina, a tobacco town like Richmond, Virginia, where the real trial was to be held. ABC assembled two groups of local people to serve as mock juries to test their case. These juries heard arguments for Philip Morris and for ABC, and the proceedings were videotaped. The mock trials were held after Philip Morris had done its discovery (the legal requirement that both sides in a trial share the evidence they would submit in court) of ABC documents but before ABC had had a chance to do the same, meaning that Philip Morris's best case was matched against ABC's worst case. Nonetheless, the results were very encouraging for ABC, with eleven of the fourteen jurors involved siding with ABC. As the trial date approached, ABC was prepared to request a dismissal of the case on the grounds that the documents in their possession "eliminated any factual dispute as to whether Philip Morris adds 'significant amounts of extraneous nicotine' " to their cigarettes.

Suddenly, however, without warning, ABC reversed course. On August 21, 1995, ABC used its evening news show to announce,

The $10 billion law suit filed against ABC News by Philip Morris and R. J. Reynolds was settled this evening with a statement. ABC News agreed that we should not have reported that Philip Morris and R. J. Reynolds add significant amounts of nicotine from outside sources. That was a mistake that was not deliberate on the part of ABC, but for which we accept responsibility and which requires correction. We apologize to our audience, Philip Morris, and Reynolds.[104]

That same night, ABC also aired the announcement in prime time during halftime on *Monday Night Football*.

Philip Morris immediately ran full-page ads in papers around the country under the blazing headline: "APOLOGY ACCEPTED." The ads showed the full text of the ABC apology and concluded with the brash commentary: "As for the group of people who eagerly embraced the 'spiking' allegation to serve their ongoing crusade against the tobacco industry—we stand ready to accept their apologies as well."[105]

John Martin, the correspondent for the *Day One* story, and Walt Boganich, his producer, refused to sign the settlement agreement, and other journalists throughout the media were outraged. Legal experts were confounded. "The evidence is overwhelming that ABC could have successfully defended this case," said John P. Coale, one of a consortium of lawyers mounting a class action suit against the tobacco companies. "This is a corporate sellout, pure and simple."[106]

Richard A. Daynard, a law school professor and chairman of the Tobacco Products Liability Project, said, "This is a triumph of bottom-line thinking over news judgement. Philip Morris has bullied a major television network into apologizing for what was essentially a true story."[107]

When asked why ABC had backed down when they seemed to have the strongest legal position, Paul Friedman rejected the use of the words "backed down." It was the policy of ABC News to apologize when they make a mistake, said Friedman.

ABC's explanation satisfied no one in the legal or journalistic professions. Anti-tobacco lawyer Ron Motley said that ABC was confident that they would prevail eventually, four or five years down the line, in the U.S. Supreme Court. The overriding factor, he said, was the immediacy of the takeover of ABC by Disney/Cap Cities. Motley was referring to the fact that just three weeks before the settlement of the lawsuit, Capitol Cities/ABC Inc. and Disney had announced their $19 billion merger. On that day, Capitol Cities/ABC chairman Thomas Murphy, who himself was to make $25 million on the deal, was asked if the pending lawsuit would affect the merger. He reportedly said that the problem would be taken care of and resolved. Three weeks later, ABC abjectly settled.

ABC executives sought to dispel speculation that the settlement was tied to the Disney deal, claiming that chairman Thomas Murphy had been uneasy about the lawsuit even before Disney had come into the picture. When Daniel Schorr asked ABC's Paul Friedman about the clear public perception of a connection between ABC's corporate ownership picture and the decision to rein in their tobacco investigation and apologize to Philip Morris, Friedman said there was no evidence of a linkage between corporate mergers and editorial policy. The impression of television newsrooms cowering before corporate power was soon to be strengthened by similar events taking place at ABC's rival network, CBS.

The popular CBS news show *60 Minutes* was putting together a Mike Wallace interview with the most important whistleblower from inside the tobacco industry, the former head of research for the Brown and Williamson tobacco company, Dr. Jeffrey Wigand. Wigand, who had devastating things to say about his former employer, was a confidential source in a developing story that *60 Minutes* producer Llowell Bergman regarded as a blockbuster. But just a few weeks after the ABC settlement, as he worked to finalize the Wigand story, Bergman was summoned to an emergency meeting at CBS corporate headquarters in Blackrock, the building on New York's 52nd Street which houses the corporation's executives and attorneys. In his thirteen years with CBS, Bergman had never been there, but this would be just the first of several meetings with his corporate bosses about the Wigand interview.

Ellen Kaden, CBS's chief corporate counsel, told Bergman that he and Mike Wallace may have been guilty of "tortious interference" by inducing Wigand to break his confidentiality agreement with Brown and Williamson. Neither Bergman nor Wallace had ever heard of tortious interference, and the notion that the press might be liable for going after an interview seemed bizarre. But Kaden, a former corporate litigator with no background in First Amendment issues, insisted that pursuing Wigand could expose CBS to legal risks in the billions of dollars. The situation was complicated, she said, by the fact that Wigand had been paid as a consultant on a previous story and that CBS had agreed to pay for any libel costs that might result from the current interview.

Bergman saw it differently. "A new rule had been created, a rule that said, or at least appeared to say, that there was a whole class of people, people who potentially had very important information, from a journalism point of view, from a public point of view, who couldn't be talked to."[108]

Prominent media lawyers could recall no case in which tortious interference had been argued successfully against a news organization. Bruce W. Sanford, an experienced media lawyer, called it "a truly eccentric argument" that was being used to "do end runs around existing First Amendment law."[109]

Even after the first meeting at Blackrock, Bergman went to Louisville, Kentucky, to talk to Wigand, but, as Mike Wallace recalls, "He got a call from the lawyers here in New York saying, 'Get out of Wigand's house. You are to do no more reporting on this. None.' "[110]

The first public suggestion that CBS had caved in to the tobacco industry came on October 17, 1995, when Don Hewitt, the always pugnacious executive producer of *60 Minutes*, meekly told the National Press Club in Washington,

> We have a story that we think is solid. We don't think anybody could ever sue us for libel. There are some twists and turns, and if you get in front of a jury in some states where the people on that jury are all related to people who work in tobacco companies, look out. That's a $15 billion gun pointed at your head. We may opt to get out of the line of fire. That doesn't make me proud, but it's not my money.[111]

The CBS lawyers never considered the First Amendment standard established in such U.S. Supreme Court cases as *New York Times v. United States* (1971), in which the *Times*'s general counsel, James Goodale, successfully argued for the publication of the Top Secret *Pentagon Papers*. In that case, the Court concluded that the *Pentagon Papers* were a historical study of American involvement in Vietnam and that their publication represented no threat to national security. When asked to compare the CBS situation with the *Pentagon Papers* case, Goodale said he saw a strong similarity. He pointed out that if the information in question is in the public interest, then the Constitution says it ought to be published. "If it's information that informs the public," said Goodale, "the First Amendment protects the publication of that type of information."[112]

CBS executives had no interest in First Amendment arguments. According to Mike Wallace, at the first meeting with Bergman, Ellen

Kaden mentioned ABC's apology and settlement of the $10 billion Philip Morris suit and said it would make things more difficult for CBS. Bergman recalls the president of ABC's news division telling him that the company would not risk its assets on this story.[113]

So the Wigand interview was scrapped. On November 12, 1995, Mike Wallace broke new journalistic ground by telling 21 million television viewers what he *could not* tell them. He acknowledged that he was gagging his own whistleblower, on orders from above. The revised version of the show contained only a brief segment of the interview with Wigand, whose identity was not revealed. Wigand's face did not appear on camera and his voice was disguised. In a "personal note" at the conclusion of the interview, Wallace said that the *60 Minutes* staff had been "dismayed that the management of CBS had seen fit to give in to perceived threats of legal action."[114]

Wallace later admitted that he had never before encountered corporate censorship quite like this. "Never before. Never before. From time to time, corporations will make their displeasure known to honchos at CBS News, but we're always protected from it."[115]

Daniel Schorr asked a subdued and reflective Mike Wallace how he had handled the frustration of censorship and the challenge to his reputation. Wallace said he finally decided not to throw the baby out with the bath water, that is, not to throw the story away by leaving CBS. He felt that if he could stay inside CBS, he might, little by little, persuade Blackrock to loosen their corporate control over CBS News. Wallace said that the capitulation of ABC News in the Philip Morris suit had changed the way in which CBS's lawyers perceived the *60 Minutes* interview. "The ABC lawsuit did not chill us as journalists from doing the story," said Wallace. "It did chill the lawyers, who with due diligence had to say, 'We don't want to, in effect, risk putting the company out of business.' "[116]

According to Eric Ober, president of CBS News, there were reasons other than the fear of tortious interference for scrapping the original interview. "We looked at the story very carefully," Ober said. "A contract is a contract. I felt for a number of reasons, both editorially and legally, that changes had to be made in the piece."[117]

A *New York Times* editorial attacked CBS for suppressing the *60 Minutes* interview, calling it an "act of self-censorship" that "sends a chilling message to journalists investigating industry practices everywhere." In rejecting the use of tortious interference to muzzle the media, the *Times* said that CBS's response to a feared suit was "exactly wrong." The *Times* noted that New York–based news organizations often face legal challenges in unfriendly state courts but they nonetheless have an obligation "to defend the journalistic franchise rather than cave in at the prospect of litigation." The most troubling part of the CBS cave-in, said the *Times*, was that the decision "was made not by news executives but by corporate officers who may have their minds on money rather than public service these days."[118]

In noting that a $5.4 billion deal between CBS and the Westinghouse Corporation was about to be approved, the *Times* article declared that some of the executives who helped kill the *60 Minutes* interview, including the general counsel, stood to gain millions of dollars in stock options and other payments once the deal was approved. "CBS and its general counsel insist that no one acted out of personal monetary interest," stated the *Times*, "but the network's action shows that media companies in play lose their journalistic aggressiveness when they let lawyers and corporate executives make decisions that ought to be the province of news executives."[119]

Like ABC, CBS had censored a tobacco story at the very moment that the network was changing hands. While CBS was dealing with the threat of a multibillion dollar lawsuit, the sale of the company to the Westinghouse Corporation was in progress. Just four days after the *60 Minutes* fiasco, the sale of CBS to Westinghouse was announced. As a result of the sale, news president Alan Ober received almost a million and a half dollars in stock options, and chief counsel Ellen Kaden received more than a million dollars in stock options as well as $3.7 million from a salary buyout and other benefits.[120]

Times columnist Frank Rich declared that the *60 Minutes* retreat was "only the latest and most visible example of a new corporate caution that is roiling broadcast news—the main source of news for most Americans." He described how ABC was betrothed to Disney as it settled its lawsuit with Philip Morris and CBS was about to merge with Westinghouse as it capitulated to Brown and Williamson. With tongue in cheek, Rich said,

The timing of ABC's and CBS's cave-ins is all, apparently, just an incredible coincidence. We're also supposed to believe it's a coincidence that ABC killed another documentary about the tobacco industry . . . shortly after Philip Morris filed its suit against "Day One." And CBS says it's yet another coincidence that its Los Angeles affiliate abruptly yanked an anti-smoking commercial last week just as "60 Minutes" took its fall. At what point do all these innocent coincidences become a chilling pattern?[121]

Mike Wallace told *Frontline*'s Daniel Schorr that it was reasonable to speculate that if the Westinghouse people were planning to buy CBS, they would not want to buy a multibillion dollar lawsuit along with it. He also said that there were concerns about Ellen Kaden's apparent conflict of interest, since she was running the merger negotiations. Journalists at CBS thought she should recuse herself from handling the *60 Minutes* story. She did not.

Martin Franks, senior vice president of CBS, said, "I categorically reject any notion that there are people here who are somehow manipulating the decisions of the corporation for their own personal gain." Still, the network had come to be a bottom-line organization under the ten years of leadership by chairman Lawrence Tisch. For Tisch, CBS was a relatively minor holding among his many corporate assets. These included the Bullova Watch Company, a subsidiary of the huge Lowes Corporation, which also controlled the Lorillard Tobacco Company. The Tisch family's tobacco interests, among them popular brands like Newport, provided between 60 and 70 percent of their total profits. Even as Tisch was selling CBS, his tobacco company was buying six new cigarette brands from Brown and Williamson, Jeffrey Wigand's former employer. None of this was known at the time by CBS journalists.

According to Walter Cronkite, "Mr. Tisch, for all his other virtues, obviously came to CBS and saw it as just another firm . . . in which profit was to be maximized and value increased toward a future sale. That was his entire approach to CBS. And we saw the results of that in a vast deterioration of programming in the news department."[122]

The most personal image of Lawrence Tisch's conflict of interest with the tobacco industry came when his son, Andrew H. Tisch, chairman and chief executive officer of Lorillard Tobacco Company, appeared with the other tobacco executives before a congressional subcommittee investigating television's allegations of nicotine manipulation. Andrew Tisch, like all the other assembled executives, swore under oath that tobacco companies were doing nothing wrong and that cigarettes represented no threat to the public health.

Llowell Bergman, producer of *60 Minutes*, concluded, "I think that we were deceived and lied to. I think that more is going on here than we even know now, unfortunately."[123]

The information suppressed by CBS lawyers was eventually re-vealed—by the *Wall Street Journal*. On January 26, 1996, using secret testimony from Wigand, the *Journal* broke the story that *60 Minutes* could not air. Only then did CBS feel bold enough to run their own interview with Wigand. Wigand, whose personal and professional life had been destroyed by his battle with the tobacco industry, later told Daniel Schorr that the power of corporate America had been dem-onstrated in the capitulation of ABC and CBS.[124]

Jane Kirtley, executive director of the Reporters Committee for Free-dom of the Press, stated in an article for the *New York Times*, "Never mind what happens to CBS, NBC and CNN. What about the small news organizations all over the country? When the big guys won't fight these battles against the likes of the tobacco company, how can the small news organizations stand up to its [sic] local equivalent, or even more unthinkable, take on the tobacco industry?"[125]

Walter Cronkite was terribly disappointed at the behavior of his for-mer network. "It seems to me that it sent a terrible message out to all broadcasters across the nation, perhaps around the world," he told *Frontline*. "Here is *60 Minutes,* the top program CBS has had on the air for almost 20 years. . . . And the management of *60 Minutes* have the power there, quite clearly, to say, 'I'm sorry, we're doing this [story] because we must do it. This is a journalistic imperative. . . . We've got to take whatever the legal chances are on it.' Well, they didn't. They felt it was necessary to buckle under the legal pressures." Cronkite said further, "Journalistic courage takes a lot of forms, and one of the important forms it takes is in the corporate environment. And, unfortunately, there are few people in that corporate environ-ment, virtually none whom I can cite on any network, that have any background of journalistic ethics or journalistic principles or journal-istic responsibility." When asked if he saw any possibility that the tele-vision networks might acquire such principles, Cronkite answered, "I don't see any hint of it on the horizon. Where would you find it?"[126]

When Mike Wallace was asked the same question, he responded, "The hope would be that no matter who owns the network . . . they'll have the courage and the sense of obligation to let the truth be told." When asked whether he had the "confidence" or just "the hope" that this would be the case, Wallace was painfully silent before answering, "The hope."[127]

A series of sensational events in 1997 vindicated the journalists at ABC and CBS, and made the corporate censorship at those networks during 1995 seem even more spineless. On March 20, 1997, in the face of a barrage of tobacco-injury lawsuits, the tobacco giant Liggett Group Inc. agreed to a settlement which would pay plaintiffs 25 percent of the company's pretax earnings for twenty-five years. Under the settlement, Liggett admitted that tobacco is addictive and harmful to health, that the firm manipulated the nicotine content of its cigarettes, and that their marketing targeted teenagers. In the wake of the Liggett settlement, the other tobacco companies, faced with their own bevy of lawsuits, made it known to plaintiffs, state governments and the White House that they would be willing to accept an industrywide settlement.

On June 20, 1997, the tobacco industry announced a tentative deal that would settle forty state lawsuits. Under the proposed agreement, the industry would pay $368.5 billion over twenty-five years, mostly for antismoking campaigns and public health programs. The tobacco companies would also be forced to accept an FDA regulation of nicotine as a drug; more prominent health warnings on cigarettes; disclosure of research on health, toxicity, addiction and drug dependance; a nationwide licensing program with penalties for selling to minors; a cigarette vending machine ban; the elimination of all outdoor billboards and signs; and a host of other programs and prohibitions. The White House, which undertook a detailed review of the proposed deal, said prospects were good for wrestling further concessions from the industry. "They have to have a settlement now," said an administration official. "They've opened Pandora's box. They can't go back to stonewalling and denial."[128]

A FRIGHTENED UNIVERSITY CENSORS CYBERSEX, 1994

In November 1994, Carnegie Mellon University (CMU) began to censor sexually explicit words and images on campus computer bulletin boards originating on the Internet. University officials were concerned that providing access to the bulletin boards could open up the university to prosecution under the state of Pennsylvania's obscenity laws. "[I]t didn't take a lawyer to read those pornography and obscenity laws to know we were really vulnerable," said Erwin Steinberg, vice provost for education. When students complained that CMU was doing the electronic equivalent of burning books, Steinberg said, "Those involved in the decision were also upset. It was a nasty decision."[129]

CMU, located in Pittsburgh, Pennsylvania, is a leader in computer technology. It was one of the first universities to join the Arpanet, the predecessor to the Internet. It was the first university to wire up its dorms, even providing Internet access in some of its bathrooms. The Internet community locates its elite Computer Emergency Response Team, the crack virus police, at Carnegie Mellon—all the more reason why CMU's 1994 attempt to ban sex from its campus computer network sent a chill along the information highway.

In the face of increasing campus pressure, the university eventually agreed to limit the ban to "pornographic" pictures, pending legal advice on the broader text ban. Steinberg said that the lawyers would offer an opinion on whether sexually explicit words would also violate the law. "If they decide they do not make us vulnerable then we will not pull the plug on them," said Steinberg, "and we will set up . . . an all-campus panel to review them. We're not backing down. We're trying to be careful."[130]

Meanwhile, the ban on pictures caused the removal of a number of topics from the "Usenet" newsgroups subscribed to by the university and available on the Internet. In reality, it was not actual pictures that were being censored. It was, to all appearances, an encoded stew of binary gibberish. A single image was represented by pages of incomprehensible keyboard characters. Those wishing to view an image would have to save the half-dozen or so pages of characters on their hard drives, splice the pages together into a single long file and use a special graphics program to see the image on the screen. Even then, such pictures did not contain enough detail to allow them to be printed.

Despite such hurdles, apparently enough students were using the controversial Usenet bulletin boards to cause the university concern. William Ames, vice president for computing services, viewed a few of the bulletin boards that included the words "sex" or "erotica" in their titles and recommended that sixty-six of them be banned. "He told me he looked at five or six of them," said Student Council President DeClan McCullagh. "The university decided to yank the b-boards without looking at them, which is censorship in the worst form. We have obscene books in our library but the university isn't burning them. The university is burning cyberbooks."[131]

Faculty reaction was quick and decisive. In an unusual move, the faculty senate unanimously approved a resolution calling on the administration to reinstall all the banned bulletin boards. The author of the resolution, computer science researcher David Touretzky, said, "I guess my biggest fear is that the university is running the risk of harming academic freedom at other schools because of the publicity surrounding the incident."[132]

Mike Godwin, staff counsel for the Electronic Frontier Foundation, said, "It's like banning Henry Miller from the library. This is a pure academic freedom issue." Godwin wrote to CMU administrators, warning, "[A]s any First Amendment lawyer can tell you, the discussion of sexual matters of any sort is constitutionally protected speech, and thus cannot be prosecuted under any state's laws, much less Pennsylvania's."[133]

The Pittsburgh chapter of the ACLU wrote to CMU President Robert Mehrabian to protest the ban, which it said was based on an incorrect reading of the state obscenity laws. "Your policy sweeps far too broadly," said the letter. "Out of fear that your students may be exposed to a few works that a court might ultimately find unprotected, you have cut off access to a large volume of protected areas and information." While complimenting CMU for its recognition of "the extraordinary potential of network communications to enhance and democratize speech," the letter warned that "if the full potential is to be reached, it is important that leaders like CMU stand strong for free and open access to information and that you resist the urge to censor."[134]

On a campus not known for its activism, a restrained student protest movement arose, claiming that CMU had abrogated its responsibility as a center for free inquiry. "I'm deeply ashamed that Carnegie Mellon capitulated so spinelessly," said one CMU student in a radio call-in debate. "Some lawyer told them they might some day be dragged into court, and they just decided, 'To hell with the First Amendment.' "[135] Presiding over an angry Student Council meeting that condemned the university's ban, council president McCullagh called the ban "the equivalent of closing down a wing of the library."[136]

In addition to demonstrating against the ban, students created an extensive on-line list of relevant readings, including press reports of the controversy, Internet links to copies of key documents and legal texts on censorship, a history of free expression, texts of banned books and references to free speech organizations. The students also provided a lengthy list of procedures for skirting the CMU ban.

It was soon revealed that Carnegie Mellon initiated its cybersex ban only after it learned that a student, Martin Rimm, was preparing to publish a study on sexual material available through computers on and off campus. Ironically, when Rimm informed CMU of the content of his study and the possible legal problems, he brought the university into a situation of vulnerability. After all, virtually every university in the nation provides access to the same Internet content, but they are doing little more than providing hardware and phone lines. They do not control the content that individual students access. CMU officials, however, had been provided with an alleged description of that content and a forewarning that it was illegal in the state *knowingly* to distribute sexually explicit material to anyone under eighteen—as many freshmen are—or to distribute obscenity at all.

"This research report made it impossible for us to say we didn't know anything about it," said vice provost Steinberg. "Obviously we can't be responsible for knowing about everything on the Internet, but if we were ever sued, it would be obvious that we knew about this."[137]

On-line columnist Todd Copilevitz wrote,

> This all seems reasonable, but consider the message it sends. What if another research project reveals that certain file libraries on the Net offer terrorist handbooks, or banned art works? They do. Will the school then remove those from the students' choices? Eventually, will researchers be hesitant to report their findings for fear it will force the school to restrict access? Universities around the country are dealing with the same issue.[138]

Rimm's unlikely "research report," prepared when he was still an undergraduate, would soon cause even more mischief. A sensational cover story based on Rimm's study appeared in the July 3, 1995, issue of *Time* magazine. *Time*'s entire cover was filled with the picture of an eerie, bug-eyed child's face, mouth agape, staring in terror, presumably at a computer screen. Under the picture was a large headline: "CYBERPORN," followed by the statement, "A new study shows how pervasive and wild it really is. Can we protect our kids—and free speech?"

The *Time* article, written by Philip Elmer-DeWitt, began,

> Something about the combination of sex and computers . . . seems to make otherwise worldly-wise adults a little crazy. . . . If you think things are crazy now, though, wait until politicians get hold of a report coming out this week. A research team at Carnegie Mellon University . . . has conducted an exhaustive study of online porn— what's available, who is downloading it, what turns them on—and the findings . . . are sure to pour fuel on an already explosive debate.

That "research team" was, of course, Marty Rimm, who declared in *Time*, "We now know what the consumers of computer porn really look at in the privacy of their own homes."[139]

The *Time* article acknowledged that most of the material on the bulletin boards in question had simply been scanned from print publications, but Elmer-DeWitt insisted that computer porn was different. "You can obtain it in the privacy of your home—without having to walk into a seedy book store or movie house," he wrote. "This is the flip side of Vice President Al Gore's vision of an information superhighway linking every school and library in the land. When kids are plugged in, will they be exposed to the seamiest sides of human sexuality? Will they fall prey to child molesters hanging out in electronic chat rooms?" Elmer-DeWitt concluded, "How the Carnegie Mellon report will affect the delicate political balance on the cyberporn debate is anybody's guess. Conservatives thumbing through it for rhetorical ammunition will find plenty."[140]

Indeed, congressional conservatives were quick to seize upon the Rimm study to justify federal legislation censoring the Internet. Senator Charles Grassley (R-Iowa) was so impressed by the conclusions of "the Carnegie Mellon study" that he had the full text entered into the Congressional Record. On June 26, 1995, he went farther. "Mr. President," began Grassley on the Senate floor, "there is an article from *Time* magazine that I ask unanimous consent to have printed in the Record at the end of my remarks. . . . My topic is cyberporn, that is, computerized pornography. I have introduced S.892, entitled the Protection of Children from Computer Pornography Act of 1995." Grassley then proceeded to praise "a remarkable study conducted by researchers at Carnegie Mellon University." He emphasized the credibility of Carnegie Mellon, adding that this was "not a study done by some religious organization." Prompted by the Rimm study, Grassley concluded, "With so many graphic images available on computer networks, I believe Congress must act . . . to help parents who are under assault in this day and age. . . . In closing, Mr. President, I urge my colleagues to give this study by Carnegie Mellon University serious consideration, and I urge my colleagues to support S.892."[141]

Senator Dan Coats (R-Ind.), whose 1995 bill proposed new penalties for obscenity and indecency in cyberspace, wrote,

On the Internet, we are confronting perversion and brutality beyond normal imagination and well beyond the boundaries of civil human discourse. A new Carnegie-Mellon study finds that 83.5 percent of pictorial images on Usenet news groups are pornographic, and nearly 50 percent of all downloads from commercial bulletin boards depict child pornography, incest, torture and mutilation. This is the wild frontier of degraded and degrading pornography, and it is available to every child with a computer and modem.[142]

But just when it seemed that nothing could stop the oppressive power of Marty Rimm's report, its fundamental flaws began to surface. Carnegie Mellon initiated an investigation of Rimm's research following the charge by angry faculty members that Rimm had spied on the private computer habits of its students, faculty and staff. It was soon discovered that no member of the CMU faculty or administration had ever read the final report carefully. It had been kept from reviewers who might have caught the errors in its methodology and its sensational tone.

Even people listed by Rimm as advisors or contributors said they had not seen a complete version of the study. George Duncan, a CMU professor cited as an advisor, said, "I had no official role in the research study that was conducted by Marty Rimm." Rimm's chief adviser and research partner said, "This was not a report I would have written; it was Marty Rimm's report."[143] As criticism grew and faculty members distanced themselves from the report, CMU's provost decided that a three-member faculty committee would determine whether Rimm had violated ethical and academic guidelines.

Scholars around the country began to question the Rimm report. Social scientists and statisticians criticized it as a poorly designed study, whose conclusion—that the majority of images exchanged on the Usenet bulletin board system were pornographic—could not be supported. Even *Time* reporter Philip Elmer-DeWitt, under increasing criticism for his unquestioning acceptance of Rimm's study, began to have his doubts. In a candid on-line exchange with computer scholars, Elmer-DeWitt initially insisted that the study was going to be covered whether he did it or not. He said it was a difficult story to write, but he had done the best he could. Critic Jon Glass responded, "There's just no way that the story as published by *Time* is anything other than a huge gift to those who want to censor the Internet."[144]

Elmer-DeWitt tried to explain his situation, saying that if he had had more time and more presence of mind, he would have called in an outside expert to review the study. Elizabeth Lipson responded, "This cannot be waved away by saying that these are the breaks the truth gets when people are in a hurry." She said if a doctor or lawyer makes errors of this magnitude, it is called malpractice. If a lawyer does it, it is called malpractice. She said if a journalist does it, "it should be called fiction, at best."[145]

John Katz said that the Rimm study was "starting to smell bad," and he asked if *Time* was having any second thoughts about it. Elmer-DeWitt said he was still not convinced that the study was fatally flawed or fraudulent, but David Kline insisted that *Time* had a duty to note in the story that serious questions about the veracity of the study and *Time*'s analysis of it had been raised by highly regarded academics.

On this point Elmer-DeWitt agreed, saying Kline had raised an important point. "I think he's put his finger on precisely where I screwed up," said Elmer-DeWitt. "Would I still go with it the way I did? No. There is nothing I wish I had more than another week to work on that story."[146]

It soon became common knowledge that the Rimm study was so flawed that it was virtually useless. For example, the much quoted claim that 83.5 percent of Internet content is pornographic was later corrected to 0.5 percent. Nonetheless, the Senate Judiciary Committee had already scheduled hearings on naughtiness on the Internet, with Marty Rimm listed as the star witness. At first, Congress tried to stay the course with Rimm, but when stories emerged that Rimm had written his own pornographic book, *The Pornographers Handbook*, the Judiciary Committee quietly dropped him from its witness list.[147]

Unfortunately, it was too late to calm the Internet porn panic that Carnegie Mellon had begun. The Internet censorship bills that had been introduced in Congress took on a life of their own. The most significant of them, the Communications Decency Act (CDA), was passed as part of the Telecommunications Act of 1996. Its constitutionality was immediately challenged, and in June 1997 the Supreme Court struck down the CDA as an abridgement of the freedom of speech protected by the First Amendment (see Chapter 3).

NOTES

1. Stanley N. Katz, Introduction to *A Brief Narrative of the Case and Trial of John Peter Zenger*, by James Alexander (Cambridge: Belknap Press of Harvard University Press, 1963), 9.

2. Ibid., 11; also *New York Weekly Journal* 2 (November 12, 1733).

3. Katz, Introduction to *A Brief Narrative*, 11; also *New York Weekly Journal* 3 (November 19, 1733).

4. Rodney A. Smolla, *Free Speech in an Open Society* (New York: Knopf, 1992), 29.

5. Vincent Buranelli, ed., *The Trial of Peter Zenger* (New York: New York University Press, 1957), 95.

6. Ibid., 70, 78–79.

7. Ibid., 70.

8. Ibid., 80.

9. Ibid., 124.

10. Katz, Introduction to *A Brief Narrative*, 34–35.

11. Carl Bode, ed. *The Editor, the Bluenose and the Prostitute: H. L. Mencken's History of the "Hatrack" Censorship Case* (Boulder, Colo.: Roberts Rinehart, 1988), 4.

12. Henry Louis Mencken, *A Book of Prefaces* (Garden City, N.Y.: Garden City Publishing Co., 1917), 232, 277–78.

13. Bode, *The Editor, the Bluenose and the Prostitute*, 45.

14. Ibid., 51–52.

15. Ibid., 52.

16. Ibid., 55.

17. "Mencken Freed on $1,000 Bond in Boston Court," *Baltimore Sun*, April 6, 1926, 1.

18. Ibid., 2.

19. Ibid.

20. Ibid.

21. "Mencken Case to Be Decided This Morning," *Baltimore Sun*, April 7, 1926, 1–2.

22. Ibid.

23. Ibid.

24. Bode, *The Editor, the Bluenose and the Prostitute*, 70.

25. "Mencken Honored at Harvard Following Victory in Court," *Baltimore Sun*, April 8, 1926, 1, 8.

26. Ibid.

27. Ibid.

28. Ibid.

29. "Mencken Returns, Rejoicing in Victory over Reformers," *Baltimore Sun*, April 10, 1926, 25.

30. "U.S. Mails Bar April Mercury; Issue Sold Out," *Baltimore Sun*, April 9, 1926, 1–2.

31. "Decision in Mercury Suit Reserved by Federal Judge," *Baltimore Sun*, April 13, 1926, 1, 6.

32. Ibid.

33. Ibid.

34. Ibid.

35. "Federal Court Enjoins Chase in Mencken Suit," *Baltimore Sun*, April 15, 1926, 1, 7.

36. "Ban on April Issue of Mercury Stands," *Baltimore Sun*, April 16, 1926, 6.

37. Bode, *The Editor, the Bluenose and the Prostitute*, 99.

38. Ibid., 130.

39. Ibid.

40. Ibid., 171.

41. Ibid., 41.

42. John Henry Faulk, *The Uncensored John Henry Faulk* (Austin, Texas: Monthly Press, 1985), 156.

43. Ibid., 158.

44. Joseph Blank, "The Ordeal of John Henry Faulk," *Look*, May 7, 1963, 81.

45. Ibid.

46. Faulk, *The Uncensored John Henry Faulk*, 157.

47. Ibid.

48. Michael C. Burton, *John Henry Faulk: The Making of a Liberated Mind* (Austin, Texas: Eakin Press, 1993), 134.

49. Blank, "The Ordeal of John Henry Faulk," 80–81.

50. Ibid.

51. Ibid., 82.

52. Ibid.

53. Burton, *John Henry Faulk*, 185.

54. Ibid., 186.

55. Ibid., 189.

56. Faulk, *The Uncensored John Henry Faulk*, 160.

57. Blank, "The Ordeal of John Henry Faulk," 87.

58. Ibid., 89.

59. Faulk, *The Uncensored John Henry Faulk*, 161.

60. Ibid.

61. Blank, "The Ordeal of John Henry Faulk," 96a.

62. Burton, *John Henry Faulk*, 168, 183.

63. Molly Ivins, "Me No Alamo," *Progressive*, June 1990, 46.

64. Herbert N. Foerstel, *Secret Science: Federal Control of American Science and Technology* (Westport, Conn.: Praeger, 1993), p. 64.

65. Bill Lueders, *An Enemy of the State: The Life of Erwin Knoll* (Monroe, Maine: Common Courage Press, 1996), 123.

66. *United States v. Progressive*, 467 F.Supp. 990(1979), at 991, 996.

67. Ibid.

68. Ibid.

69. "The Way the Press Saw It," *Progressive*, May 1979, 44–46.

70. Quoted in Ellen Alderman and Caroline Kennedy, *In Our Defense* (New York: Morrow, 1991), 52.

71. Ibid.

72. "U.S. Labels Three Films Propaganda," *Washington Post*, February 25, 1983, A6.

73. Mary McGrory, "Justice Department's Boos Make Film Subjects Boffo Box Office," *Washington Post*, March 1, 1983, A3.

74. Robert McFadden, "3 Canadian Films Called 'Propaganda' by U.S.," *New York Times*, February 25, 1983, C4.

75. Deborah Caulfield, "U.S. Labels 3 Canada Films as Propaganda," *Los Angeles Times*, February 25, 1983, 27.

76. Ibid.

77. Cass Peterson, "U.S. Labels Three Films Propaganda," *Washington Post*, February 25, 1983, A6.

78. "Film Ruckus, in Slow Motion," *New York Times*, March 6, 1983, A27.

79. Ibid.

80. Anthony Lewis, "Afraid of Freedom," *New York Times*, March 3, 1983, A27.

81. McGrory, "Justice Department's Boos," A3.

82. Cass Peterson, "Canada Asks State Department to Reverse Decision on 3 Films," *Washington Post*, February 26, 1983, A2.

83. "U.S. Denounced for Labeling 3 Canadian Films as Propaganda," *Chicago Tribune*, February 26, 1983, 2.

84. House Committee on the Judiciary, Subcommittee on Civil and Constitutional Rights, *Canadian Films and the Foreign Agents Registration Act*, Oversight Hearings, 98th Cong., 1st sess., March 18, 1983, 54.

85. Ibid.

86. Ibid.

87. Ibid.

88. Ibid.

89. Ibid.

90. Ibid., 54–55.

91. Ibid., 56–57.

92. "Canada Film Orders Spark Lawsuits, Bill," *News Media and the Law* 8, no. 1 (January/February 1984): 8–9.

93. *Block v. Meese*, 793 F2d 1303, 1313–14 (D.C. Cir. 1986).

94. *Meese v. Keene*, 107 Sup. Ct. 1862, 1871–74, 1877–78 (1987).

95. Ibid.

96. Ibid.

97. Ibid.

98. Rodney A. Smolla and Stephen A. Smith, "Propaganda, Xenophobia, and the First Amendment," *Oregon Law Review* 67, no. 2 (1988): 255.

99. Ava Marion Plakins, "Heat Not Light: The Foreign Agents Registration

Act after *Meese v. Keene,"Fordham International Law Journal* 11 (1 October 1987): 205.

100. Author's interview with Helen Caldicott, April 16, 1997, Long Island, N.Y.

101. "Philip Morris Suit Against ABC News Seeks $10 Billion, Alleges Defamation," *Wall Street Journal*, March 25, 1994, B12.

102. "Smoke in the Eye," *Frontline* television series, April 2, 1996.

103. Ibid.

104. *ABC World News Tonight* television series, August 21, 1995.

105. "Apology Accepted," advertisement placed by the Philip Morris Company, *Washington Post*, August 24, 1995, A16.

106. "ABC News Settles Suits on Tobacco," *New York Times*, August 22, 1995, A1.

107. Ibid.

108. "Smoke in the Eye," *Frontline*.

109. " '60 Minutes' Ordered to Pull Interview in Tobacco Report," *New York Times*, November 9, 1995, A1.

110. "Smoke in the Eye," *Frontline*.

111. " '60 Minutes' Ordered to Pull Interview," A1.

112. "Smoke in the Eye," *Frontline*.

113. Ibid.

114. "CBS Executives Killed Story, '60 Minutes' Broadcast Says," *New York Times*, November 13, 1995, B8.

115. "Smoke in the Eye," *Frontline*.

116. " '60 Minutes' Ordered to Pull Interview," A1.

117. Ibid.

118. "Self-censorship at CBS," *New York Times*, November 12, 1995, E14.

119. Ibid.

120. "Smoke in the Eye," *Frontline*.

121. Frank Rich, "Fear and Favor," *New York Times*, November 15, 1995, A23.

122. "Smoke in the Eye," *Frontline*.

123. Ibid.

124. Ibid.

125. " '60 Minutes' Case Part of a Trend of Corporate Pressure, Some Analysts Say," *New York Times*, November 17, 1995, B14.

126. "Smoke in the Eye," *Frontline*.

127. Ibid.

128. "Clinton's Feelings Vary on Tobacco Settlement," *Washington Post*, June 28, 1997, A8.

129. "CMU Handcuffing Cyberspace Sex," *Pittsburgh Post-Gazette*, November 4, 1994, A1.

130. "CMU Bans Sex Pictures but Delays on Words," *Pittsburgh Post-Gazette*, November 8, 1994, A1.

131. "Censorship on the Internet," *Newsletter on Intellectual Freedom*, March 1995, 57.

132. John Schwartz, "School Gives Computer Sex the Boot," *Washington Post*, November 6, 1994, A26.

133. Ibid.

134. "Reinstate Computer Sex Material, ACLU Urges in Letter to CMU Head," *Pittsburgh Post-Gazette*, November 9, 1994, B4.

135. Philip Elmer-Dewitt, "Censoring Cyberspace," *Time*, November 21, 1994, 104.

136. "Censorship on the Internet," 29.

137. Todd Copilevitz, "Techno-smut on Campus," *Dallas Morning News*, December 4, 1994, F3.

138. Ibid.

139. Philip Elmer-DeWitt, "Cyberporn," *Time*, July 3, 1995, 38–42.

140. Ibid.

141. *Congressional Record*, Senate, 104th Cong., 1st sess., June 26, 1995, no. 105: S9017–S9021.

142. Dan Coats, " 'Dark Side' of the Internet," *Washington Post*, June 6, 1995, A23.

143. "New Concerns Raised over a Computer Smut Study," *New York Times*, July 16, 1995, 22.

144. "How *Time* Fed the Internet Porn Panic," *Harpers*, September 1995, 11–15.

145. Ibid.

146. Ibid.

147. Al Kamen, "In the Loop," *Washington Post*, July 24, 1995, A19.

Three

A Chronological History of Media Censorship Cases

The legal history of media censorship is abundant. It contains exciting stories of individuals and institutions willing to act against prevailing law in the name of free expression. In some cases their action forced the courts to expand First Amendment protections to cover the media. Even when their legal struggles failed in court, they inspired others to pursue victory at a later date.

This chapter examines the case history of media censorship chronologically. It would, of course, be tidier to separate cases by media type—press, motion pictures, broadcast media, and the Internet—but there is enough of a common thread in their legal history to make a single chronology useful. Indeed, because the courts did not extend First Amendment protections beyond newspapers until the mid-twentieth century, we can discuss early media law in that exclusive context.

As described in detail in Chapter 2, the trial of John Peter Zenger (1735) was the great prerevolutionary legal test of the freedom of the American press. Here, in colonial New York, the seeds of constitutional press freedom were sown in a trial that caught the imagination of common people throughout the colonies. Though the case did not become formal legal precedent, it presaged the spirit and intent of the founders in protecting the popular media from governmental repression.

Zenger was indicted for "seditious libel," the common law crime of criticizing the king or his public officials. He was jailed in an effort to close or suppress the newspaper, but his wife Anna took up the battle. By continuing to publish the offending newspaper during the nine months that her husband was confined in jail, she saved the *Weekly Journal* and became the world's first woman newspaper publisher.

News of Zenger's acquittal spread quickly throughout the American colonies, and privately owned newspapers soon availed themselves of the new freedom. Journals of information and opinion proliferated, and by the time the colonies won their independence a new relationship between the citizen and his government had emerged. The press had become a constitutionally protected institution in the new nation.

The common law tradition of seditious libel, wielded historically against the press, did not die easily, even in the newly independent, fiercely libertarian United States of America. For example, in *People v. Croswell* (1804), the Republicans prosecuted a New York Federalist editor for seditious libel against President Thomas Jefferson.

UNITED STATES V. HUDSON AND GOODWIN, 1812

Not until 1812, in *United States v. Hudson and Goodwin*, did the Supreme Court, in considering another action for libel against the president, rule that there was no federal common law crime of seditious libel. The case arose when the *Connecticut Courant* printed an article accusing the president and Congress of having secretly provided two million dollars to Napoleon Bonaparte in order to accomplish a treaty between the United States and Spain. The publishers of the *Courant* were charged with libel, but the Circuit Court of the United States was divided on whether it had common law jurisdiction to try the case.

The issue went to the Supreme Court, which said that jurisdiction to try "any particular act done by an individual in supposed violation of the peace and dignity of the sovereign power" could only be acquired through legislative action making it a crime, affixing a punishment and designating the court that would have jurisdiction. In conclusion, the Court declared, "Certain implied powers must necessarily result to our courts of justice from the nature of their institution. But jurisdiction of crimes against the state is not among those powers."[1]

MUTUAL FILM CORPORATION V. INDUSTRIAL COMMISSION OF OHIO, 1915

For more than a century, the Supreme Court had little further opportunity to interpret press freedoms or the First Amendment generally, primarily because of the prevailing view that the Bill of Rights served only to protect citizens from federal infringement, not from state laws or policy. Needless to say, many states exercised systematic restraint on freedom of expression during this period, and the newer media technologies were particularly affected. Many states established motion-picture censorship boards which exercised an iron hand in controlling film content. For example, in 1913, the state of Ohio passed a statute creating a Board of Censors that had to approve all motion pictures in advance of their exhibition in that state. The statute said that only films of "moral, educational or amusing and harmless character" would be approved by the board, and exhibitors were required to pay a fee to have such a judgement rendered on their films.

Ohio exhibitors complained in court, and the case eventually reached the Supreme Court, where the nascent film industry was treated with virtual contempt. In *Mutual Film Corporation v. Industrial Commission of Ohio* (1915), the Court stated, "[N]ot only the State of Ohio but other States have considered it to be in the interest of the public morals and welfare to supervise moving picture exhibitions. We would have to shut our eyes to the facts of the world to regard the precaution unreasonable or the legislation to effect it a mere wanton interference with personal liberty."

In their brief, the film exhibitors declared that

> motion pictures constitute part of the "press" of Ohio within the comprehensive meaning of that term. They play an increasingly important part in the spreading of knowledge and the molding of public opinion upon every kind of political, educational, religious, economic and social question. . . . The censorship law cannot be sustained as a proper exercise of the police power, because it directly contravenes the constitutional guarantees of freedom of publication and liberty of the press.

The Court disdainfully disposed of such First Amendment claims for motion pictures.

> We need not pause to dilate upon the freedom of opinion and its expression, and whether by speech, writing or printing. They are too certain to need discussion—of such conceded value as to need no supporting praise. . . . Are moving pictures within the principle, as it is contended they are? . . . The first impulse of the mind is to reject the contention. We immediately feel that the argument is wrong or strained which extends the guarantees of free opinion and speech

to the multitudinous shows which are advertised on the billboards of our cities . . . and which seeks to bring motion pictures and other spectacles into practical and legal similitude to a free press and liberty of opinion. It cannot be put out of view that the exhibition of moving pictures is a business, pure and simple, originated and conducted for profit, like other spectacles, not to be regarded as part of the press of the country, or as organs of public opinion.[2]

It would be thirty-five years before the Court saw fit to revisit its disdainful judgement of the film industry.

FROHWERK V. UNITED STATES, 1919

Even the traditional press was being treated rudely by the Court during this period, as the xenophobia surrounding World War I revived the legacy of seditious libel, the common law notion that criticism of government was a crime. This wartime hysteria produced a trio of disturbing Supreme Court cases: *Frohwerk v. United States* (1919), *Abrams v. United States* (1919), and *Schenck v. United States* (1919). *Frohwerk v. United States* (1919) involved a series of articles published in a small German-language newspaper in Missouri. The articles criticized the war effort and opposed sending American troops to Europe. For writing these articles, Frohwerk was convicted under the Espionage Act and sentenced to a fine and ten years in prison. The Supreme Court upheld the conviction, with Justice Oliver Wendell Holmes writing for a unanimous Court.

ABRAMS V. UNITED STATES, 1919 AND SCHENCK V. UNITED STATES, 1919

Just a few months later, in *Abrams v. United States* (1919), the Court upheld the use of the Espionage Act of 1917 to impose a twenty-year jail sentence for printing and distributing a leaflet urging a strike considered by the government to be damaging to the war effort. The Espionage Act imposed criminal liability on anyone who, while the country was at war, made statements intended to interfere with the success of the American military's efforts.

A similar prosecution, which occurred in *Schenck v. United States* (1919), involved the prosecution of Charles Schenck for producing leaflets characterizing World War I as a capitalist conspiracy engineered by Wall Street. Justice Oliver Wendell Holmes, speaking for the Court, admitted that in ordinary times Schenck's pamphlets would be protected by the First Amendment, but in time of war Schenck's words could create "a clear and present danger" that Congress had a right to prevent.

GITLOW V. NEW YORK, 1925

After World War I, bolshevism came to be regarded as a major threat to entrenched political and financial interests in the United States, and the courts were inclined to uphold the suppression of any leftist political expression. In *Gitlow v. New York* (1925), the Supreme Court upheld the prosecution of an individual for disseminating a left-wing leaflet.

NEAR V. MINNESOTA, 1931

In the late 1920s and 1930s, when the Supreme Court held that the basic guarantees of the First Amendment extended to the states under the Fourteenth Amendment's due process clause, federal courts began to recognize jurisdiction over state legislation that violated freedom of speech and press. The Court found that First Amendment guarantees were implicit in the concept of "ordered liberty" and applied those guarantees against the states in such cases as *Near v. Minnesota* (1931). In *Near*, the Court examined a Minnesota statute prohibiting the publication of "malicious, scandalous, and defamatory newspapers." In its landmark opinion, the Court placed the criticism of public officials outside the "indecencies" subject to censorship.

The case arose when the Minnesota legislature enacted a bill ostensibly intended to control the state's scandal sheets, the forerunners of today's supermarket tabloids, but its real purpose was to shut down the *Deluth Rip-Saw*, a small weekly that continually embarrassed public officials. The new law permitted a judge to close permanently any publication he deemed "obscene, lewd and lascivious" or "malicious, scandalous, and defamatory." After the death of the controversial publisher of the *Rip-Saw*, Minnesota officials turned their sights onto another sensational rag, the *Saturday Press*, whose publishers, Howard Guilford and Jay Near, alleged complicity between local officials and organized crime. Police Chief Frank Brunskill, a constant target of their attacks, tried to keep the *Saturday Press* off the streets, and District

Attorney Floyd Olson filed a complaint charging that the *Saturday Press* had defamed Brunskill and other officials.

A cooperative local judge promptly issued a temporary restraining order. The order was appealed to the state supreme court, where Near's lawyer, Thomas Latimer, argued that the statute was unconstitutional on First Amendment grounds and that his clients had been denied their rights to due process, including a trial by jury. The state supreme court upheld the constitutionality of the statute, stating that "our constitution was never intended to protect malice, scandal, and defamation." In October 1928, the case went back to the lower court to decide whether the *Saturday Press* had indeed violated the statute. Publisher Near enlisted the aid of Colonel Robert McCormick, publisher of the *Chicago Tribune* and chairman of the Committee on Freedom of the Press of the American Newspaper Publishers Association (ANPA).

On April 24, 1930, the ANPA passed a resolution attacking the Minnesota gag law as "one of the gravest assaults on the liberties of the people . . . since the adoption of the Constitution." In the meantime, the restraining order on the *Press*, which had kept the paper from publishing for more than two years, was declared a "perpetual injunction."

In 1930 the U.S. Supreme Court accepted Near's petition and agreed to hear the case. The following year, McCormick's personal attorney, Weymouth Kirkland, told the Court, "So long as men do evil, so long will newspapers publish defamation." He argued that gagging the press was unconstitutional unless the danger it suppressed "threaten[ed] the destruction of the state politically, morally, industrially, or economically. History is evidence that it is better to suffer from such an evil than from the manifold evils which arise when the press is fettered."[3]

Minnesota's deputy state attorney general claimed that the suppression of the *Saturday Press* was not a prior restraint, but a punishment, after the fact, for defamation. The conservative bloc on the Court supported the state's right to regulate the press, but the venerable Justices Oliver Wendell Holmes and Louis Brandeis led the narrow majority in ruling the law to be an unconstitutional prior restraint. In describing the controversial publishers of the *Saturday Press*, Justice Brandeis said, "These men set out on a campaign to rid the city of certain evils. Now, if that is not one of the things for which the press chiefly exists, then for what does it exist?"[4]

In his written opinion, Justice Hughes declared, "The object of the statute is not punishment in the ordinary sense, but suppression of the offending newspaper or periodical. . . . The statute not only operates to suppress the offending newspaper or periodical but to put the publisher under an effective censorship." In distinguishing between English common law and America's constitutional liberties, Hughes quoted James Madison's view that "the great and essential rights of the people are secured against legislative as well as executive ambition. . . . This security of the freedom of the press requires that it should be exempt not only from previous restraint by the Executive, as in Great Britain, but from legislative restraint also."[5]

GROSJEAN V. AMERICAN PRESS CO., 1936

After *Near*, the Supreme Court broadly questioned reliance on common law principles to construe the First Amendment. In *Grosjean v. American Press Co.* (1936), the Court declared, "The predominant purpose of [the First Amendment] here invoked was to preserve an untrammeled press as a vital source of public information." In order to realize that goal, said Justice George Sutherland, "It is impossible to concede that by the words 'freedom of the press' the framers of that amendment intended to adopt merely the narrow view then reflected by the law of England that such freedom consisted only in immunity from previous censorship."[6]

Though press freedoms were enhanced in the 1930s, these were difficult times for radio, now the popular medium of choice. Like motion pictures, radio was given little respect by the courts. The Federal Radio Commission, later named the Federal Communications Commission (FCC), had been created by the Radio Act of 1927 to cover the technical aspects of station management and the assignment of licenses. But the Radio Act had also stated: "No person within the jurisdiction of the United States shall utter any obscene, indecent, or profane language by means of radio communication." The Communications Act of 1934 retained the Radio Act's wording in this regard, and the FCC soon became a heavy-handed censor. During the 1930s, the commission frequently revoked station licenses as a means of censoring their programs. Two of these cases reached the court of appeals in 1935, which affirmed the decisions of the FCC.

In considering the punishment of station KGEF (Los Angeles), the appeals court said, "This is neither censorship nor previous restraint, nor is it a whittling away of the rights guaranteed by the First Amendment, or an impairment of their free exercise. Appellant . . . may not, as we think, demand, of right, the continued use of an instrument of commerce . . . except in subordination to all reasonable rules and regulations Congress, acting through the Commission, may prescribe."[7]

In rejecting the appeal of station KFKB (Milford, Kansas), the court implied that any censorship short of prior restraint was within the FCC's power.

> Appellant contends that the attitude of the Commission amounts to a censorship of the station contrary to the provisions of Section 29 of the Radio Act of 1927. This contention is without merit. There has been no attempt on the part of the Commission to subject any part of the appellant's broadcasting matter to scrutiny prior to its release. . . . [T]he Commission has merely exercised its undoubted right to take note of appellant's past conduct, which is not censorship.[8]

Thus a radio station could be put out of existence and its owner deprived of his livelihood for expression which, if printed in a newspaper, would be protected by the First Amendment.

NATIONAL BROADCASTING COMPANY V. UNITED STATES, 1943

In 1943 the Supreme Court upheld the constitutionality of federal regulation of broadcasting, relying upon the unique technical nature of the airwaves and the social characteristics of the medium. In *National Broadcasting Company v. United States*, the Court concluded: "Freedom of utterance is abridged to many who wish to use the limited facilities of radio. Unlike other modes of expression, radio inherently is not available to all. That is its unique characteristic, and that is why, unlike other modes of expression, it is subject to governmental regulation. Because it cannot be used by all, some who wish to use it must be denied."[9]

Even as the Court limited First Amendment guarantees for radio communication, it was moving toward greater protection for magazines and films. Because magazines have always relied heavily on mail subscriptions, they are vulnerable to censorship through postal regulations. Indeed, the notorious history of master censor Anthony Comstock (see Chapter 1) demonstrates how the manipulation of postal regulations, particularly the second-class mailing privilege, can suppress periodicals. In 1943 certain issues of *Esquire*, a rather tame "men's magazine," offended the postmaster general, who revoked the magazine's second-class permit. "A publication to enjoy these unique mail privileges," he explained, "is bound to do more than refrain from disseminating material which is obscene or bordering on the obscene. It is under a positive duty to contribute to the public good and the public welfare."[10]

HANEGAN V. ESQUIRE, 1946

The denial of *Esquire*'s mail privileges was appealed, and, in *Hanegan v. Esquire* (1946), the Supreme Court ruled that the postmaster general had no power to determine whether the contents of a magazine served the public good or welfare. In writing for the Court, Justice William O. Douglas stated,

[T]o withdraw the second-class rate from this publication today because its contents seemed to one official not good for the public would sanction withdrawal of the second-class rate tomorrow from another periodical whose social or economic views seemed harmful to another official. The validity of the obscenity laws is recognition that the mails may not be used to satisfy all tastes. . . . But Congress has left the Postmaster General no power to prescribe standards for the literature or the art which a mailable periodical disseminates.[11]

JOSEPH BURSTYN, INC. V. WILSON, 1952

Just a few years later, a landmark Supreme Court decision would bestow First Amendment protection, earlier denied, to motion pictures. The film *The Miracle* had been licensed for exhibition in New York in 1949 and 1950, but its portrayal of a peasant woman who imagines that her pregnancy is an immaculate conception drew protests from Catholics around the country (see Chapter 1). After being condemned by the Legion of Decency as "a sacrilegious and blasphemous mockery of Christian religious truth," its license was withdrawn. A distributor for the film sued to regain its license, and the New York Supreme Court ruled that the city license commissioner had exceeded his authority in censoring the movie.

The full Board of Regents then held a new hearing, and on February 16, 1951, the board determined that the film was indeed "sacrilegious" and, under the New York Education Law, could not be licensed for exhibition. The license was once more withdrawn, moving the case on to the Supreme Court. In *Joseph Burstyn, Inc. v. Wilson* (1952), the Court issued a threefold decision: (1) Motion pictures are included within the free speech and press guarantees of the First Amendment; (2) the New York Education Law, which prohibited the exhibition of any film without a license, was void as a prior restraint on protected expression; and (3) films may not be censored on the basis of "sacrilege."

Speaking for the Court, Justice Tom Clark declared:

[T]he present case is the first to present squarely to us the question whether motion pictures are within the ambit of protection which the First Amendment, through the Fourteenth, secures to any form of "speech" or "the press." It cannot be doubted that motion pictures are a significant medium for the communication of ideas. They may affect public attitudes and behavior in a variety of ways, ranging from direct espousal of a political or social doctrine to the subtle shaping of thought which characterizes all artistic expression. The importance of motion pictures as an organ of public opinion is not lessened by the fact that they are designed to entertain as well as to inform.

Clark rejected the state's claim that motion pictures may be censored because they possess a greater capacity for evil than other modes of expression.

Even if one were to accept this hypothesis, it does not follow that motion pictures should be disqualified from First Amendment protection. . . . We conclude that expression by means of motion pictures is included within the free speech and free press guarantee of the First and Fourteenth Amendments. To the extent that language in the opinion in *Mutual Film Corporation v. Industrial Commission of Ohio* (1915), is out of harmony with the views here set forth, we no longer adhere to it.[12]

SUPERIOR FILMS V. DEPARTMENT OF EDUCATION OF OHIO, 1953

State courts now began to question local film censorship laws. Courts in Kansas and Pennsylvania declared such laws to be unconstitutional, and the Massachusetts Supreme Court ruled that laws that allowed mayors to deny a license to show a film on Sunday constituted a prior restraint, in violation of the First and Fourteenth Amendments.

In *Superior Films v. Department of Education of Ohio* (1953), the Supreme Court relied on the *Burstyn* (1952) decision to once again reject the use of review boards to censor films. Justice William O. Douglas delivered the Court's judgment:

> Certainly a system . . . which required a newspaper to submit to a board its news items, editorials, and cartoons before it published them could not be sustained. Nor could book publishers be required to submit their novels, poems, and tracts to censors for clearance before publication. Any such scheme of censorship would be in irreconcilable conflict with the language and purpose of the First Amendment.
>
> Nor is it conceivable to me that producers of plays for the legitimate theatre or for television could be required to submit their manuscripts to censors on pain of penalty for producing them without approval. . . . The same result in the case of motion pictures necessarily follows as a consequence of our holding in *Joseph Burstyn, Inc. v. Wilson* . . . that motion pictures are "within the free speech and free press guaranty of the First and Fourteenth Amendments."
>
> Motion pictures are of course a different medium of expression than the public speech, the radio, the stage, the novel, or the magazine. But the First Amendment draws no distinction between the various methods of communicating ideas. On occasion one may be more powerful or effective than another. The movie, like the public speech, radio, or television, is transitory—here now and gone in an instant. . . . Which medium will give the most excitement and have the most enduring effect will vary with the theme and with the actors. It is not for the censor to determine in any case. . . . In this Nation every writer, actor, or producer, no matter what medium of expression he may use, should be freed from the censor.[13]

KINGSLEY INTERNATIONAL PICTURES V. REGENTS OF THE UNIVERSITY OF THE STATE OF NEW YORK, 1959

In *Kingsley International Pictures v. Regents* (1959), the Supreme Court revisited the same New York motion picture censorship law that it had found unconstitutional in *Burstyn* (1952). New York had tinkered with the law in an attempt to pass constitutional muster and, this time, used it to deny a license to the movie *Lady Chatterley's Lover*. The distributor petitioned the regents of the University of the State of New York for review of the decision, but the regents upheld the denial of a license on the grounds that "the whole theme of this motion picture is immoral under said law, for that theme is the presentation of adultery as a desirable, acceptable and proper pattern of behavior."

The judgement was appealed and eventually reached the Supreme Court. During oral argument, Ephraim London, attorney for the appellant, initially sought a declaration from the Court that "the entire film licensing system be declared unconstitutional as a prohibitive form of prior restraint of communication."

Justice John Harlan asked, "You mean across the board?"

London answered, "Yes, Your Honor. . . . Across the board, without any question relating to the application in this particular case."

When Justice William Brennan prodded London on the same issue, London softened his position. "If the relief sought, namely, that the entire system is unconstitutional, is not granted," said London, "we seek a determination that the statute is void and that it authorizes the suppression of a film on the ground that it is immoral."

London claimed that the term "immoral" was so vague as to permit the suppression of protected speech. In addition, he said, the statute permitted the suppression of ideas and advocacy, in violation of the constitutional guarantee of free speech.

London said that the licensing law was particularly offensive because "one must come hat in hand in order to secure permission to exercise his right of expression."

Charles Brind, speaking on behalf of the New York Board of Regents, explained how the motion-picture licensing system worked. Justice Potter Stewart then asked Brind whether the New York legislature could also place newspapers under the power of prior censorship.

Brind responded, "Well, it might, if they set up standards."

Justice Brennan asked, "What about comic books?"

Brind answered, "There has been discussion of comic books in the legislature. . . . Legislation hasn't been passed for that kind of a procedure yet."

Justice William O. Douglas asked whether the state was authorized to censor the book from which the movie had been made. Brind said that there was no authority granted to deal with books, the theatre or television—only movies.

Justice Felix Frankfurter asked, "If a movie house showed a picture without a license, you would have power to go in and get an injunction against the showing?"

"That is correct," said Brind.

Justice Stewart asked, "And you could institute criminal proceedings?"

"That is right," answered Brind.

"Regardless of merit of that particular movie?"

"That is right," said Brind, "under the present statute."[14]

When oral argument concluded and the Court reached a decision, the case produced a rare consensus among the justices, all of whom agreed that the movie could not be barred by New York State. Speaking for the Court, Justice Stewart said, "What New York has done . . . is to prevent the exhibition of a motion picture because that picture advocates an idea—that adultery under certain circumstances may be proper behavior. Yet the First Amendment's basic guarantee is of freedom to advocate ideas. The State, quite simply, has thus struck at the heart of constitutionally protected liberty."

Because the movie had been censored in a way that violated the First Amendment so directly, Stewart simply cited *Joseph Burstyn, Inc. v. Wilson*, (1952), saying there was no need to consider the state's authority to require licensing of films prior to exhibition. "Nor," said Stewart, "need we here determine whether, despite problems peculiar to motion pictures, the controls which a State may impose upon this medium of expression are precisely coextensive with those allowable for newspapers, books, or individual speech. It is enough for the present case to reaffirm that motion pictures are within the First and Fourteenth Amendments' basic protection."[15]

NEW YORK TIMES V. SULLIVAN, 1964

In 1964, in *New York Times v. Sullivan*, the Supreme Court overturned a libel judgement against the *New York Times* and, in the process, established the premise that the First Amendment guarantees to the press the freedom of expression necessary to inform the citizenry. The case originated in 1960 after the *Times* published a full-page advertisement/article titled "Heed Their Rising Voices," which criticized police in Montgomery, Alabama, for their brutal treatment of black demonstrators and appealed for funds to support the civil rights movement. No government official or member of the police was identified by name, but L. B. Sullivan, a city commissioner, charged that criticism of the police constituted libel of him in his capacity as commissioner of public affairs. Sullivan instituted a civil libel action against the *New York Times* and the religious organizations that sponsored the ad, and a jury awarded Sullivan $500,000 in damages. After the state supreme court of Alabama affirmed the award, the *Times* appealed to the Supreme Court.

Justice William Brennan's opinion for the Warren Court rejected the contention that the ad was commercial speech not protected by the First Amendment. Brennan said the ad communicated information about "a movement whose existence and objectives are matters of highest public interest and concern." He quoted *Roth v. United States* (1957), the case establishing the controlling obscenity standard at that time, asserting that the First Amendment "was fashioned to assure unfettered interchange of ideas for the bringing about of political and social changes desired by the people." Therefore, said Brennan, civil libel actions by government officials against citizens must be considered "against the background of a profound national commitment to the people that debate on public issues should be uninhibited, robust and wide-open, and that it may well include vehement, caustic, and sometimes unpleasantly sharp attacks on government and public officials."

Brennan's opinion fashioned the constitutional rule that public officials may not recover damages for libel unless they prove that the offending statement was made with "actual malice," which he defined as "knowledge that it was false or with reckless disregard of whether it was false or not." Brennan concluded,

> Raising as it does the possibility that a good-faith critic of government will be penalized for his criticism, the proposition relied on by the Alabama courts strikes at the very center of the constitutionally protected area of free expression. We hold that such a proposition may not constitutionally be utilized to establish that an otherwise impersonal attack on governmental operations was a libel of an official responsible for their operations.

Justices Hugo Black, William O. Douglas and Arthur Goldberg would have gone even farther. Black and Douglas argued that libel actions by public officials against criticism of their official conduct were completely prohibited. Goldberg declared: "In my view, the First and Fourteenth Amendments to the Constitution afford to the citizen and to the press an absolute, unconditional privilege to criticize official conduct despite the harm which may flow from excesses and abuses."[16]

ESTES V. TEXAS, 1965

Just a few years later, the first Supreme Court recognition of First Amendment protection for television came, ironically, in a case which approved of the exclusion of television cameras from courtrooms. In *Estes v. Texas* (1965), the Court overturned the swindling conviction of Billy Sol Estes, a much-publicized financier with alleged political connections, after concluding that television cameras had disrupted his trial and had deprived him of his right to due process. However, in delivering the opinion of the Court, Justice Charles Evans Hughes went out of his way to emphasize that courts were not discriminating against television when they routinely allowed newspaper reporters into courtrooms. "The television and radio reporter has the same privilege," said Hughes. "All are entitled to the same rights as the general public. The news reporter is not permitted to bring his typewriter or printing press. When the advances in these arts permit reporting by printing press or by television without their present hazards to a fair trial we will have another case."[17]

GINZBURG V. UNITED STATES, 1965

During the next few years, a spate of Supreme Court cases addressed significant aspects of magazine censorship. In *Ginzburg v. United States* (1965), the Court found publisher Ralph Ginzburg guilty of sending obscene materials through the mails, including copies of a magazine titled *EROS*, a newsletter titled *Liaison*, and a book. The unusual thing about the decision was that it invoked the federal obscenity statute while concluding that the content of the material in question was probably *not* obscene. The statute in question, the old Comstock Act, had been used historically to label materials "unmailable" and, as such, had targeted magazines, which depended on mail subscriptions for their survival.

In delivering the Court's opinion in *Ginzburg*, Justice William Brennan stated, "Our affirmance of the convictions for mailing *EROS* and *Liaison* is based upon their characters as a whole, including their editorial formats, and not upon particular articles contained, digested, or excerpted in them. Thus we do not decide whether particular articles, for example, in *EROS*, although identified by the trial judge as offensive, should be condemned as obscene whatever their setting."

Brennan went so far as to claim that the nature of the magazine's advertising could be used as a basis for determining the obscenity of its content. "We perceive no threat to First Amendment guarantees," said Brennan, "in thus holding that in close cases evidence of pandering may be probative with respect to the nature of the material in question and thus satisfy the *Roth* [obscenity] test."

Justice Potter Stewart's dissent declared,

> The Court today appears to concede that the materials Ginzburg mailed were themselves protected by the First Amendment. But, the Court says, Ginzburg can still be sentenced to five years in prison for mailing them. Why? Because, says the Court, he was guilty of "commercial exploitation," of "pandering," and of "titilation." . . . Neither the statute under which Ginzburg was convicted, nor any other federal statute I know of makes "commercial exploitation" or "pandering" or "titilation" a criminal offense.

Dissenting Justice William Harlan agreed.

> In fact, the Court in the last analysis sustains the convictions on the express assumption that the items held to be obscene are not, viewing them strictly, obscene at all. . . . While the precise holding of the Court is obscure, I take it that the objective test of *Roth*, which ultimately focuses on the material in question, is to be supplemented by another test that goes to the question whether the mailer's aim is to "pander" to or "titilate" those to whom he mails the questionable matter.[18]

REDRUP V. NEW YORK, 1967 AND *TANNENBAUM V. NEW YORK*, 1967

Censors have always suppressed the media in the name of America's youth, and in 1967 and 1968 three Supreme Court cases addressed this issue with respect to magazines. In *Redrup v. New York* (1967), the Court issued a short and unsigned per curiam (by the court as a whole) decision reversing the convictions of newsstand owners for selling obscene magazines. The decision made reference to Justice William Brennan's view that the state's power to suppress obscenity was limited to materials made available to minors or unconsenting adults. However, another per curiam decision that same year, in *Tannenbaum v. New York* (1967), affirmed the conviction of a cigar store owner who sold a "girlie" magazine to a seventeen-year-old youth.

GINSBERG V. NEW YORK, 1968

The question of magazine sales to minors was addressed squarely the following year in *Ginsberg v. New York* (1968). Sam Ginsberg, a stationery store owner, had sold a "girlie" magazine to a sixteen-year-old boy, and he was convicted of violating New York's Exposing Minors to Harmful Materials law. The purchase had actually been arranged in advance by a group hoping to initiate a prosecution under a law prohibiting the sale to anyone under seventeen of "any picture which depicts nudity and which is harmful to minors or any magazine which contains such pictures."[19]

The case was appealed to the Supreme Court, where, during oral argument, Emanuel Redfield, representing Ginsberg, asked, "[W]here in the Constitution can you justify a restraint based on the age of the reader?" Redfield complained that "in order to prosecute anybody [under this statute], you'd have to do what you did in this case, and that is involve the youngsters in the criminal court. The youngster in this case . . . acted as a decoy in a case that was specially framed for the purpose of enforcing this law."

William Cahn, representing the state of New York, told the Court that "taken as a whole . . . these magazines, although not obscene insofar as adults are concerned, when taken into consideration in the juvenile area, are harmful to minors."[20]

Justice William Brennan wrote the opinion for the Court, which sustained Ginsberg's conviction, though it recognized that the magazines in question were not obscene and could be made freely available to adults. In his concurring opinion, Justice Potter Stewart stated, "We conclude that we cannot say that the statute invades the area of freedom of expression constitutionally secured to minors. . . . [A] State may permissibly determine that . . . a child—like someone in a captive audience—is not possessed of that full capacity for individual choice which is the presupposition of First Amendment guarantees."

In his dissent, Justice Abe Fortas declared,

> The Court certainly cannot mean that the States and cities and counties and villages have unlimited power to withhold anything and

everything that is written or pictorial from younger people. But here it justifies the conviction of Sam Ginsberg because the impact of the Constitution, it says, is variable, and what is not obscene for an adult may be obscene for a child. . . . I do not disagree with this, but I insist that to assess the principle—certainly to apply it—the Court must define it. . . . This is not a case where, on any standard enunciated by the Court, the magazines are obscene, nor one where the seller is at fault. Petitioner is being prosecuted for the sale of magazines which he had a right under the decisions of this Court to offer for sale, and he is being prosecuted without proof of "fault."[21]

RED LION BROADCASTING V. FCC, 1969

In *Red Lion Broadcasting v. FCC* (1969), the Court addressed the constitutionality of the "fairness doctrine," the FCC requirement that radio and television broadcasters cover public issues on their stations and that they present each side of those issues. The Court ruled that the FCC's fairness doctrine was a legitimate exercise of congressionally delegated authority which did not violate the First Amendment. In delivering the Court's opinion, Justice Byron White explained, "The broadcasters challenge the fairness doctrine and its specific manifestations in the personal attack and political editorial rules on conventional First Amendment grounds. Their contention is that the First Amendment protects their desire to use their allotted frequencies continuously to broadcast whatever they choose, and to exclude whomever they choose from ever using that frequency."

Justice White concluded:

Because of the scarcity of radio frequencies, the Government is permitted to put restraints on licensees in favor of others whose views should be expressed on this unique medium. But the people as a whole retain their interest in free speech by radio and their collective right to have the medium function consistently with the ends and purposes of the First Amendment. It is the right of the viewers and listeners, not the right of the broadcasters, which is paramount.

Where there are substantially more individuals who want to broadcast than there are frequencies to allocate, it is idle to posit an unabridgeable First Amendment right to broadcast comparable to the right of every individual to speak, write, or publish. . . . A license permits broadcasting, but the licensee has no constitutional right to be the one who holds the license or to monopolize a radio frequency to the exclusion of his fellow citizens.[22]

NEW YORK TIMES V. UNITED STATES, 1971

The spectacular *Pentagon Papers* case, *New York Times v. United States* (1971), affirmed the right of the press to publish "secret" government information. At issue in the case was a classified 7,000-page Pentagon report on U.S. involvement in the Vietnam War that was allegedly "stolen" from the government by a former Pentagon employee, Daniel Ellsberg, and provided to the *New York Times*. Ellsberg had withheld substantial portions of the *Pentagon Papers* from the *Times* in order to avoid releasing sensitive information.

On June 13, 1971, the *Times* began publishing a series of articles based on the secret Pentagon study, and the following day U.S. Attorney General John Mitchell warned the *Times*, "Further publication of information of this character will cause irreparable injury to the defense interests of the United States." Mitchell claimed that publication of the *Pentagon Papers* was "directly prohibited by the provisions of the Espionage Law." The newspaper responded, "The *Times* must respectfully decline the request of the Attorney General, believing that it is in the interest of the people of this country to be informed of the material contained in this series of articles." The next day, the *Times* resumed its series on the *Pentagon Papers*, but the lead story was the government's attempt to censor the series.[23]

On June 15, 1971, the Department of Justice obtained a temporary restraining order preventing further publication of the *Pentagon Papers*, the first such act of prior restraint of a major newspaper in the history of the republic. The lead counsel at the *Times*, the venerable Louis Loeb, and his prominent partner Herbert Brownell declined to defend the *Times* in court. Indeed, they had opposed publishing the papers from the start. But the newspaper's in-house counsel, James Goodale, followed the advice of his journalists, not that of his more cautious legal colleagues.

The *Times* prepared for battle by assembling a legal team consisting of Goodale, First Amendment specialist Floyd Abrams, and constitutional scholar Alexander Bickel.

Before the attorneys for the *Times* appeared in New York for the scheduled hearing on the order, Daniel Ellsberg supplied a second copy of 4,000 pages from the *Pentagon Papers* to the *Washington Post*.

On June 18, the *Post* began publishing its own series on the papers, causing the Justice Department to seek another restraining order in federal court in Washington. Federal District Judge Gerhard Gesell denied the government's request, citing the Supreme Court ruling in *Near v. Minnesota* (1931) forbidding prior restraint on publication. Government lawyers immediately appealed Gesell's ruling to a three-judge panel of the U.S. Court of Appeals for the District of Columbia, which reversed Gesell's ruling and issued a temporary restraining order on the *Post*. The case was sent back to Gesell for a full hearing on the evidence.

Meanwhile, the *Times* argued its case in federal district court in New York against U.S. Attorney Whitney North Seymour, Jr. Seymour told the court that the "stolen" papers were Top Secret documents vital to the national defense and not protected by the First Amendment. Alexander Bickel responded with explicit reference to the Supreme Court's opinion in *Near*, in which the Court declared prior restraint unconstitutional except in rare cases such as the "publication of the sailing dates of transports or the number or location of troops." But nothing in these papers, said Bickel, bore any resemblance to such information. Bickel maintained that Congress never intended the Espionage Act to be used against the press, and he claimed that the mundane secrets in the papers were public information appropriate to the civic debate on Vietnam policy.

On June 19, Judge Murray Gurfein delivered a seventeen-page opinion supporting the right of the *Times* to publish the papers, but Appeals Court Judge Irving Kaufman allowed the restraining order to continue until the full appeals court could hear the case.

In Washington, Judge Gesell was similarly unconvinced that the *Post* should be restrained from publishing, but here also the appeals panel carried over its previous restraining order until the full court could hear the case.

It now became necessary for the two appeals courts to convene simultaneously in Washington and New York to address the restraining orders on the *Post* and the *Times*, respectively. By this time, further leaks had resulted in publication of parts of the *Pentagon Papers* in several other national newspapers. Clearly, the Justice Department could not stop the story from mushrooming around the country, but the *Post* and the *Times* continued to honor their restraining orders.

U.S. Solicitor General Irwin Griswold argued the government's case at the *Post*'s hearing in Washington. Despite Griswold's claim that publication of the papers would threaten confidential American diplomacy, the appeals court ruled seven to two against the government, noting the massive and spreading character of the leak.

In New York, the Second Circuit Court of Appeals was more accommodating to the government, voting five to three to send the case back to Judge Gurfein for a secret hearing at which the government would be given a chance to show which parts of the *Pentagon Papers* might compromise national security.

Griswold appealed the D.C. circuit's ruling against the government, and the *Times* appealed the New York decision. Restraining orders on both newspapers were continued, pending resolution in the Supreme Court. Chief Justice Warren Burger and Justices John Harlan, Byron White, and Harry Blackmun wanted to maintain the injunctions against both papers until the Court could review the cases in the fall. Justices Hugo Black, William O. Douglas, William Brennan, and Thurgood Marshall wanted to allow both newspapers to publish the contested documents immediately. Justice Potter Stewart was the swing vote at this early stage. He notified Chief Justice Burger that, unless the Court granted an immediate hearing of the cases, he would vote to remove the restraining order. Burger had no choice but to agree, and oral argument in both cases was set for the next morning.

The Court's first act was to delay sending the *Times* case back to Judge Gurfein, but, pending a judgement in the case, it also prohibited the *Times* and the *Post* from publishing anything in the government's special appendix or anything that the government chose to identify by five o'clock that afternoon as posing "grave and immediate danger" to the national security if disclosed. The list of such items that the government submitted was so sweeping that the two newspapers felt obliged to print nothing, rather than a radically truncated version of the *Pentagon Papers*.

Lawyers for both sides were now faced with the task of writing their briefs and preparing for oral argument in just twenty-four hours. Solicitor General Erwin Griswold submitted a sealed brief that examined the threats posed by publication of the documents, including the claim that publication would reveal intelligence activities and compromise the future capacity of the United States to negotiate an end to the war and the release of prisoners of war. The brief argued for an injunction barring both newspapers from publishing the material identified by the government, pending new hearings in the district courts.

On June 30, 1971, just two weeks after the case began, the Supreme

Court voted six to three to strike down the government's prior restraint on the newspapers as a violation of the First Amendment. Voting with the majority were Justices Black, Brennan, Douglas, Marshall, Stewart and White. Voting with the minority were Justices Blackman and Harlan and Chief Justice Burger. Justice Brennan's brief per curiam opinion expressed the Court's judgement that any prior restraint on expression bears a "heavy presumption against its constitutional validity" and the government "thus carries a heavy burden of showing justification for the enforcement of such a restraint." The opinion concluded that "the Government had not met that burden."

In addition to the brief per curiam opinion, there were nine individual opinions. Justices Black and Douglas joined each other's opinions, as did White and Stewart. Harlan's dissenting opinion was joined by Burger and Blackmun.

Justice Black was the most forceful and passionate in declaring that "every moment's continuance of the injunctions against these newspapers amounts to a flagrant, indefensible, and continuing violation of the First Amendment." He said that accepting prior restraint under *any* circumstances "would make a shambles of the First Amendment." The purpose of the press, he said, was "to serve the governed, not the governors," and thus must the press "remain forever free to censure the Government" and to "bare the secrets of government and inform the people."

Black regarded the Pentagon Papers as "current news of vital importance to the people of this country," and he declared that the newspapers should be commended for their "courageous reporting" of this information. "In reporting the workings of government that led to the Viet Nam war," he said, "the newspapers nobly did precisely that which the Founders hoped and trusted they would do."[24]

Justice Douglas shared Black's position, stating that the First Amendment leaves "no room for governmental restraint on the press." He explained that it was "common knowledge that the First Amendment was adopted against the widespread use of the common law of seditious libel to punish the dissemination of material that is embarrassing to the powers that be." Douglas concluded that the case "would go down in history as the most dramatic illustration of that principle."[25]

Justice Brennan, unlike Black and Douglas, did not claim an absolute prohibition of governmental prior restraint, but he did conclude that "every restraint in this case, whatever its form, has violated the First Amendment." This was so because the government had offered only "surmise" and "conjecture" as evidence of the need for injunctive relief. Brennan did offer a legal standard for determining when governmental prior restraint could be tolerated. "[O]nly governmental allegation and proof that publication must inevitably, directly and immediately cause the occurrence of an event kindred to imperiling the safety of a transport already at sea can support even the issuance of an interim restraining order." Because proof that publication must "inevitably" bring harm is virtually impossible, Brennan's standard is widely regarded as indistinguishable from the position of Black and Douglas.[26]

TIME, INC. V. HILL, 1974

Just three years later, in *Time, Inc. v. Hill* (1974), the Supreme Court gave its first explicit recognition to free press guarantees for magazines when it applied the *New York Times v. Sullivan* (1964) precedent to a libel action against *Life* magazine. The Hill family had sued *Life* for publishing an inaccurate account of a hostage incident they had suffered in 1952. A jury awarded them compensatory and punitive damages, and an appeals court ordered a new trial at which only compensatory damages were awarded. The Supreme Court reversed the award, saying constitutional guarantees of free expression could tolerate sanctions only against "calculated" falsehood.

Justice William Brennan, who delivered the Court's opinion, stated,

> The question in this case is whether the appellant, publisher of *Life Magazine*, was denied constitutional protections of speech and press. . . . We hold that [such protections] preclude the application of the New York statute to redress false reports of matters of public interest in the absence of proof that the defendant published the report with knowledge of its falsity or in reckless disregard of the truth. The guarantees for speech and press are not the preserve of political expression or comment upon public affairs, essential as those are to healthy government.

As had been attempted in years past with respect to motion pictures, the prosecution claimed that magazines were an inferior medium because of their commercial character. The Court rejected such a view by citing *Burstyn* (1952) and concluded, "That books, newspapers, and magazines are published and sold for profit does not prevent them from being a form of expression whose liberty is safeguarded by the First Amendment."[27]

FEDERAL COMMUNICATIONS COMMISSION V. PACIFICA FOUNDATION, 1978

In 1978 the courts addressed the authority of the FCC to censor indecent language on radio. The case was precipitated by a single complaint lodged with the FCC against a New York radio station for the broadcast of a twelve-minute monologue, "Filthy Words," from an album by humorist George Carlin. The FCC subsequently issued a declaratory order ruling that the program had been "indecent" and defined indecency to include "language or material that depicts or describes, in terms patently offensive as measured by contemporary standards for the broadcast medium, sexual or excretory activities or organs."[28] The FCC also warned the station that its programming would be scrutinized when its license came up for renewal. The owner of the New York station, Pacifica Foundation, appealed the FCC's ruling, which was then overturned by the U.S. Court of Appeals.

U.S. Court of Appeals judge Edward A. Tamm said the FCC order in the Pacifica case violated the no-censorship provision of the Communications Act and was "overbroad" in that it "sweepingly forbids any broadcast of the seven words (from the George Carlin monologue) irrespective of context or however innocent or educational they may be." In his concurring opinion, Chief Judge David Bazelon said that the FCC "incorrectly assumes that material regulatable for children can be banned from broadcast."[29]

The FCC appealed the decision to the Supreme Court. In *Federal Communications Commission v. Pacifica Foundation* (1978), the Court held that the Carlin broadcast was indecent because of the repetitive and deliberate use of words that refer to excretory or sexual activities during an afternoon broadcast that could be heard by children. Because the Court addressed just seven particular "indecent" words, it provided little guidance on how to recognize other indecencies. The FCC therefore chose to apply its indecency concept narrowly to the repetitive use of Carlin's seven dirty words under similar broadcast circumstances. For example, the FCC determined that a broadcast similar to Carlin's monologue would be permissable after 10 P.M. This attempt to sweep the problem under the rug would have short-term success, but within a decade the problem of indecency on the airwaves would be back in the courts.

FALWELL V. FLYNT, 1988

The high court had occasion to judge another kind of indecency, a satirical advertisement in *Hustler* magazine. In November 1983, Larry Flynt, the outrageous publisher of *Hustler*, published a full-page parody of a liquor ad showing evangelist Jerry Falwell's photograph accompanied by a fictitious interview with him. The *Hustler* ad mimicked the well-known Campari liqueur ads in which celebrities use sexually suggestive language to discuss the "first time" they tasted Campari. In *Hustler*, the satirical interview had Falwell identify his "first time" as having occurred in an outhouse with his mother. At the bottom of the ad was the disclaimer: "Ad parody—not to be taken seriously."

Falwell filed suit in federal district court, seeking $45 million in damages for the unauthorized use of his name and likeness, for false and defamatory statements and for the intentional infliction of "severe emotional anguish and distress."

When *Falwell v. Flynt* went to trial, Judge James Turk instructed the jury to consider just two counts: libel and the infliction of emotional distress. Falwell's attorney, Norman Grutman, attempted to prove that Flynt's ad represented "actual malice," the standard for libel of public figures established in *New York Times v. Sullivan* (1964). Alan Isaacman, Flynt's attorney, said the ad could not be libelous because no reasonable person could believe that the satirical interview was true. The jury agreed that the ad was too absurd to be the basis for libel, but it nonetheless found that Falwell had suffered emotional distress, for which it awarded him $100,000 in compensatory damages and $100,000 in punitive damages. Flynt appealed the jury's award, and Falwell appealed the judge's elimination of the charge of unauthorized use of his photograph.

At the time the appeal was heard, a number of press organizations, including the ANPA and the Reporters Committee for Freedom of the Press, filed briefs supporting Flynt. On August 5, 1986, the appeals panel issued a unanimous ruling upholding the lower court's judgement. In particular, the damage award to Falwell was upheld under the judgement that emotional distress can be inflicted even when there is no libel. Flynt appealed to the Supreme Court.

This would be Flynt's second case before the Supreme Court. In his first, in 1983, he had caused an uproar by spewing expletives at the justices, causing him to be physically ejected from the courtroom. This time, the Court was packed with spectators, many of whom anticipated another fireworks show. Instead, they were treated to a constitutional battle of major proportions.

Flynt's attorney, Alan Isaacman, addressed the justices: "This case raises as a general question whether the Court should expand the areas left unprotected by the First Amendment and create another exception of protected speech. . . . [T]he question becomes: 'Is rhetorical hyperbole, satire, parody, or opinion protected by the First Amendment when it doesn't contain assertions of fact and when the subject of the rhetorical hyperbole is a public figure?' "

Falwell's attorney, Norman Grutman, declared, "Deliberate, malicious character assassination is not protected by the First Amendment to the Constitution. . . . By the defendant's own explicit admission, the publication before this Court was the product of a deliberate plan to upset the character and integrity of the plaintiff, and to cause him severe emotional disturbance."[30]

But when Justices John Paul Stevens and Antonin Scalia questioned the applicability of *Sullivan* to this case, it became clear that uncharted First Amendment territory was being entered. Justice Byron White told Grutman, "If these were factual statements . . . you could win under *New York Times [v. Sullivan]* anytime."[31] But, since a jury had firmly established that the parody was not factual, another standard would have to be used.

On February 24, 1988, Chief Justice William Rehnquist delivered the Court's unanimous opinion that the *Hustler* parody was protected under the First Amendment. "This case presents us with a novel question involving First Amendment limitations upon a State's authority to protect its citizens from the intentional infliction of emotional distress," wrote Rehnquist.

> Respondent would have us find that a State's interest in protecting public figures from emotional distress is sufficient to deny First Amendment protection to speech that is patently offensive and is intended to inflict emotional injury, even when that speech could not reasonably have been interpreted as stating actual facts about the public figure involved. This we decline to do.
>
> Were we to hold otherwise, there can be little doubt that political cartoonists and satirists would be subjected to damage awards with-

out any showing that their work falsely defamed its subject. . . . "Outrageousness" in the area of political and social discourse has an inherent subjectiveness about it which would allow a jury to impose liability on the basis of the jurors' tastes or views. . . . We conclude that public figures and public officials may not recover for the tort of intentional infliction of emotional distress by reason of publications such as the one here at issue without showing in addition that the publication contains a false statement of fact which was made with "actual malice."[32]

The significance of the *Hustler* decision for all the media was captured by legal scholar Rodney Smolla.

The Supreme Court's opinion in *Falwell v. Flynt* is a triumphant celebration of freedom of speech. . . . Thomas Jefferson taught us that a little rebellion now and then is a good thing. Rebellion is often raucous and disturbing, indecorous and indecent. But it can also ring true, in the way that only George Carlin, Garry Trudeau, Richard Pryor, or Robin Williams can ring true. That Jeffersonian side of us is good for the soul.[33]

HAZELWOOD V. KUHLMEIER, 1988

Another 1988 Supreme Court decision, this one addressing censorship in public schools, showed the willingness of the courts to support virtually any controls on the media in the name of protecting our children. In *Hazelwood v. Kuhlmeier* (1988), the Court invoked the principle of judicial restraint when it allowed a Missouri school principal to censor articles on pregnancy and divorce from a student newspaper produced as part of a high school journalism class. "The First Amendment rights of students in the public schools are not automatically coextensive with the rights of adults in other settings," said the Court. "A school need not tolerate student speech that is inconsistent with its 'basic educational mission,' even though the government could not censor similar speech outside the school."

The Court did caution, however, "It is only when the decision to censor a school-sponsored publication, theatrical production, or other vehicle of student expression has no valid educational purpose that the First Amendment is so 'directly and sharply implicate[d]' as to require judicial intervention to protect students' constitutional rights."[34]

In many ways, *Hazelwood* contradicted the Court's declaration in *Tin-*

ker v. Des Moines Community School District (1969) that students do not shed their constitutional rights at the schoolhouse gate. Justice Byron White, writing for the *Hazelwood* Court, used the "public forum" doctrine to distinguish this case from *Tinker*. That doctrine says the degree of First Amendment protection on public property, such as a school, differs depending on the use of that property. In the "traditional" public forum, such as a park or a street, the government has no power to restrict expression on the basis of its content. The government can create a "limited" public forum by designating certain restrictions on the property, but the limited public forum is entitled to the same First Amendment protection as a traditional public forum.

A "closed" forum, on the other hand, exists on public property that does not operate as a traditional or restricted public forum. Examples would include certain government-supported activities, including curricular activities in public schools. Here, said the Court, the government can regulate speech so long as it is "reasonable." In *Hazelwood*, the Court declared that the high school newspaper in question was a closed forum, and that school officials were entitled to regulate its content in any reasonable manner. The court concluded that "educators do not offend the First Amendment by exercising editorial control over the style and content of student speech in school-sponsored expressive activities so long as their actions are reasonably related to legitimate pedagogical concerns."[35]

Although the trend since *Hazelwood* has been for lower courts to reject claims of First Amendment protection against official censorship of the student press, or of any student expression that is related to the curriculum, this view has been challenged in the courts and in the schools. Indeed, throughout the 1990s, the student press has continued to deal with official censorship in imaginative ways (see Appendix A).

ACTION FOR CHILDREN'S TELEVISION V. FCC, 1988

In recent years, the protection of children from indecency on the airwaves has remained the most significant area of official control of media expression in the broader society. The FCC continued to increase the frequency and scope of its regulation of indecent programming during the 1980s, and on April 29, 1987, the FCC released its Indecency Policy Reconsideration Order, allowing indecent programs to be aired only between midnight and 6 A.M. The order was appealed by a group of petitioners, including Action for Children's Television, as well as commercial networks, associations of broadcasters and journalists, and public interest groups. The petitioners argued that the FCC's definition of indecency was unconstitutionally vague and overbroad, and that the new hours during which indecent broadcasting was banned would effectively prohibit adult access to material protected by the First Amendment.

In *Action for Children's Television v. FCC* (1988), the appeals court held that the FCC's definition of indecency was not overbroad, but found that the restriction of such programming to the hours from midnight to 6 A.M. was unreasonable. The court therefore returned the case to the FCC for reconsideration of these hours. Soon after the court's decision, Congress passed a bill introduced by Senator Jesse Helms (R-N.C.), which required the FCC to promulgate regulations to enforce a twenty-four-hour-a-day ban on indecent broadcasting. The Helms Amendment, as it was called, was implemented by the FCC on December 21, 1988, but the action was again appealed by seventeen media and citizen groups led by Action for Children's Television, which sought an injunction against the twenty-four-hour ban. The D.C. Circuit Court of Appeals initially granted the stay, but later remanded it pending an FCC report documenting its ban.

The FCC report, released on August 6, 1990, claimed the twenty-four-hour ban was necessary to protect the nation's children, defined to be minors seventeen and under. The report said that alternative methods, such as ratings, warnings or lockout devices, would not totally remove the risk of exposing children to indecency.

On May 17, 1991, the appeals court struck down the twenty-four-hour ban, concluding that it violated constitutional protections on free speech. At issue here was the constitutionality of both the FCC's 1987 indecency standard and the Helms Amendment, which attempted to apply that standard on a twenty-four-hour basis. The court felt compelled by the Supreme Court's *Pacifica* (1978) ruling to uphold the FCC's definition of "indecency," but the controls on indecent programming had to be carefully crafted.

In affirming the right of adult access to indecent material, the appeals court stated: "Broadcast material that is indecent but not obscene is protected by the First Amendment; the FCC may regulate such material only with due respect for the high value our Constitution places on freedom and choice in what the people say and hear."[36]

The court thus concluded that the Helms Amendment was unconstitutional, but that, within reasonable restrictions, the FCC's indecency standard did not violate the First Amendment. As the result of this decision and a similar Supreme Court ruling, the FCC was led to reduce its indecency ban to the hours from 6 A.M. to midnight, but this was once again struck down by the appeals court in Washington, D.C. The FCC then proposed a new 6 A.M. to 10 P.M. ban, which was eventually approved by an appeals court. In early January 1996 the Supreme Court refused to review that ruling, rejecting arguments made by the broadcasting industry, the news media and free speech advocates. FCC Chairman Reed Hundt said that the decision vindicated the FCC's indecency policy.

The court judgements in these skirmishes between the FCC and radio broadcasters were assumed to apply to broadcasting in general, that is, to television. But the conservative character of the television networks made these cases virtually irrelevant to the television industry. After all, the idea of George Carlin's "Seven Dirty Words" ever appearing on a television broadcast was absurd. Cable television, however, was another matter.

TURNER BROADCASTING SYSTEM V. FEDERAL COMMUNICATIONS COMMISSION, 1994

The Supreme Court first addressed the extent of First Amendment protections for cable television in early 1994, when, in *Turner Broadcasting System v. Federal Communications Commission*, it examined the question of whether Congress could require cable systems to set aside one-third of their channels for local broadcasters, called "must-carry" regulations. The cable companies had appealed a 1993 decision made by a district court that found that the must-carry regulations did not violate the First Amendment because they did not target programming content. The cable companies claimed that the government was indeed trying to regulate the content of protected speech. During oral arguments, Justice David H. Souter declared that cable television might, for legal purposes, be defined as somewhere between a newspaper and telephone services, both an originator and a carrier.

On June 27, 1994, the Court rendered a unanimous landmark decision that stated that cable television was entitled to virtually the same constitutional guarantees of free speech as newspapers and magazines. Though the Court did not strike down the must-carry regulations, as the cable companies had sought, it set up new legal ground rules for cable and wire-based communications systems that provide more First Amendment protection from government interference than is available to broadcasters. The Court distinguished cable systems from broadcast systems, whose "spectrum scarcity" has been used to justify heavy regulation. Historically, the courts have accepted the government's claim that since there are only a finite number of frequencies on which to broadcast, the FCC must allocate and oversee them in the public interest.

"Cable television does not suffer from the inherent limitations that characterize the broadcast medium," said Justice Anthony Kennedy. "Indeed, given the rapid advances in [technology], soon there may be no practical limitation on the number of speakers who may use the cable medium." Kennedy, joined by all of the other justices, said a cable regulation should be upheld only if it furthers an "important or substantial" government interest, a standard slightly below the level of protection accorded newspapers, but greater than that accorded broadcasters.[37]

DENVER AREA EDUCATIONAL TELECOMMUNICATIONS CONSORTIUM, INC. V. FCC, 1996

Cable television, nevertheless, soon came under federal pressure to curb its sexually explicit programming. In early 1996, in *Denver Area Educational Telecommunications Consortium, Inc. v. FCC,* the Supreme Court heard arguments over the constitutionality of 1992 "indecency" restrictions sponsored by Senator Jesse Helms (R-N.C.). These restrictions on cable programming were comparable to the earlier indecency provisions imposed on the broadcast media by the Helms Amendment. Under that law, a cable company could ban programming that it "reasonably believes describes or depicts sexual or excretory activities or organs in a patently offensive manner as measured by contemporary standards." The government claimed that, though the law allows cable operators to block indecent programs, it does not "significantly encourage" them to do so, and therefore any programming censorship could not be attributed to the government. During oral arguments, Justice Ruth Bader Ginsburg said that the provision authorizing cable companies to block indecent programming, unless a subscriber makes a written request to the contrary, makes it difficult and uncomfortable for a person to access protected speech.

On June 28, 1996, the Supreme Court voted five to four in the *Denver* case to strike down the section of the law that allowed cable companies to refuse to air indecent material—defined as sexually explicit or "patently offensive"—on "public access" channels, those required by local governments. The justices also voted six to three to strike down the section of the act that required subscribers to "leased access" channels—those paid for by independent programmers—to submit a written request before "indecent" programs could be received. In explaining why the Court struck down the two provisions, Justice Stephen Breyer declared that they violated the First Amendment because "they are not tailored to achieve the basic, legitimate objective of protecting children from exposure to patently offensive material." By a vote of seven to two, however, the Court upheld sections of the law allowing cable operators to refuse "indecent" programming on these "leased access" channels.[38]

ACLU V. RENO, 1997

Another more publicized censorship provision, contained in the giant Telecommunications Act of 1996, was the Communications Decency Act (CDA), intended to control expression on the Internet, the fledgling media technology that had been considered virtually uncensorable. In 1995 Senator James Exon (D-Neb.) had introduced a bill regulating electronic communications, amending an existing law by changing the word "telephone" to "telecommunications devices." The Exon bill extended criminal liability to anyone who makes available any "comment, request, suggestion, proposal, image or other communication" that is found to be "obscene, lewd, lascivious, filthy or indecent." The penalties under Exon's act of 1995 included fines of up to $100,000 and two years in jail and applied even to messages exchanged privately between adults.

Despite heavy opposition from public interest groups, the bill, folded into a major telecommunications deregulation package, easily passed through committee and went on to the full Senate. In June 1995 the bill passed the full Senate by an overwhelming vote of eighty-four to sixteen. The House bill was a considerable improvement over the Senate bill, but it still included a provision that would make it a crime to use offensive terms about "sexual or excretory activities or organs" in computer communications with anyone believed to be under eighteen years of age.

By the end of 1995, the congressional tide had turned against the moderates and free speech advocates, and House lawmakers agreed to apply to computer networks the existing sexual content laws designed for broadcasting and telephone conversations. Like the earlier Senate bill, the House bill provided prison sentences and heavy fines for anyone who "knowingly" transmits obscene or indecent material to minors or to public areas of the Internet where minors might see it.

On February 1, 1996, Congress overwhelmingly passed the Telecommunications Act of 1996, including the CDA, which imposed heavy criminal penalties for Internet indecency. The bill defined indecency as any communication "that, in context, depicts or describes, in terms patently offensive as measured by contemporary community standards, sexual or excretory activities or organs."

President Bill Clinton signed the full bill just a week after its passage, but many in Congress and elsewhere were uncomfortable. A group of public service organizations, including the American Civil Liberties Union (ACLU) and the Electronic Frontier Foundation, prepared their own lawsuit, *ACLU v. Reno* (1996), challenging the Internet indecency provisions on constitutional grounds. Chris Hansen, the ACLU's lead counsel in the case, said,

> Our chances of success depend fundamentally on how the judges come to see the Internet—will they view it as analogous to the print medium, or to broadcasting? We argue that the Internet should be analyzed as another element of the public square, rather than a new variant of a broadcast medium. . . . If the judges understand that even though a computer monitor may resemble a television, the Internet has more in common structurally with the printing press, our chances of obtaining a preliminary injunction are strong.[39]

The Justice Department said it would defend the indecency standard in the legislation and would defend similar statutes against constitutional challenges, so long as they were consistent with Supreme Court rulings in this area.

On February 15, in response to the ACLU suit, U.S. District Judge Ronald Buckwalter blocked government enforcement of the Internet decency provision. Buckwalter said his order applied only to the ban on "indecent materials," not to the provision against "patently offensive" material. Civil liberties lawyers were somewhat confused by the ruling, since the words "patently offensive" appear within the bill's definition of "indecent materials."

As provided in the telecommunications bill, the chief judge for the U.S. Court of Appeals for Eastern Pennsylvania named a three-judge panel to rule on the challenge to the indecency provision, after which the matter could be appealed directly to the Supreme Court. The Clinton administration defended the indecency provision, claiming that it applied only to communications to minors. The plaintiffs argued that Congress failed to consider the least restrictive means to block indecency from minors, which would be software designed for parental control of Internet access. Plaintiffs contended that the law as written would chill free speech on-line, including material with literary or educational value that deals with issues such as sexuality, reproduction, human rights and civil liberties.

On February 26, another group of organizations and businesses filed suit under the umbrella of the American Library Association (ALA). The suit, which for the first time included all the major on-line companies as well as the trade and professional associations of newspaper publishers, editors and reporters, was filed in the same court as the ACLU suit and combined with it. The draft ALA complaint maintained that the on-line medium in which people seek information differs from the broadcast model that gave rise to the indecency standard. The complaint noted: "The speech at issue in this case . . . does *not* include obscenity, child pornography, or other speech that lacks First Amendment protection even for adults."[40]

On June 12, 1996, the special three-judge panel addressing *ACLU v. Reno* declared that the Internet restrictions in the CDA violated the constitutional guarantee of free speech. Judge Stewart Dalzell concluded:

> Cutting through the acronyms and argot that littered the hearing testimony, the Internet may fairly be regarded as a never-ending world-wide conversation. The Government may not, through the C.D.A., interrupt that conversation. As the most participatory form of mass speech yet developed, the Internet deserves the highest protection from government intrusion. . . . Just as the strength of the Internet is chaos, so the strength of our liberty depends upon the chaos and cacophony of the unfettered speech the First Amendment protects. For these reasons, I without hesitation hold that the C.D.A. is unconstitutional on its face.[41]

The opinion granted First Amendment protections to the Internet that are equal to, if not stronger than, those afforded to print material.

The court accepted the plaintiffs' contention that parents could best protect their children from objectional on-line material by using readily available software to screen Internet content. The availability of such tools, said the judges, meant that the CDA failed to employ the least restrictive means to regulate speech, as required by the Constitution. Chief Judge Dolores K. Sloviter wrote,

> Those responsible for minors undertake the primary obligation to prevent their exposure to such [indecent] material. Instead, in the C.D.A., Congress chose to place on the speakers the obligation of screening the material that would possibly offend some communities. Whether Congress's decision was a wise one is not at issue here. It was unquestionably a decision that placed the CDA in serious conflict with our most cherished protection—the right to choose the material to which we would have access.

Judge Ronald Buckwalter wrote, "I believe that the challenged provisions are so vague as to violate both the First and Fifth Amendments. . . . In addition, I believe that technology as it currently exists . . . cannot provide a safe harbor for most speakers on the Internet, thus rendering the statute unconstitutional under a strict scrutiny analysis." Nonetheless, Judge Buckwalter left the door open for other legislative attempts to regulate the Internet, saying, "I believe it is too early in the development of this new medium to conclude that other attempts to regulate protected speech within the medium will fail a challenge."[42]

Judge Dalzell, on the other hand, was decisive in rejecting future attempts to recraft the CDA. He declared that the CDA's disruptive effect on Internet communication and its broad reach into protected speech "not only render the Act unconstitutional but would also render unconstitutional any regulation of protected speech on this new medium."[43]

Even before the panel's ruling, government lawyers had said they would appeal any adverse decision to the Supreme Court, and President Clinton said he remained convinced that the Constitution allowed laws like the CDA to protect children from exposure to objectionable material. Senator Exon, who introduced the bill that became the CDA, said he expected to win approval for the bill in the Supreme Court, but Laurence Tribe, a constitutional expert at Harvard Law School, disagreed. He had argued a 1989 case in which the Supreme Court unanimously ruled that a federal ban on "indecent" telephone messages violated the constitutional right to free speech. The same principles, according to Tribe, applied with respect to the CDA. "The Internet is the telephone writ large," he said.[44]

The final judgement on the CDA was, of course, left in the hands of the Supreme Court, which, on June 26, 1997, struck down the CDA as an abridgement of " 'the freedom of speech' protected by the First Amendment." The seven-to-two opinion actually had the strength of unanimity on the issue of constitutionality, since even the minority opinion, signed by Justice Sandra Day O'Connor and joined by Chief Justice William Rehnquist, concurred in part and supported much of the majority's approach. O'Connor said the CDA was an attempt to create "adult zones" on the Internet, but she said that "portions of the C.D.A. are unconstitutional because they stray from the blueprint our prior cases have developed for constructing a 'zoning law' that passes constitutional muster."

The majority opinion, written by Justice John Paul Stevens, was a forceful rejection of the CDA and a ringing endorsement of the democratic potential of the Internet. "[O]ur cases provide no basis for qualifying the level of First Amendment scrutiny that should be applied to this medium," wrote Stevens.

> The vagueness of the CDA is a matter of special concern for two reasons. First, the CDA is a content-based regulation of speech. The vagueness of such a regulation raises special First Amendment concerns because of its obvious chilling effect on free speech. . . . Second, the CDA is a criminal statute. In addition to the opprobrium and stigma of a criminal conviction, the CDA threatens violators with penalties including up to two years in prison for each act of violation. The severity of criminal actions may well cause speakers to remain silent rather than communicate even arguably unlawful words, ideas, and images.

Stevens stated further,

> Given the vague contours of the coverage of the statute, it unquestionably silences some speakers whose messages would be entitled to constitutional protection. . . . [T]he CDA lacks the precision that the First Amendment requires when a statute regulates the content of speech. In order to deny minors access to potentially harmful speech, the CDA effectively suppresses a large amount of speech that

adults have a constitutional right to receive and to address to one another. . . . The general, undefined terms "indecent" and "patently offensive" cover large amounts of nonpornographic material with serious educational or other value. Moreover, the "community standards" criterion as applied to the Internet means that any communication available to a nationwide audience will be judged by the standards of the community most likely to be offended by the message.

Stevens concluded, "The CDA, casting a far darker shadow over free speech, threatens to torch a large segment of the Internet community. . . . The interest in encouraging freedom of expression in a democratic society outweighs any theoretical but unproven benefit of censorship."[45]

Civil libertarians and the business community were elated by the strongly worded opinion. Jerry Berman of the Center for Democracy and Technology, called the decision "the Bill of Rights for the 21st century."[46]

PLAYBOY ENTERTAINMENT GROUP V. UNITED STATES, 1997 AND SPICE ENTERTAINMENT COMPANIES V. RENO, 1997

Another Supreme Court ruling affecting cable television programming came in 1997, when the Court allowed the government to begin enforcing a law that requires cable operators to scramble the signals of certain sexually explicit programs so that children cannot inadvertently see them. In two combined cases, *Playboy Entertainment Group v. United States* and *Spice Entertainment Companies v. Reno*, the Court summarily affirmed a three-judge panel's denial of an injunction implementing the law, without issuing an opinion or a recorded vote.

The law in question, part of the massive Telecommunications Act signed by President Bill Clinton in February 1996, requires cable operators to completely block sexually oriented programs from nonsubscribing homes or, if that is not feasible, to transmit such programming only between 10 P.M. and 6 A.M. The cable operators complained that because complete scrambling is prohibitively expensive, they would be forced to transmit sexually oriented material only at night, violating their free speech right to show such programs to adults during the day. Denying the injunction, they said, would have devastating conse-

quences for the ability to provide constitutionally protected adult programming.

NOTES

1. *United States v. Hudson and Goodwin,* 1 Cranch 32, 34 (1812).

2. *Mutual Film Corporation v. Industrial Commission of Ohio,* 236 U.S. 230,
236–38, 242–44 (1915).

3. *Essential Liberty: First Amendment Battles for a Free Press,* preface by Joan
Konner, introduction by Harrison E. Salisbury, essays by Francis Wilkinson,
afterword by Floyd Abrams (New York: Columbia University Graduate School
of Journalism, 1992), 14–25.

4. Fred W. Friendly, untitled essay in *Essential Liberty: First Amendment Battles
for a Free Press* (New York: Columbia University Graduate School of Journalism,
1992), 27.

5. *Near v. Minnesota,* 283 U.S. 697, 711, 714 (1931).

6. *Grosjean v. American Press Association Company,* 297 U.S. 233 (1936), at
248–50.

7. Louis Caldwell, "Freedom of Speech and Radio Broadcasting," *Annals
of the American Academy* 177 (January 1935): 179–207.

8. Ibid.

9. *National Broadcasting Company v. United States,* 319 U.S. 190, 226 (1943).

10. Leon Hurwitz, *Historical Dictionary of Censorship in the United States* (Westport, Conn.: Greenwood Press, 1985), 94.

11. *Hanegan v. Esquire,* 327 U.S. 142, 158 (1946).

12. *Joseph Burstyn, Inc. v. Wilson,* 72 Sup. Ct. 777, 780 (1952).

13. *Superior Films v. Department of Education of Ohio,* 346 U.S. 587, 588–89
(1953).

14. Leon Friedman, ed., *Obscenity: The Complete Oral Arguments Before the Supreme Court in the Major Obscenity Cases* (New York: Chelsea House, 1983), 67–
85.

15. *Kingsley International Pictures Corp. v. Regents of the University of the State of
New York,* 360 U.S. 684, 688–90 (1959).

16. *New York Times v. Sullivan,* 376 U.S. 254, 266–70, 280, 298 (1964).

17. *Estes v. Texas,* 381 U.S. 532, 540 (1965).

18. *Ginzburg v. United States,* 383 U.S. 463, 474, 487, 494 (1966).

19. Hurwitz, *Historical Dictionary of Censorship,* 132.

20. Friedman, *Obscenity,* 287–88, 294.

21. *Ginsberg v. New York,* 390 U.S. 629, 649–50, 673–74 (1968).

22. *Red Lion Broadcasting Company v. Federal Communications Commission,* 395
U.S. 367, 386–89 (1969).

23. *Essential Liberty,* 65.

24. *New York Times Company v. United States*, 403 U.S. 713 (1971) at 717.

25. Ibid., at 721–24.

26. Ibid., at 726–27.

27. *Time, Inc. v. Hill*, 424 U.S. 374, 376, 387–88, 397 (1974).

28. *Pacifica Foundation*, 56 FCC 2d 94 (1975).

29. *Federal Communications Commission v. Pacifica Foundation*, 438 U.S. 726 (1978).

30. Rodney A. Smolla, *Jerry Falwell v. Larry Flynt: The First Amendment on Trial* (Urbana: University of Illinois Press, 1990), 264, 278.

31. Ibid., 284.

32. *Hustler Magazine, Inc. v. Falwell*, 108 Sup. Ct. 876 (1988).

33. Smolla, *Jerry Falwell v. Larry Flynt*, 303.

34. *Hazelwood School District v. Kuhlmeier*, 108 Sup. Ct. 562, 571 (1988).

35. Ibid.

36. *Action for Children's Television v. Federal Communications Commission*, 852 F2d 1332 (D.C. Cir. 1988).

37. *Turner Broadcasting System v. Federal Communications Commission*, 114 Sup. Ct. 503 (1969).

38. *Denver Area Educational Telecommunications Consortium, Inc. v. Federal Communications Commission*, 116 Sup. Ct. 2374 (1996).

39. Chris Hansen, untitled article, *ACLU Spotlight*, Spring 1996, 3.

40. "Coalition to File Suit over Internet Rules," *Washington Post*, February 26, 1996, A4.

41. *American Civil Liberties Union v. Reno*, 929 F. Supp 824 (E.D. Pa. 1996), at 883.

42. Ibid., at 857–59.

43. Ibid., at 867.

44. "Ruling Declares Internet a Complex Medium That Will Be Hard to Regulate," *New York Times*, June 13, 1996, B10.

45. *American Civil Liberties Union v. Reno* (1997), in *United States Law Week*, 65 LW 4715, at 4723–27.

46. "1st Amendment Applies to Internet, Justices Say," *New York Times*, June 27, 1997, A1.

Four

Voices from the Media

The determination with which media professionals have opposed censorship, often at great personal cost, has been made clear in the previous chapters, but their personal strength and intellectual conviction can best be revealed in their own words. The six individuals interviewed here are representative voices from newspapers, magazines, motion pictures, broadcasting and the Internet.

Paul Jarrico: The Hollywood Inquisition

Paul Jarrico was among Hollywood's busiest screenwriters during the 1930s and 1940s. His early credits include *No Time to Marry* (1938), *Beauty for the Asking* (1939), *The Face Behind the Mask* (1941), *Tom, Dick and Harry* (1941), *Song of Russia* (1943), *Thousands Cheer* (1943), *The Search* (1948) and *The White Tower* (1950). He was also one of Hollywood's radicals, a not uncommon category in that community. He had served in the armed forces, moreover, during World War II, when the United States and its Communist ally, the Soviet Union, formed a united front against fascism. But after the allied victory over Nazi Germany and its axis allies, the Cold War began to cast a chill over leftist expression, making talented individuals like Paul Jarrico politically unacceptable in Hollywood. A conspiracy of conservative politicians and craven Hollywood producers introduced "blacklisting," the systematic process that fired and exiled some of America's best actors, writers and directors simply because of their politics. After the initial Hollywood Ten (see Chapter 1) were jailed for defying the House Un-American Activities Committee (HUAC) hundreds more, including Jarrico, were targeted.

When Jarrico was denied work as a screenwriter, he formed an independent production company in an attempt to bypass both the blacklist and the stifling political control of the Hollywood studios. The aim of the new company was to use blacklisted talent to produce films about the working men and women of America. In the process, quipped Jarrico, they hoped to commit a crime worthy of the punishment they had already received. The company's first film, *Salt of the Earth* (1954), was also its last, due to a coordinated film industry boycott which denied professional services during filming and blocked it from being shown in all but about a dozen theaters in the country. Although it went on to win international prizes and was hailed as a classic in many parts of the world, it is still barely known in the United States.

When I spoke with Jarrico in May 1997,[1] he showed little bitterness about his long ordeal, but he recalled the details clearly. He described his subpoena before the HUAC and his consequent firing, without notice, by the studio for which he worked.

"I didn't anticipate being turned away from the RKO lot," said Jarrico, "but I was not all that surprised. I was dodging a subpoena from the Un-American Activities Committee at the time. It was a little difficult, because it had been publicized that they were looking for me, along with a group of others. They knew I was working at the studio, so the idea that they had to search the city for me was ridiculous.

"They arrived at my home the evening before the studio turned me away, trailed by some newspaper people. I played it as though I had been there all the time, and asked why they had such trouble finding me. A newspaper reporter asked me what I would do now that I had been summoned before the Committee, and I made a statement that has been repeated and printed a number of times. I said I would go before the Committee, but if I had to choose between crawling in the mud with Larry Parks [an actor who gave HUAC the names of alleged Communists in Hollywood] or going to jail like my courageous friends of the Hollywood Ten, you could be sure I would choose the latter. That was printed in the next morning's papers, and when I got to the studio, the guards had been instructed not to let me onto the lot."

Jarrico had done nothing wrong. Why did the studio feel the need to take action against him? "Because of Howard Hughes [owner of RKO]," he said. "Howard Hughes was a nut."

I wondered whether the studio mogels really believed all of that HUAC nonsense, or whether they were just frightened businessmen. "That goes way back," explained Jarrico, "much earlier than my particular case, which was in the spring of 1951. In the fall of 1947, the Hollywood Ten had denied the right of the Committee to inquire into their politics and their associations. They stood on the First Amendment and wound up in prison after the Supreme Court had refused to hear their appeals. When they were finally leaving prison in the spring of 1951, the Committee hit again, and I was among the group that I call the Second Wave, which turned the Hollywood Ten into the Hollywood Hundreds.

"So the studios had initiated the blacklist in 1947. There was no mystery about it. If you didn't cooperate with the Committee, which meant giving names, because that's the way the Committee defined 'cooperation,' you were blacklisted. And since I made it clear that I was not going to cooperate with the Committee, it was only a question of time. If there was any drama in my being turned away by the studio, it was only because it occurred immediately after I was subpoenaed." If Howard Hughes was behind RKO's politics, did he pull all the political strings? "He owned RKO," said Jarrico, "and interfered only to see that he had a continuing supply of girls and that nothing 'Red' could be produced. But he was not an active head of production."

"The other studios were just as bad. They just didn't do it in quite such a crude way. Anyone who refused to cooperate was fired and never hired again, not for many, many years. I was a fairly well known radical in Hollywood, more than some of the others. But, in one way or another, it happened to everyone who refused to cooperate."

I asked whether Jarrico had any legal recourse against such arbitrary action. "I sued the studio and they sued me," he said. "I sued them for breaking my contract, and for denying me a credit on a picture that I was working on at that time. It went into production almost immediately after I was fired, and although Hughes had ordered that the script be rewritten entirely so that none of that poisonous Jarrico stuff remained, they were unable to do that. The Writers Guild, which has control of credits, awarded me a credit after arbitration, and Howard Hughes said, 'Over my dead body, I'm not going to put his name on my screen.' This despite the fact that another RKO picture I had written, *The White Tower*, was already in distribution.

"He sued the Guild, and I sued him, and he sued me for violating the morals clause of my contract. In court, I said that standing on one's constitutional rights was not immoral, but the judge ruled that I had indeed placed myself in public obloquy. He then shook my hand, saying it was a pleasure to be associated with me. There were a lot of ironies in this situation."

After Jarrico had been disposed of by the studio, how did he survive? "One of the ironies of the blacklist," said Jarrico, "was that they took away our passports at the same time that they prevented our employment. I had already been to Europe several times, and I knew I could get work there, but I couldn't get out of the country. So some of us organized a company to use the talents of the blacklisted. We had several scripts in preparation, with several good blacklisted writers working on them. Then, more or less by accident, I happened to come across this strike in New Mexico in which the women had taken over the picket line. I came back from New Mexico full of excitement about what I had seen and sold my colleagues in our company on making this our first project.

"So I produced *Salt of the Earth*. Herbert Biberman directed it, and we persuaded Michael Wilson to write it. He was, we felt, the best blacklisted writer among us. He went down there while the strike was still in progress and observed and wrote. He sent back a treatment, and with our feedback and criticism it just grew out of the actual situation. This was our way of fighting back. It was a conscious effort to use the talents of the blacklistees and to say things that we had never been able to say as Hollywood filmmakers, and to try to counterattack. We felt we were doing something good and important. We didn't realize that it would become a classic, but we thought that if the market was open to us, we could make money with the picture and plow it back into making other pictures with content."

Thus, ironically, the blacklist was directly responsible for a film that is still in heavy demand on campuses and small theaters, but when it was made, the film itself was blacklisted. I asked Jarrico if he anticipated the enormous difficulties he would encounter in getting the film distributed.

"No," he said, "we didn't think we would have as much trouble as we had. We were sending material to a big laboratory in Hollywood and they were sending back the rushes for examination. We were proceeding in a normal way to make a movie—until the stuff hit the fan. They discovered that people who had been kicked out of Hollywood had the effrontery to be making a movie. Then all hell broke loose. About three weeks after we started shooting, we were denounced on the floor of Congress by a member of the Un-American Activities Committee, who told his colleagues that we were making a new weapon for Russia, that we were shooting not far from Los Alamos, and where you find atom bombs you find Communists. This kind of crap was broadcast on the local stations and suddenly the laboratory in Hollywood would no longer develop any of our film. It happened very, very quickly.

"Newspaper reporters descended on us. Airplanes were buzzing our sets. Our star, who had come up from Mexico, was arrested and held for deportation on the flimsiest of charges. There were numerous examples of a concerted effort to stop the film. After many obstacles, we managed to finish the film, but it didn't make any money, because we couldn't get any distribution. We lost our shirts, and we didn't make any other films."

Once again, Jarrico turned to the courts for justice but found little. "We sued the entire motion picture industry, including the studios and the various service companies, laboratories, sound studios and so on for conspiracy to prevent the making of the film, of which they were indeed guilty under the antitrust laws. It dragged through the courts for eight years, as studio lawyers tried to make communism the legal issue. Our point was that we had a right to make an independent film, whether we were Communists, gangsters, or anything else.

"In the fall of 1964, ten years after the film was first exhibited in New York, there was a ten-week trial in district court in New York. We lost. The jury was sympathetic, as they later told us, but they felt that we had not proved conspiracy. The spokesmen for the studios and companies involved admitted that they had refused to service our production, but they claimed they didn't do it in collusion. According to the judge's instructions, we failed to prove collusion, and we lost. Essentially, we lost because we were unable to subpoena Howard Hughes. We were forced to drop him from among the defendants, preventing us from introducing a letter he had written to a congressman on the Un-American Activities Committee. The congressman had written to Hughes, asking, 'What can we do to stop these people?' and Hughes outlined the entire conspiracy in his response.

"Hughes said that the filmmakers could be stopped because they did not have the equipment, the technical facilities and the technical people to complete a film on their own. He said we could be stopped in the laboratories, in the mixing studios, and so on. He outlined the whole damn thing. But we could never get that into the evidence or testimony.''

Since his attempt as an independent film producer failed, financially at least, Jarrico had to find other ways to survive. ''I did what most blacklisted writers did,'' said Jarrico. ''I worked on the black market and managed to support myself. You know, phony names, pseudonyms, fronts, any way to conceal one's identity.

''In 1958, when the Supreme Court ruled that the State Department did not have the right to withhold our passports, I took off for Europe, despite the fact that the black market was beginning to flourish here. Even though the producers in Europe knew who I was and hired me very consciously, they still insisted that I use pseudonyms because they didn't want to jeopardize their access to the American market.''

In order to understand the sordid role of the studios in a decade of McCarthyism, it is necessary to acknowledge the fear that stalked the nation. ''The studios were afraid of losing their audience,'' said Jarrico. ''They were afraid of boycotts. They knew that the Red Scare had made many people unwilling to attend movies created by Reds or people accused of being Reds. The fear was palpable, and it wasn't only in the film industry. It included radio and TV, of course, but it went beyond the entertainment industry. The same thing was happening in schools, universities, and government. People were fired wholesale, simply on suspicion of leftist associations. It was happening in unions as well, where either the union expelled the Reds or the union itself was expelled from the AFL/CIO.''

I asked Jarrico how the political hysteria came to an end. ''Things began to change, slowly,'' he said. ''The blacklist didn't end with a bang, but with a whimper. The Un-American Activities Committee lost popular support as its behavior became increasingly outrageous. There was less and less fear as the years went by. People came to realize they really had nothing to be afraid of. They had been cowards, basically for business reasons.

''Then the industry began to experience some real problems. The rise of television put the fear of God in them, a real fear. Then the courts required the studios to divest, to give up control of their own theaters and distribution companies. That created havoc in the industry. The foreign market was also increasingly closed to American films, as foreign countries put up barriers to protect their own industry. And of course, by this time the blacklist had drained the American film industry of some of its best talent. This, and the pervasive fear within the industry, brought about a perceptible change in the kind of pictures being made. They started making big screen epics, adventure films, musicals, and generally vapid films. It may be a little unfair, but it is said that the films of the 1940s are epitomized by *Casablanca* and the films of the 1950s by *Pillow Talk.*

"The blacklist began to crumble in 1956 or '57 when Jules Dassin made two pictures, *Rififi* and *Never on Sunday,* which United Artists backed and distributed, though they set up a dummy corporation as the distributing company. The pictures were distributed very successfully and there were no picket lines. So the fear of adverse public reaction was shown to be clearly unmerited. Dassin was the first to break the blacklist, though that honor is often given to screen-writer Dalton Trumbo who, in 1960, received credit under his own name for two very big pictures, *Spartacus* and *Exodus.*"

And what is Jarrico doing today?

"I'm doing the same thing I've done all my life," he said. "I write and I hustle. I'm a screenwriter and I have been for an awfully long time. I'm currently active on the Guild committee that's restoring credits to blacklistees. In some cases it's obvious, but we do a lot of detective work, investigating whether credits were indeed earned. If people worked under a consistent pseudonym that was on file with the Guild, we simply restore their own names as having earned the credit. The producers have been more or less cooperative. They won't go back and change the prints they already have, but if they go into new markets with an old picture, say home video or laser disk, they have promised to make the change in credits."

For a man who endured the worst period of political censorship in American history, Jarrico shows little bitterness. "I'm not really typical of most of the blacklistees," he said, "because I was pretty well fed up with what I was able to do in Hollywood before I was blacklisted. I had already started to try to make independent films with content. I had been to Europe, trying to put together a deal to make a picture. I failed to get it off the ground, but nevertheless I was already looking for ways to make films outside of the Hollywood system. So for me, it wasn't quite as big a blow as it was for many others. I did manage to make a living during the 17 years when I could not receive a credit under my own name. Also, I guess I'm a generally sanguine person."

I asked Jarrico what he thought about the current flurry of interest in Hollywood morality being expressed by political figures like Bob

Dole. "Of course there's a very real danger there, but that has been continuous. I gave a lecture in Denmark last year in which I pointed out that just one year after films began to be projected, instead of viewed through peep-holes, some of the gyrations in Fatima's dance were being erased to make it less sexual. They were already altering the film technically. So censorship has been there from the beginning.

"The power of film to express cultural values was recognized immediately, and the effort to prevent the expression of values that were opposed by the religious right, or whatever it was called at that time, began immediately. There were local censorship boards, state censorship boards, and an effort to set up a mechanism within the industry to police itself. This went on until the mid-1960s, when the various protest movements helped to liberate Hollywood. Of course, the government is still imposing standards upon the film industry and all the other means of communication."

Though Jarrico suffered personally and professionally from the Red Scare, he sees no possibility of a new McCarthyism. "It won't take that form," he said. "The fear that was palpable in the late 1940s and early 1950s, especially during the McCarthy period, was unique. You could feel that fear. But a generation of social protest, including the civil rights movement, has changed that. Today, Americans are more willing to stand up to their government."

Howard Morland: Telling the H-Bomb Secret

Antiwar activist Howard Morland was known to few beyond his grassroots network until he wrote an article for *Progressive* magazine in 1979 purporting to tell "The H-Bomb Secret." The article provoked a government injunction against publication and a landmark First Amendment court case, described in Chapter 2. Morland, a layman with little formal training in science, had initially intended merely to educate his fellow antinuclear activists about the military half of the nuclear industry. In 1977 he found it puzzling that the unintended dangers of nuclear power could foster greater public opposition than the deliberate production of nuclear weapons, which entailed all of the environmental and safety risks of nuclear reactor operation, plus the danger of nuclear war. He concluded that access to information was the difference.

Morland suspected that any industrialized nation could quickly determine the design concept for the H-bomb. He noted that every encyclopedia contained a schematic drawing of a generic thermonuclear weapon, or H-bomb, with a short explanation of how it worked, and he concluded that the real reason for maintaining the classification of a now widely known "secret" was to bias policy decisions and stifle public debate.

Morland had been an Air Force pilot in Vietnam before his activist days, and subsequent to his work for *Progressive* magazine he wrote a book, *The Secret that Exploded* [1981], documenting his confrontation with the federal government. He spent the next decade working as a lobbyist and researcher for grassroots groups. Today he lives in Virginia, spends most of his time doing carpentry, and says his only political activity is his responsibility as president of the local Neighborhood Association.

When I spoke with Morland on April 10, 1997, he began by describing the path that led to his article on the H-bomb.

"I came to this experience more as an antinuclear, antiwar activist, than as a journalist," he said. "I had done virtually no formal writing before the *Progressive* article. I had been an Air Force pilot in the Vietnam War and for a while after leaving the service I was fairly alienated from the whole of American society. I was pretty much a peace activist, advocating nuclear disarmament and nonintervention overseas, but I didn't really know very much about the bomb.

"I grew up in Chattanooga, Tennessee, which is 90 miles downstream from Oak Ridge, where the main H-bomb factory is located. My high school football team played against theirs. I was steeped in the nuclear mystique, because it's one of the more interesting things that happens in eastern Tennessee. By the 1970s I knew a lot about the downside of nuclear power, because I had read a book called *Perils of the Peaceful Atom*, by Richard Curtis [1970]. In New Hampshire, where I was going to graduate school, I joined a group called the Clamshell Alliance, which was protesting the construction of the Seabrook nuclear power plant. There were about 2,000 of us at the construction site on May Day, 1977, and 1,400 of us were arrested in a civil disobedience action.

"A month later I joined a demonstration at the Electric Boat plant in Groton, Connecticut, where General Dynamics makes nuclear submarines, including the Trident ballistic missile submarine. There were only 200 people there, and I wondered why so many fewer people protested the global doomsday machine, which was far more dangerous and sinister than the power plant. I decided that if there were as much information published about nuclear weapons as there is about nuclear power, people might protest against them in force.''

I asked Morland how his political views led to the H-bomb article.

"I still thought of myself as a patriotic person," he said. "I didn't see the bomb-makers as evil, but somehow our political leaders had stumbled into this policy of nuclear deterrence, which I thought was ultimately suicidal. The dangers of our nuclear policy had been pointed out numerous times, and no one had ever censored the expression of that view, but we had difficulty effectively communicating a sense of urgency to the general public. I eventually considered publishing the H-bomb secret in a way that might provoke government censorship. I was certain that if the government did take the bait, it would look foolish in the end and we would look clever. Everyone would be talking about the very issue that we had wanted to bring before the public. I thought common-sense and the Bill of Rights would prevail against government censors.''

I asked what academic training Morland had received to qualify him for such a technical analysis of the H-bomb.

"I started off as a physics major in college," he said, "but I changed. I took two courses, introductory physics and quantum mechanics. That's all. So I was certainly not a scientist, though even today my favorite magazines are *Scientific American* and *Discovery*. I consider myself a scientifically literate layman.

"I didn't even know there was an H-bomb secret until I read a book by Herbert York, the first director of the Lawrence Livermore Lab, titled *The Advisors*. It described the internal debate over what kind of H-bomb to build. Edward Teller wanted an unlimited superbomb and Robert Oppenheimer wanted a smaller, fusion-boosted battlefield bomb. When Stanislav Ulam solved the main technical problem with the superbomb, Oppenheimer found the design concept so 'technically sweet' that he agreed to support building the superbomb.''

Morland was fascinated with this "technically sweet" idea that had seduced Oppenheimer.

"I assumed it was nifty," he said, "but that it would not change my own opinion about H-bombs. I felt I had enough knowledge of nuclear physics to figure it out; all I had to do was collect all of the public information and weed out what was incorrect. It took me about a year to conclude that the essence of the H-bomb secret is something called 'radiation implosion.'

"I was aware of the fact that three college students had made designs for A-bombs which the government immediately classified Secret. There was an MIT student who did it for the Nova program on CBS. There was a Princeton student who did it as a term paper, and there was a student from Harvard. In each case, the students gained a good deal of publicity. I realized that if I could come up with the H-bomb secret and get the government to declare it classified, as it did with those three students, I could get a certain amount of notoriety out of it. But these students had all agreed to keep their work secret. They had essentially been co-opted and joined the club. My goal, on the other hand, was to provide this information to antiwar activists like the Clamshell Alliance to help organize demonstrations at the bomb plants."

At this point, Morland was not yet thinking in terms of publishing.

"I was thinking of a slide show," he said, "which was the first way I actually put the material together. Then Sam Day, the former editor of the *Bulletin of the Atomic Scientists*, who was then working for *Progressive* magazine, approached me. Sam hired me to do research for a series of articles on the H-bomb. He was the person who got permission for me to visit the bomb plants. He talked to one of the lab directors and received permission to visit all the major factories. I managed somehow to convince him that I could make better use of some of the factory visits than he could, so he told the DOE [Department of Energy] that he was going to send me in his stead.

"On the first day of my visits I told them, 'Look, I don't know what's classified and what's not, so I want to be able to ask any question that comes to mind. You can choose to answer or not.' They agreed. I often framed my question in such a way that their reaction would either validate my assumptions or lead me to a better approach. Soon they were on to me, and I received a phone call from DOE saying that I was stepping across the line."

At that point Morland wasn't even sure that the *Progressive* was interested in publishing the H-bomb secret, because it was so technical. Even if the magazine was willing to publish it, would the government allow it? Morland talked to Erwin Knoll, the editor of *Progressive*, who immediately jumped at the idea of publishing the article. "I told him that if I discovered the secret, I didn't want the government to classify it and prevent its publication," said Morland. "He agreed."

Now Morland and Sam Day began working together on the article. "Sam's approach was a little different from mine," recalled Morland. "He framed the article in terms of, 'I'm going to tell you a secret that's going to knock your socks off.' He mixed in anecdotes about why the secret was important and how the government uses secrecy. All the technical information was still there, but he added some hype. I suspected that the sensationalized language was more likely to provoke a response from the government censors, which I had mixed feelings about.''

I asked Morland if he had anticipated the chain of events that would ensue from publication of the article. "I didn't know exactly what to expect," he said. "I assumed that if the government acquired my article and classified it, essentially endorsing its accuracy, they would then succeed in suppressing it. On the other hand, if the government chose not to classify the article, we could publish it, but no one would know whether we had it right or not. We wouldn't have the same credibility as if we had been anointed by the government. I wanted both worlds. I wanted the government to 'endorse' my research by classifying it, but I also wanted to distribute it. That was a quandary, because I assumed that if the government classified my article, I could be criminally prosecuted for distributing it. I thought I would lose in court, and I didn't want to do that. Even though I had committed civil disobedience in the past, I didn't want to be on trial for my life.''

But hadn't the Pentagon Papers case demonstrated that the press could publish classified information with impunity? "Yes," said Morland, "but that was a very expensive trial, and I had no money. Also, that case was settled in favor of the *New York Times*, but in a separate case, Daniel Ellsberg was tried criminally and faced the possibility of spending the rest of his life in jail. Unlike Ellsberg, I was functioning as an agent of the press, but I wasn't sure I wanted to bet my life on the press privilege. Ellsberg was freed on a technicality. The government had engaged in misconduct relating to the trial. But I couldn't count on the government making the same mistake in prosecuting me. I was very conflicted, and just before we published the article I spent a whole weekend talking to Daniel Ellsberg in California, trying to figure out what my options were and what should be done.''

I wondered how the government discovered the contents of Morland's article before publication.

"There were certain people I was trying to dig the secret out of," said Morland, "and one of those people was George Rathjeans at MIT, recently retired. He knew the H-bomb secret, and at one point I showed him a preliminary drawing of how I thought the bomb worked. I concluded from his general attitude that if I showed him a correct description, he would probably turn me in. When I showed some later drawings to a couple of his graduate students, one of them told him about my progress. Rathjeans then succeeded in getting Sam Day to send him a copy of my complete drawings and descriptions."

If Rathjeans was likely to warn the government of Morland's work, why would Sam Day confide in him?

"Sam said they didn't have any way of technically evaluating my work to determine whether I was right or not," explained Morland. "So that was the excuse for sending it to Rathjeans. When Rathjeans received the material, he promptly sent it on to the classification officer at DOE. I knew that if it was published before the government saw it, they would officially ignore it. I also knew that if we gave them a chance to stamp it classified, then anything we did after that would be an act of civil disobedience. So sending it to Rathjeans was, in a sense, the first step in the scenario of civil disobedience. Of course, we then risked not being allowed to publish it without severe criminal penalties."

Indeed, once the government got hold of the manuscript, it threatened legal action against the magazine. Morland and Erwin Knoll had little time to develop a response. "It was too late to get a regular issue out," said Morland. "Our options were to print it immediately as a leaflet, before the government classified it, or allow it to be classified and then challenge the government in court. I advised Erwin to go ahead and print an extra edition of the magazine to preempt government censorship. We could quickly print the article, put a cover on it, mail it to subscribers or just pass it out on the streets of Milwaukee. Erwin said, 'No, this will make an ideal test case and we will challenge them in court.'

"Erwin said they would be willing to cover all my costs for legal and civil prosecution, if it came to that, and they guaranteed that they would not let the article be suppressed. They would defy the order not to publish, even if they lost in the Supreme Court."

And so the legal battle began. The *Progressive* had its attorneys, but Morland did not yet have a lawyer. "Erwin decided that I should not meet the world without a lawyer," recalled Morland. "It took a couple of days, and during that time I went into hiding. The first filing of the case was *U.S. v. Howard Morland*, but because I was in hiding, the next filing was *U.S. v. Progressive*."

Morland was just as happy to have the focus removed from him, making it a prior restraint case rather than a criminal case.

"We tried to stage manage my coming out," said Morland. "I was going to appear on *60 Minutes*, but Yasser Arafat beat me out. So my coming out was on the *Today Show* about a week after the case began. After that I attended the court proceedings and gave interviews, but I was always protected by the lawyers."

As predicted, once the government declared Morland's article classified, a restraining order was issued preventing the magazine from publishing it. In an unusual move, the government also chose to classify Morland's freshman physics textbook, claiming that the underlining he had put in it while studying for a test in 1961 might be of help to a bomb-maker. "The government argued that if someone were to look at my censored affidavit and the accompanying exhibits, they would be able to fill in some of the blank spots using my underlined textbook."

I asked how that underlining could be relevant, when it was done for a freshman test almost twenty years earlier.

"That was one of many absurdities in the case," Morland said.

Unlike the Pentagon Papers case, in which the published material had been classified by the Executive Branch under a Presidential Executive Order, the material in the *Progressive* case had been declared secret under a statute, the Atomic Energy Act. Morland understood the distinction quite well. "That's one of the things that made the case interesting," he said. "I had examined the Atomic Energy Act, and saw that it declared *all* information related to nuclear technology to be classified unless it was specifically declassified. So the act cast its net broadly over all atomic research. I thought, this is totally absurd. The notion of classifying a whole subject area was completely out of date, absurd and ridiculous. The act's provisions are so broad and vague that you couldn't tell what was and wasn't classified.

"I was delighted with the idea of challenging that statute, though the case didn't proceed far enough to have a ruling on its constitutionality. In the end, we were arguing that even though this information is classified under the Atomic Energy Act, we have the right to publish it because the information had already been published elsewhere. It's ironic that this premiere test case of the First Amendment, a case taught in schools today, established the right to publish a story because we were scooped."

In an effort to prove that the "secret" in Morland's article was publicly available, the *Progressive* issued a public challenge for someone else to duplicate Morland's research. The *Milwaukee Sentinel* responded by sending a reporter to the library to see if he could figure out what the government was suppressing in the *Progressive* case.

"He basically got it," said Morland, "and the *Sentinel* published the secret. But the government claimed that the *Sentinel* didn't contain as much detail as I had provided. Still, the whole purpose for publishing the article was being obscured.

"It's unfortunate that the defense of our legal right to publish became the whole story. I didn't set out to prove that the secret was in the public domain. I set out to do a sort of in-your-face piece of guerilla theater to cause a commotion, to get people thinking and break down the wall of secrecy. To me it was irrelevant whether I dug this thing out of public sources or some guy slipped me a blueprint when I was walking through the plant. I thought the point was that we needed to seriously discuss the issue and pursue nuclear disarmament. We deserved to have an understanding of the fusion bomb if we were to discuss its use. The government had made an icon of this secret, a secret that clearly could be reinvented by any government that wanted to devote resources to it. Whether I got the secret by legal or illegal means didn't matter, because it was a bogus secret."

Nonetheless, Morland acknowledged that the government lost confidence in its own case as it discovered the wealth of material on the fusion bomb that was available in the public literature. "They dropped their case after a nuclear hobbyist, Chuck Hansen, published a letter containing the secret," said Morland. "He essentially duplicated my research without access to my materials. Hansen included drawings which he produced on his kitchen table, tracing concentric circles from the jars in his cupboard. The Hansen letter got the government to throw in the sponge, but none of us believed that was the real reason they dropped the case. The judges were openly ridiculing the government's case in court, making fun of the government's lawyers and cracking jokes. The audience was laughing. It was humiliating for them. Everyone assumed that the three-judge appeals panel was going to rule in favor of the magazine, forcing the government to appeal to the Supreme Court. They didn't want to do that, so they used the Hansen letter as an excuse to drop the case."

Morland said that because the case was declared "moot," many people thought that nothing had been accomplished. He disagreed. "Quite the contrary," he said. "The government had the option of dropping the case at any time. I thought that during the first week or so we began to severely embarrass their case. The fact that they hung on as long as they did just meant that our propaganda mill had six months to work instead of two weeks. I didn't really think that they would give the Supreme Court a chance to rule against them."

I asked Morland how he thought the Supreme Court would have ruled on it? "I don't know," he said, "but I had a chance to ask William Rehnquist that question. The *Progressive* case was being used as the 'moot' court case for the Georgetown University Law School about a year after our case ended. Georgetown students essentially reargued our case in front of a three-judge panel, one of whom was Justice Rehnquist. This was before he had been named Chief Justice. I don't recall whether they actually decided the issue or whether they simply awarded a prize for the best argument. But Rehnquist and the others sat on the case, heard the arguments, and awarded a prize to one of the students. When it was all over, I caught Rehnquist as he was leaving. I introduced myself and said, 'I can't help asking what you would have done if this had reached the Supreme Court.' He laughed and said, 'Well, we're always glad when the really hard cases don't get to the Supreme Court.' "

If the case had gone to the Supreme Court, would they have addressed the constitutionality of the Atomic Energy Act?

"I seriously doubt it," said Morland. "They would probably have handled it much the same way that they handled the Pentagon Papers. In that case they said it was all right to publish this classified study because it was essentially harmless political speech. But they did not challenge the basic power of the national security state.

"I think it likely that they would have done the same thing in the *Progressive* case. They would have agreed to the publication of my article because it was already in the public domain. But those nine justices were not the people to defy both the legislative and executive branches. We would not have emerged with a ruling that the Atomic Energy Act was unconstitutional. But our limited victory makes such a ruling more possible today. The Atomic Energy Act was ridiculed, like one of those blue laws or sodomy laws that never gets enforced. It's still on the books, but it doesn't have the same kind of power over society that it did. So if someone baits the trap again and gets the government to make the Atomic Energy Act vulnerable to a Court ruling, they would have a better chance today than we did then."

Does that mean that if a similar article were published in the future, the government would be unlikely to seek an injunction?

"The story of the H-bomb has been retold many times in increasing detail," said Morland, "the latest being Richard Rhodes' book on the hydrogen bomb, *Dark Sun* [1995]. It's still hard to pry information out of the government, but I don't see any indication that the government would again reach out and censor private authors and journalists who are speculating on this subject. I believe, essentially, that the issue has been resolved in our favor."

Peter Sussman: Committing Journalism

After serving for almost thirty years in a variety of editorial positions for the *San Francisco Chronicle*, Peter Sussman has been an instructor, lecturer and freelance writer, editor and researcher since 1994. His awards include the Media Alliance's Elsa Knight Thompson Award for Special Achievement (1988), the James Madison Freedom of Information Award (1989), the Scripps Howard Foundation National Journalism Award (1989), the Society of Professional Journalists' Freedom of Information Award (1990), the Bill Farr Freedom of Information Award (1990), Honorable Mention for the James Aronson Award for Public Conscience Journalism (1992), the Hugh M. Hefner First Amendment Award (1992), and the PEN/Newman's Own First Amendment Special Citation (1993). His important book, *Committing Journalism* (1993), coauthored with prison inmate/journalist Dannie Martin, was well received by the major review publications. More recently, Sussman authored "Crimes of Silence" in *Censored 1997: The News That Didn't Make the News* (1997).

In recent years, Sussman has used his publications and the courts to fight the power of the federal prison system to censor the writing of inmate-journalists, and he has campaigned to reverse the California ban on face-to-face news media interviews with prisoners. In our interview, held on June 27, 1997, Sussman outlined the startling statistics on incarcerated Americans, the highest per capita prison population in the world. Given the fact that the American press covers acts of crime in more detail than any other press in the world, I wondered why the nature of the prison system, its rules, its environment and its effects were of such meager interest to the press.

"One reason has to do with economic class," said Sussman. "Just as election campaigns are not aimed at the poor, because they don't vote in comparable proportion to the middle class, news is skewed toward those who buy newspapers and those to whom advertisers wish to market. It's increasingly a matter of niche marketing.

"Another reason has to do with journalists, the people who work at the newspapers. The news is always going to reflect the attitudes and backgrounds of the people who write it. That's why diversity is so essential in journalism.

"There's plenty of evidence, too, that the news media buy into and perpetuate politicians' fear-based mythology about crime and its perpetrators. The stereotypes help win elections, and they help sell papers too. Unfortunately, the press has generally allowed the lowest-common-denominator politicians to define the debate.

"And finally, newspapers don't cover prisons adequately because they sense that the public doesn't want to hear about them. The public seems less interested in prisons as places where criminals are rehabilitated, or even punished, than as places to get criminals out of their sight. We ran into that attitude when we talked with one of the governor's legislative councils here in California about our bill to overturn the state's ban on prison interviews. We were told that the reason the governor wanted to ban interviews with prisoners was that he didn't see any reason why he should have to see 'those people' on his television set. It's that simple."

Sussman's campaign for legislation to reverse the prison interview ban in California brought his attention to a case that he says represents the kind of press censorship common in the secretive world of prisons. He described the case of two San Diego prisoners who were sent to the "hole" on suspicion of criticizing a prison program to the news media.

"Papers handed to the prisoners made it clear that it was not only their suspected contact with the media that got them in trouble. Part of their punishment, believe it or not, was based on the fact that a news story appearing on a local television station and apparently attributed to the prisoners was 'negative.' One of the prisoners was formally accused of 'sabotage' for attempting to 'impugn the credibility' of a prison industry program 'by contacting the news media.'

"What the two prisoners were suspected of telling the TV reporters was that workers in a prison factory were ordered to remove 'Made in Honduras' labels from T-shirts and replace them with 'Made in USA' labels before they were sold. In any case, two people were silenced on suspicion of criticizing the operation of a government program, and wasn't it for just such situations that the freedom-of-the-press and freedom-of-speech clauses were included in the First Amendment? To make it all the more galling, it was impossible for the news media, and through them the public, to get to the bottom of the controversy because of the two-year-old ban on interviewing prisoners in person."

Prison authorities often cite "prison security" as justification for all manner of restrictions on communication with the press. I asked Sussman whether the "prison security" justification suggested a connection with the national security state, akin to military censorship and controls on battlefield reporting.

"These regulations are certainly political," he said. "They manipulate the notion of domestic security in the same way that military regulations invoke national security, and with the same questionable validity. If you evaluate the legitimate security needs of the prison system, you find that security is enhanced by allowing press interviews. For example, if there is a prison riot, the first thing the prisoners want to do is tell their grievances to the media. Allowing interviews acts as a safety valve by letting the word get out to the public about often legitimate grievances in the prison. Even the Supreme Court ruling in *Pell v. Procunier*, which upheld an earlier ban on prison interviews, justified it only so long as there were alternative means of getting the word out. It must be shown that inmates can speak with their lawyers or their families, who can then pass the word on to the press.

"But that process itself," said Sussman, "amounts to a child's game of telephone. It's hearsay, and anyone can tell you that what the court is encouraging here is the most dangerous thing in any prison: rumor. The regulations encourage rumor and discourage the give-and-take questioning that constitutes a press interview. Such an interview process winnows out truth from fabrication or misunderstanding. When you pass on undigested hearsay, it is dangerous to prison security."

I told Sussman that these prison regulations also reminded me of the paternalistic censorship policies in public schools. The government and the Supreme Court apparently regard both prisons and schools as unique institutions outside the free speech protections of the broader society.

"That's true," said Sussman. "This is predicated on the notion that institutional officials, the 'experts,' know best how to deal with those under their care. The judges say we cannot know or evaluate what goes on in the prison system, so we must believe the people who run the prisons. Let them tell us what regulations they need, and we will approve them. That's what it amounts to."

I pointed out to Sussman that another of the interviewees in this chapter, Howard Morland, said the public could not make informed political decisions about nuclear weapons and the weapons industry unless they understood more about the weapons themselves. Is there a parallel with the prison system?

"That's exactly the argument I use," said Sussman. "I've pointed out that today in California we are voting directly on issues of crime and punishment through the initiative process, without the benefit of informed debate. The primary example is the 'Three Strikes' initiative, in which the people voted for specific prison terms as punishment for particular crimes. We're doing that with no way of knowing the effect of prison on those people or on the crime rate. The public does not have a clue. It's an exact parallel with the weapons industry."

The case that first led Sussman to examine the First Amendment rights of inmates involved Dannie Martin, a prisoner who was sent to the "hole" because Sussman published one of his essays in the *San Francisco Chronicle*. Sussman told me the source of the prison's claimed authority for punishing Martin.

"The regulation in question says a prisoner is not allowed to write for a newspaper or magazine under a byline or for compensation," said Sussman. "It also says a prisoner may not act as a reporter. No one knows what 'acting as a reporter' means. As far as compensation is concerned, a prisoner can be paid for handicrafts produced in prison or for working in prison industries. They just can't make money writing for newspapers. And the byline provision is nonsense. As an editor at the *Chronicle*, it was I, not the Bureau of Prisons, who determined what byline appeared on an article."

I asked Sussman why, given the regulation against prisoners acting as reporters or writing under a byline, I can still find occasional articles in my local newspaper that were written by prisoners.

"They must be from state prisons," explained Sussman. "You can't do it in a federal prison. We were fighting the Federal Bureau of Prisons. Evidently there is not a byline rule in most state departments of correction. Let me add, there are some inmates in federal prisons who have managed to publish. If you're not stepping on the warden's toes and the writing is not considered a threat to institutional bureaucrats, sometimes they will look the other way. For example, Denny McClain, the former major league pitcher, wrote for a sports publication when he was in federal prison. In fact, we had a declaration from him for our case. He said he was told that as long as he didn't muck with the warden or anything, they didn't care about his publishing. So they use the regulation to penalize inmates for crossing some invisible line. There's no way to know where that line is.

"I believe it's political, and in fact, later court testimony confirms that the byline rule originated with the federal prisons' attempt in the 1970s to silence imprisoned antiwar activists such as the Berrigan brothers. Dannie Martin wrote articles for me at the *San Francisco Chronicle* for two years before he was punished for it. Are you going to tell me that the officials didn't know that these incredibly popular articles were appearing in the *Chronicle*? Of course they knew, but it wasn't until he criticized the warden that they suddenly 'discovered' the regulation and threw Dannie in the hole."

The story of Dannie Martin has been covered extensively in a book, *Committing Journalism*, jointly authored by Sussman and Martin, but I asked Sussman to review his association with Martin.

"Dannie was a prisoner at the Federal Correctional Institution at Lompoc, California," said Sussman. "In 1986, he sent me a freelance article while I was the editor of the *Chronicle*'s 'Sunday Punch' section. It was a well-written piece on AIDS in prison, which gave the feel of the prison and addressed an issue that was of great interest to my readers. So far as I know, it was the first article on AIDS in prison, where, obviously, all of the risk factors are present in spades.

"I had never heard of Dannie before, but it was a very important story, so I ran it. The headline said something about providing the view from a prison cell. It was clearly an opinion piece, not a news story. Dannie subsequently began sending me other articles, some of which I ran and some not. Every one of his pieces that I ran said that this was how it looks to the prisoner. His pieces were not masquerading as impartial news stories."

At one point, Sussman accompanied Martin before his parole board and described Martin's work for the *Chronicle*.

"So did the authorities know Dannie was writing under a byline? Sure they did," said Sussman. "I told them, and nothing was said. I even gave the parole board some of his articles to look at. Nonetheless, after two years of writing pieces for the *Chronicle*, Dannie was punished for 'acting as a reporter.' Suddenly, prison officials pretended they had just discovered a crime. He had written a story about rising tensions in the prison, and he was put in the hole two days later. We publicly protested his situation, and he was released from the hole in a few days. The warden said his main concern about Dannie's writing was that he had not been shown the articles in advance of publication. I told the warden it was my understanding that he considered the articles illegal, but I said I would be happy to show future articles to him in advance if he would promise not to suppress them or retaliate against Dannie. He agreed.

"But while Dannie and I were editing a piece he had written while he was in the hole, Dannie was whisked out of the prison and charged with violating prison regulation 540.20B, called the Inmate Reporter Rule. The authorities learned about the article in progress through wiretaps on our phone conversations, during which we discussed editing of the story about his solitary confinement. The warden had reneged on his promise to me that he would not punish Dannie for his writing. We immediately sued, and we were joined by the ACLU and the *Chronicle*. We sued the Bureau of Prisons, the warden and other officials for deprivation of the civil rights of both the prisoner and the newspaper.

"We convinced a judge to issue a temporary restraining order and a preliminary injunction, allowing us to continue running Dannie's articles under his byline and to pay him for those articles. Then, to everyone's surprise, we lost when the court made its final ruling. The same judge who had issued the restraining order threw up his hands and said we had to leave the matter to the experts. We appealed, but I was uncertain about what to do next. I talked to Dannie, and he wanted to continue publishing under his name, but I said I had no way of protecting him. I ended up running his stories without paying him, and with a byline that simply said, 'By a federal prisoner.' I felt very much like a South African editor under apartheid."

Did Sussman regard this as bowing to federal authority?

"I didn't want to set a precedent by suggesting that the court could control a newspaper," said Sussman, "but I couldn't run the byline without causing Dannie to be punished. I decided to add a note saying, 'Under a recent federal court ruling, prisoners are not allowed to write under their bylines in newspapers or magazines, and the *Chronicle* has chosen not to use the author's name in order to protect him from further punishment.' I picked the word 'chosen' deliberately to show that the government couldn't *order* us not to run a byline.

"Despite our precautions, the publisher of the *Chronicle* received a letter from the director of the Bureau of Prisons in Washington, saying that he thought one article had violated the spirit, if not the wording, of the judge's order, because it was printed in the news section—as if the government can tell a newspaper where to publish an essay. We never answered that letter and nothing ever came of it. We've also been told that this rule doesn't apply to letters to the editor. That means that if Dannie writes the same thing and we publish it on the letters to the editor page, it's OK, but if we publish it on the op ed page it's illegal. Clearly, the government believes that it can tell us what page we can run an item on.''

I asked Sussman what came of the court case.

''There was an appeals court hearing that was terrific,'' he said. ''One of the judges on the Ninth Circuit told the government's lawyer that he didn't understand why Dannie could write for, say, the *New Yorker*, but not for *Time* or *Newsweek*. The lawyer said, 'For one thing, the *New Yorker* is a monthly.' The judge said, 'No, it's a weekly.' The flustered attorney, who had been flown in from Washington to make these points, said, 'In any case, it's not as newsy as the others, and since the Bureau of Prisons has to draw a line somewhere, they have decided to go after the news media.' After the hearing, one of our attorneys told me that he had only one thing written in his note pad: 'They decided to go after the news media.'

''This regulation applies specifically to the news media, and does not apply to books or other publications. So in court we asked questions like, 'Could Dannie draw a picture of a guard beating an inmate? Could he sign that picture? Could he sell it?' The answers were all yes. But could he write, 'Guard Beats Prisoner' in the *Chronicle*? No.''

Despite the encouraging tone of the appeals hearing, six months later when Dannie was released on parole, the appeals court had still not issued a ruling. The government then hustled to the court with a demand that the case be ruled moot because Dannie was no longer a prisoner. The appeals court agreed.

''That was a largely conservative appeals court panel,'' said Sussman, ''and I believe they welcomed the opportunity to declare the issue moot. The facts of the case were such that I believe they would have been forced to support us if it had come to a decision.''

I asked Sussman how he and Martin came to write their book.

''While Dannie was still in prison I had received a call from Doubleday saying they were interested in a book of Dannie's writing,'' he said. ''They did not offer a very good deal, and they were not interested in the broader First Amendment story, so Dannie and I eventually arranged for a book with Norton. It was the book we wanted to write, including the First Amendment aspects, the crackdown and so on. After that book, Dannie wrote a novel, and he has a second novel coming out in a few months. He has a third novel already completed."

Despite his continuing success as a writer, Dannie Martin is having difficulty adjusting to life outside of prison.

"Dannie was actually back in prison when the book was published," said Sussman. "He was sent back for a parole violation for driving under the influence. He got out after a year and has been out for several years now."

I asked Sussman about the case of another convict/journalist, Mumia Abu-Jamal. Unlike Martin, Abu-Jamal had been a journalist before he went to prison.

"The fact that he was a journalist who stepped on a lot of toes may have had something to do with the way his case was treated," said Sussman, "but more significant is the fact that he went before a terrible judge, a prosecutor's judge. Since his conviction, his treatment has been directly affected by the fact that he is a journalist. The government tried to shut off his writing, and in addition to the direct, official censorship, there was a climate of intimidation. The Fraternal Order of Police in Philadelphia has done everything in their power to intimidate those in the media who would run his pieces or give him voice in any way. They went so far as to drop leaflets from the air onto the Addison Wesley corporate headquarters near Boston to prevent them from publishing his book. Addison Wesley did not cave in."

Abu-Jamal is best known for his radio commentaries, and I asked about reports that some radio stations had caved in.

"Yes, that's true," said Sussman, "and I was on one radio program on the day some stations caved. It was absolutely extraordinary. The *Democracy Now* program on Pacifica Radio, which had been broadcast by Temple University's station in Philadelphia, was interviewing me and Kyle Niederpruem, the Freedom of Information chair of the Society of Professional Journalists, about inmate publishing and related issues. As part of the program's package that day they were also beginning a series of recorded commentaries by Mumia Abu-Jamal. Then, while we were on the air, the moderator said she was receiving word that Temple University had pulled the plug on the show. We were asked for our response. We were dumbfounded. Apparently fifteen minutes before air time, Temple cancelled their entire contract with *Democracy Now* and Pacifica.

"It was a political decision; it was censorship. They had run the show every day, but now, under pressure, they cancelled. Because Temple controlled the feed to eleven or twelve other stations, *Democracy Now* lost one third of its outlets. The program was now effectively blacked out in Pennsylvania, Delaware, and southern New Jersey.

"There was a lawsuit over Abu-Jamal's right to publish, charging that he was being targeted specifically because of his writings and commentaries. The Society of Professional Journalists did an amicus brief in that case, and there were a number of publishing groups involved. The lawsuit was successful in preventing the authorities from singling out Abu-Jamal. The ruling said they could not tailor the regulations specifically to prohibit his writings, to deny him visitors or interviews and so on. Unfortunately, after being defeated in court, the state decided to prohibit interviews with *all* prisoners in the state of Pennsylvania. I'm told that locally it is known as the Mumia Rule. Theoretically, we won the case, in the sense that they cannot single out a prisoner and prevent him from publishing. But in the end, the state had the last laugh."

Daniel Schorr: Challenging Broadcasting's Corporate Masters

Daniel Schorr began his career in journalism in 1946 as a foreign correspondent in Europe for the *Christian Science Monitor* and the *New York Times*. His work brought him to the attention of Edward R. Murrow in 1953, who asked him to join his CBS News team in Washington, D.C. In 1955 Schorr opened the CBS bureau in Moscow and two years later did a groundbreaking interview with Nikita Khrushchev. Schorr soon became a fixture on CBS television. His coverage of the Nixon administration earned him a place on Richard Nixon's official "enemies list." He always regarded it as an honor to be one of Nixon's enemies, and he recently remarked, "Thank God I was one of them."[2] Schorr was investigated by the FBI in 1971 and called before the House Ethics Committee in 1976 for releasing a classified report. As the result of such bold attempts to inform the public, Schorr was suspended by and then left CBS. In 1979 Schorr helped Ted Turner launch the Cable News Network (CNN), and he remained there for six years, until a dispute over his editorial independence caused him to resign. In recent years, Schorr has been associated more with radio than television, and he is currently senior news analyst for National Public Radio (NPR).

Schorr has been described as "one of the last of the oldtimers still on the air: a reporter recruited for television from print journalism. He considered makeup silly, hated waiting for camera angles and relentlessly hustled to get his stories on the air. He was controversial, difficult, pushy and annoying as hell."[3]

Though Schorr still does occasional important documentaries for public television, he is not reluctant to criticize television. He says he was once advised, "The secret of success on television is sincerity. If you can fake that, you've got it made." Schorr believes that television allows people to experience events without knowing their meaning. "It goes to that part of the brain that deals with emotions," he said. "It is not intellectual experience, because television is not really a medium to convey ideas, thoughts and information."[4]

Schorr has won numerous awards and honors during his long career. In 1991 he was feted at the Smithsonian Castle by 150 friends and admirers who celebrated his seventy-fifth birthday. Among the prominent friends attending "An Evening with Dan Schorr: Confessions of a Journalist at 75" were Supreme Court Justice Harry Blackmun, Senators Howard Metzenbaum and Paul Simon, former CIA Director William Colby, and Schorr's colleagues at NPR. In 1996 Schorr won a coveted Gold Baton, the highest honor of the annual Alfred I. Du-Pont–Columbia University Awards for broadcast journalism.

In June 1997, I spoke with Schorr about the problems of free expression on television and radio. Schorr believes that many factors have contributed to making television the most conservative and self-censored of all the media, but he feels that the network structure has exercised the greatest influence.

"Networks don't really exist by themselves," he said, "other than the five or six stations that they own. For the most part, they are dependent for their markets on acceptance by their affiliates, who, if they are sufficiently upset by network programming or policy, could change their affiliation if they wanted to. Therefore, any regional tendency to disagree with national policy is something that the networks in the past have been very very sensitive to.

"Going back to an early example of this, CBS newsman Howard K. Smith had a programming fight with his CBS boss Bill Paley that resulted in Smith being fired or forced to resign. Smith was doing a *CBS Reports* show on civil rights, and Paley tried to censor it because he had complaints from several southern stations that didn't want to carry it. It resulted in a big dispute in which Howard Smith left CBS. To me it was an indication of why networks tend to be so much more conservative.''

I wondered whether the fact that television came into being along with the Cold War had anything to do with its conservative political character. Schorr agreed.

"It is true that television suffered from the Cold War mentality," said Schorr. "Even before the McCarthy era, the tendency was to blacklist and pursue people in television, and such action seemed to go much more heavily against CBS than against the other networks. The late Winstin Burdett, for many years a CBS correspondent in Italy, had during the Russo-Finnish War allowed himself to get involved in something that was later characterized as espionage for the Soviet Union. In the end, Burdett was called before a Senate subcommittee to confess not only his own past, but to name others. It's a very long and complicated story, but the result of it was that CBS felt very defensive and politically vulnerable.

"John Henry Faulk, a radio and TV personality at CBS, was another political casualty of the McCarthy era. He was blacklisted for several years. He wrote a book [*Fear on Trial*, 1963] before he died, telling what it was like to work for a 'chicken' network during the red-baiting period.''

Schorr recalled his own experience at CBS during this period. "There's an anecdote I can tell you," he said, "that will perhaps illustrate the sensitive political climate better than anything else. In 1955, I opened a CBS bureau in Moscow, which had been closed by [Joseph] Stalin years before. I opened the bureau, and after spending some time in a hotel, I did what was normally done, which was to propose a budget for the bureau. The budget was to include a combined office/apartment, a translator provided by the government, a chauffeur provided by the government, a car, and so on. It was indeed a normal budget for a bureau. For a long, long time I didn't hear anything back, and I kept asking if the budget had been approved. Here I was just hanging out at the hotel. I wanted to get settled.

"Well, nothing happened, until finally the head at CBS News, Sig Mickelson, came to Moscow and told me, with great embarrassment, that he had not been able to get the budget through the board of CBS. By this time it was early 1956. He said it was all right as far as CBS News was concerned, but not for the board. A couple of members of the board, now get this, had decided that it was too soon after

[Senator Joseph] McCarthy to have a Moscow Bureau listed in the CBS directory. That probably tells the story of those times better than any generalization I could give you."

I asked Schorr why radio does not display the same kind of timidity that is seen in television today. He said radio had originally been vulnerable to the same network forces, but that things had changed.

"For one thing," he said, "the stakes in radio are much smaller. For another thing, in recent years radio has become much more local. There are still networks, there is still the CBS Radio Network, and I believe NBC [the National Broadcasting Company] and Mutual combined into a network, but they don't really have a powerful influence over the radio market any more. Radio is now, by and large, local, and fits into local traditions and mores. Local stations are accepted by their audience or they are not. On local radio, if you get a good rating and make money, you will not experience severe political censorship. The people who have investments in radio today are much more interested in deriving profit than in pursuing ideological goals. As a result, local stations can reach accords and accommodations much more easily than the networks can."

I asked Schorr whether he agreed with the view that concentrated corporate power was the source of television's current problems.

"I think that's right," he said, "but let's make a careful distinction about how that has developed. In the early days, there were pressures brought by corporations as advertisers, the sponsors of programs. It is generally believed that Edward R. Murrow's landmark series *See It Now* was cancelled because it went after Joe McCarthy. In those days *See It Now* was sponsored across the board by Alcoa [Aluminum Company of America], and shortly after the McCarthy show Alcoa withdrew its sponsorship and the show died. Alcoa claimed they were merely looking for a more consumer-oriented show, a different type of advertising. But it is generally believed that they withdrew their sponsorship of *See It Now* specifically because of the program on Joe McCarthy. A lot of people, pressured by anticommunists, wrote letters of complaint and organized protests against the show, resulting in its demise. Eventually the program returned with a new title, *CBS Reports*, but that was really a very dark day.

"Later there was difficulty with a CBS program called 'Guns of August,' which dealt with the perils of gun ownership. The American Rifle Association went after CBS advertisers with the result that commercials were removed from the program. CBS announced that the show would run as what is called a 'sustaining program,' meaning without commercials, because CBS did not wish to embarrass other sponsors by selling time to them. That was typical of the era of advertiser pressure on the networks, an era which I think has more or less come to an end.

"When you speak now of corporate pressure, you are referring to a wholly new phenomenon, the tendency of news media generally to be controlled by giant corporations. If you examine some of these large conglomerates like Time-Warner or Murdoch, you will find that they have broad economic interests that will often conflict with the journalistic commitment of their networks. Let me give you an example of how that works. Ted Turner is now allied with Time-Warner. Turner had earlier commissioned a documentary film to go on TNT [Turner Network Television], one of his cable networks, dealing with Anita Hill and the confirmation hearings on Justice Clarence Thomas. The film was based on a book, and it made the point that there were several important witnesses who were never called to those hearings, witnesses who might have completely changed the outcome. It would have been a dramatic and controversial show.

"The documentary was in production, about half finished, when Turner called and said he wanted work suspended on that film. Why? Because the Time-Warner empire was fighting a case on the 'must carry' rule that would be judged by the Supreme Court [see Chapter 3]. The Time-Warner people were afraid that if their Anita Hill documentary ran, they would lose one vote on the Supreme Court, Clarence Thomas. The story was told in great detail in *Variety*, and I looked into it and did a commentary on it.

"That, I believe, is the wave of the future. If you are dealing with networks whose owners, and the owners of those owners, have economic interests that may militate against your doing an expose or an investigative report on any given subject, that I think is the great fear for the future."

Indeed, Schorr had illustrated this problem in an important television documentary on the power of the tobacco industry to influence television news [see Chapter 2].

"That was on *Frontline*, the Public Broadcasting Corporation," said Schorr. "Such a show could not have run on the commercial networks. After all, the targets of the show were CBS [the Columbia Broadcasting System] and, to a lesser extent, ABC [the American Broadcasting Companies]. We revealed that the journalistic staff of *60 Minutes* almost went into a state of rebellion after CBS lawyers, representing CBS Inc., cancelled an investigative interview with a tobacco insider, claiming fear of a lawsuit by the tobacco industry. What the attorneys didn't reveal was that the boss of CBS and its majority stockholder, Larry Tisch, owned a cigarette company, Lorillard. Our documentary explored the deep suspicion that, in cases like this, where the top corporate office has economic interests that may dictate what stories they cover, the network will submit to corporate pressure and sacrifice a story.

"In the end, the negative publicity about the incident turned out to be so damaging for CBS that *60 Minutes* was eventually allowed to do the interview. By that time CBS was owned by Westinghouse and Tisch was out. But that is the kind of danger that we face in the future. For these big conglomerates, journalistic enterprises represent a relatively small portion of their overall business and therefore will have to yield to the economic interest of the larger enterprise."

I wondered whether investigative reporters like Schorr would always have to turn to public television to air such stories.

"Yes," said Schorr, "or public radio, for that matter. That's why I think public television and radio have become increasingly important, because we can no longer trust the commercial media to serve the public interest."

But surely there is some way to save the commercial media from the stifling effect of corporate control. I asked whether some massive antitrust action would be required.

"No," said Schorr. "We are stuck with our wonderful First Amendment. Someone once said, 'Freedom of the press belongs to anyone who owns one,' and that is, generally speaking, true. I don't have a First Amendment right to force any radio or television network to carry anything I would like them to carry. The First Amendment is the property of those who own the carriers. Therefore, if you start antitrust suits, they will be fought with First Amendment defenses. They will say, you can't tell us what to broadcast. We own this television network, or we own this outlet on cyberspace. The First Amendment may have been written in the first place for little one-man printing presses like Zenger's. But today we have evolved to a point where the people who exercise the First Amendment are the very conglomerates we're worried about.

"If you start trying to deal with the problem through antitrust suits or legislation, you will be backed into the hopeless corner of having the First Amendment used against those who are dedicated to the First Amendment. Antitrust action can be used to prevent media mergers and conglomerates only if it is determined that they act anti-competitively, that by suppressing competition they prevent the truth from being told. But the truth is a relative thing, and there is no legal way of protecting the truth."

What, then, is the way out of this corporate mess?

"The way out of it always ends up to be diversity," said Schorr. "I don't know if you're familiar with the book *Technologies of Freedom* [1983] by Ithiel de Sola Pool. He was a very wise and far-sighted man who worked at MIT and wrote this important work before he died about eight or nine years ago. He foresaw that if things continued as they were going, we would have increasing restrictions on our freedoms. However, he said increased competition and diversity could begin to balance such forces. Satellite communications, computerized communications, and all the rest are competing with each other, and in the end, for competitive reasons, what one of them doesn't do, another will do. And so I believe that, aside from public television and public radio, we will have to find our answers in a multiplicity of means of communication, through radio, television, and especially in cyberspace."

Walter Cronkite: Journalistic Courage, Then and Now

From the age of six, when he dashed around his Kansas City, Missouri, neighborhood spreading the news of President Warren G. Harding's death, it was clear Walter Cronkite would be a newsman. Three years later he was peddling the Kansas City *Star*. He was editor for his high school newspaper, and during his years in college he worked as a campus reporter for the Houston *Post* and as a sports reporter for a local radio station.

Cronkite joined United Press (UP) in 1937 and was given many important reporting assignments during World War II. He was one of the correspondents accredited to American forces after the Japanese attack on Pearl Harbor and he was among the first newsmen on the scene during the invasion of Normandy. He was dropped with the 101st Airborne Division into the Netherlands, was with the Third Army during the Battle of the Bulge, and he covered the German surrender of northwest Europe.

After the war, he covered the Nuremberg trials and later was stationed in Moscow as UP's chief correspondent for Russia. In July 1950, he joined CBS as a member of the network's Washington news staff, where he presided over the flowering of a fledgling medium. In 1952 he covered the first presidential nominating convention to be carried nationwide by television and in 1962 became managing editor and anchorman of *The CBS Evening News with Walter Cronkite.*

Cronkite has received numerous awards during his long career and was inducted into the Television Academy Hall of Fame in 1985. He has written extensively, and his books include *Challenges of Change* (1971) and his 1996 bestseller *A Reporter's Life.* In that book Cronkite describes his personal and professional odyssey from newspaper reporter to America's original anchorman with CBS News. He retired from the anchor position when he reached the age of sixty-five, later to express his disappointment with the tendency of all the network managements to dilute hard news with entertainment. "They are out of a culture which thinks of profits as movie profits," says Cronkite of television management. "They don't think in terms of responsible journalists because they're not journalists."[5]

Cronkite said if he were a young lad today, he probably would not go into network news. "The bottom line has become all-definitive," he declared. "When I was fortunate to help pioneer this medium, news was a loss leader for prestige purposes. . . . Today, very good journalists in broadcasting news are handicapped in doing work they'd like to do."[6]

In *A Reporter's Life,* Cronkite describes President Richard Nixon's "conspiracy against the press," noting, "I was somewhat embarrassed that I did not make his news media 'enemies list,' which was part of the campaign. He was quoted somewhere as saying that I was the best of a bad lot. I am not sure I would put that on my escutcheon."[7]

On September 23, 1997, I asked Walter Cronkite whether the tight political control of television's early days in the 1950s was inevitable for a medium born during the origins of the Cold War.

"No," said Cronkite, "I don't think it was inevitable. I think that the Cold War made those political pressures inevitable, and people in television were made to feel that it was their obligation to control the medium's political content. But it was a certain cowardice on the part of the media managers who permitted this oppressive political current to grow to the proportions that it did. At the first suggestion by sponsors or outside groups that the management of the medium should

yield to political pressure, they should have shown the courage to simply say, 'That's not the way we do business.' It was their fault that the
political chill on television grew to the degree it did. So the pressures
were inevitable, but it was just unbelievable that the network managers
should have yielded to them."

I mentioned John Henry Faulk's ordeal (see Chapter 2) during the
blacklisting period of the 1950s, and I asked whether Cronkite recalled
such things occurring with any frequency.

"Oh yes," he said. "It happened all the time in the 1950s. Faulk
was an obvious hero, because he fought back. He won, in a sense, but
he lost years of work in his prime. Still, he won the ideological battle."

I suggested to Cronkite that, to this day, television was the most
constrained and conservative of all the media formats. He disagreed
when it came to entertainment programming, saying, "It seems to me
that I've heard everything on television today that I ever want to hear."

With regard to news programming, I offered the recent example of
the tobacco industry's forcing CBS's *60 Minutes* to cancel an interview
with tobacco expert Jeffrey Wigand until after a newspaper had printed
the same information.

"I suppose it is true that television news is less aggressive than the
newspapers," said Cronkite. "In news generally, the newspapers are
inclined to open up stories that television would not yet have picked
up. That's the nature of the beast. Newspapers are better news gath-
erers than television is. We don't have the same kinds of staffs that
newspapers have to do that job. So the print media do assume a certain
leadership role in covering stories that television cannot match."

I asked Cronkite for his response to the recent willingness of ABC
and CBS television to scuttle stories on the tobacco industry on the
advice of network lawyers.

"We know that story at CBS only too well," said Cronkite. "But we
have to be a little cautious in suggesting that in all cases the network
lawyers have the last say. I think the reason that story made such a big
splash in the papers is that it was *60 Minutes* that caved in, the most
popular show in CBS television history."

Cronkite had been featured on a 1996 Public Broadcasting System
(PBS) documentary that criticized corporate control over television
news, and I asked him whether he thought things were getting better
or worse in that regard.

"I haven't fought the daily battle on the evening news desk since
1981," said Cronkite, "but I have a sense that it is worse today. That

sense is based primarily on the fact that in so many areas the corporate authority is far less sympathetic to the needs of broadcast news and its independence than was the pioneering management under the [William] Paleys, [David] Sarnoffs, and [Leonard] Goldensons. I think that the journalistic commitment on the part of those in the news departments is probably the same, but they are under much tighter restrictions today. I believe journalistic courage is an individual thing. There were people in my day who were willing to yield quickly to any lawyer's phone call, but the decision to alter a story had to go to higher authority, at which point they were told that we didn't do things that way."

I asked Cronkite whether television was uniquely vulnerable to corporate pressure.

"I would not think so," he said. "They're no worse or better than the other media. I think all the media share this vulnerability to a degree. You can't paint with too broad a brush. There are newspapers that, because of their financial strength, can withstand this sort of pressure much better than can a newspaper that is tottering financially. The same thing is true of a radio or television station. A small-market station with a lot of competition, one that is not a great money-maker, is more likely to yield to a local advertiser, just as a struggling newspaper would. Their financial vulnerability may cause a publisher or broadcast manager to yield where they would not if they had greater financial strength."

I noted that the tobacco industry scandals that hit ABC and CBS during 1996 seemed to flow from impending financial mergers that led the corporate people to reject any controversial news stories.

"That's just another form of boardroom pressure on the news departments," said Cronkite.

But if these mergers continue, I asked, will not the reduced competition increase the pressures on media news departments?

"I would think so," said Cronkite. "There are a lot of dangers that flow from decreased competition in the media business. On the other hand, the argument has been made that these conglomerates might reach a stage where they feel profits are assured, at which point the boards and top management might be a little more willing to accept their responsibility to the public."

Some media critics like Mark Crispin Miller (see Introduction) have suggested that nothing short of sweeping antitrust legislation could prevent corporate strangulation of the media. I told Cronkite that Daniel Schorr had rejected this approach as an infringement on the First Amendment rights of media owners, and I asked him what his solution would be.

"I recently made a speech or two that described my formula," said Cronkite. "It may sound idealistic, but I think it is much more pragmatic than it appears at first glance. I have suggested an educational campaign for the shareholders and board members of these media corporations that would emphasize their responsibility to the public. Indeed, the financial analysts and stockbrokers should be taught that newspaper and broadcasting stocks involve the vesting of a public responsibility with the shareholders. When buying such stocks, shareholders should understand that they are making a major contribution to the principle of a free press, the stalwart of our democracy. Shareholders should be taught to expect a reasonable return on their investment, but not treat newspaper or broadcasting stocks in the same fashion that they treat industrial or commercial stocks, demanding ever-increasing returns to a ridiculous degree. This is where the problem lies today, it seems to me.

"In the case of broadcasting, unfortunately, the network news departments are little more than the tails of the entertainment dog, and there is really no way to separate the economic interests of the entertainment industry from those of the news departments. Because entertainment businesses own the networks, we in news are not very high in their consideration of where to make money. In that regard, one is reminded of Don Hewitt's seemingly ridiculous suggestion years ago that we in the news departments should try to buy out our departments from the broader corporate owners. It turns out, it was a great idea. We could really run a department the right way and make it a success in the process. And those who invested in us would know that their income might be limited by the necessity to spend adequately to cover the news properly."

I asked Cronkite whether the Internet offered a promising new model for the media.

"I look upon the Internet as a great hope for the media, but a potential threat as well," said Cronkite. "The great hope is that it provides democratic access, it gives everyone a voice to say what they want to say. There's never been such a medium before. The closest thing to it was in the old days of the pamphleteer, when anyone who could get hold of a small printing press could circulate his views. But the danger on the Internet is the lack of accountability for those who speak anonymously on this new medium. Anonymous communication can be dangerous when rumor or flights of imagination are represented as fact.

"On the other hand, the anonymous Internet pamphleteer may soon be forgotten when the novelty wears off and people come to recognize authoritative sources such as the *New York Times* Web site, the *Washington Post* site, *CBS* and so on. One of the encouraging things about the Internet is the proliferation of news Web sites, allowing people who would not otherwise read a newspaper to actually read some news."

I asked whether corporate pressure would soon be brought to bear on the Internet as well as the other media.

"Of course it will," said Cronkite. "We can expect corporate pressure forever. It is simply the expression of self-interest by people who have something at stake. In the old days it was the little guy who stormed into the newspaper office with his horse whip because he didn't like something said in the paper. Today it's the tobacco interests threatening suit. They're always going to try to influence the press. The point is, the press has to be courageous enough to withstand such assaults."

Jerry Berman: Forging the Digital Bill of Rights

Jerry Berman is the cofounder and executive director of the Center for Democracy and Technology (CDT), an independent, nonprofit public interest policy organization whose mission is to develop and implement public policies to protect and advance individual liberty and democratic values in new digital media. The CDT marshals legal, technical and public policy expertise on behalf of civil liberties goals, including the protection of free speech in on-line and interactive media, communications privacy in a global network environment, public access to electronic government information and universal access to the Internet.

Prior to founding the CDT in 1994, Berman was the executive director of the Electronic Frontier Foundation, and he had earlier served for ten years as the chief legislative counsel to the American Civil Liberties Union (ACLU). Today Berman has become the media's spokesman of choice on all matters related to the Internet and electronic communication. He has appeared on the *Lehrer News Hour* discussing everything from the V-chip to the Communications Decency Act (CDA). Perhaps most significant, he has developed strong ties with Congress and the White House, exercising a moderating influence on both, while educating them on the unique promise of the Internet and its need to remain free of government regulation.

When I interviewed Jerry Berman on July 23, 1997, he described his organization, the CDT, as "the Internet advocacy organization, whose goal is to see that the new digital era is consistent with democratic values." He said, "Our focus is on the Internet, but we are looking for convergence. This is a new communications medium which we think represents the right model for all electronic media."

I asked Berman to comment on which of the previous media were most comparable to the Internet.

"The closest is the newspaper," he said. "I've always called the Internet a kind of electronic Gutenberg. The old argument that anyone could start a newspaper, as opposed to a radio or television station, now applies to the electronic media. You can start a web page and compete with PBS or CDT or AOL [America Online]. You can publish a magazine. The costs of entry are very low, and web technology makes it very easy to do graphics and display. So anyone in the world can be a recipient and a publisher of information.

"The Internet's First Amendment can also be best compared with that of newspapers. The Supreme Court saw it that way. We argued in court that the Internet is not a scarce medium like radio or television, and it's not a one-to-one communications system like the telephone. It is a one-to-many and many-to-many medium."

How did the Internet come to be regarded as virtually uncensorable? "The Internet was, in many ways, an accident," said Berman. "It was developed by government money to be a defense research network. It's a network of networks with no central control point. The reason for that is that the government wanted to be sure the network could survive a nuclear attack. If one point in the network went down, you could route around it. It's a packet-switching network, and the technology was developed so that it had no central control that could be knocked out. The Internet has grown beyond the original research purpose, and is now commercialized, but its inherent resistance to control remains. Web technology has given it a user-friendly interface, and it has become a new delivery mechanism that is different from the mass media. It is the central, driving force in the communications revolution. It is a very open platform to which many have access, using the computer as the publishing mechanism.

"Just a few years ago, the President [Clinton] and Vice President [Gore] spoke of the Information Superhighway, with all the metaphors of government control, including 'two-way traffic' with information going through 'toll booths.' We are no longer talking about that paradigm. We're talking about electronic commerce and many-to-many communications. The Internet can support a lot of niche markets, not just entertainment."

I told Berman that many media experts feared that the same media conglomerates that were tightening their control over mass media content would eventually absorb the Internet. He didn't agree.

"The difference here," said Berman, "is that while Microsoft and IBM [International Business Machines] and AT&T [American Telephone and Telegraph] may be big players in the Internet, they are making money on the Internet because of its openness. Microsoft is a big player, but it doesn't control access to the network and it's not developing in a way that would allow it to do that. The future of this mass medium is to give everyone a low cost access point to the network. Certainly people will make money on it, but the model for making money is many communicating with many. You don't go to Microsoft and ask permission to go on the Internet."

I asked Berman about the prominent Internet censorship incident at Carnegie Mellon University a few years ago, the notorious Marty Rimm study (see Chapter 2), and the effect it has had on other campuses.

"The Marty Rimm study on 'cyberporn' certainly had a negative and quite misleading effect on the popular perception of the Internet. *Time* magazine wrote a scary cover story based on the Rimm study, and a lot of members of Congress used it as ammunition during the CDA battle. It took a lot of work by our organization and the Electronic Frontier Foundation and others to show that the Rimm study was, to put it mildly, unscientific. The study was eventually discredited, and it took a lot of ammunition away from those who wanted to regulate the Internet. But there are still problems on some campuses. Remember, universities have their own institutional integrity. They must balance their right to control the curriculum and determine Internet access points against the First Amendment rights of the students using their computers.

"Carnegie Mellon thought they might be liable under state obscenity laws for the content on certain Internet newsgroups. The question of who is liable in the chain of command is a very thorny issue that hasn't yet been resolved. We believe that liability should fall on those who publish, not on the access providers. That's the reasonable rule, but it's still being hammered out in law and practice. If Internet providers are held liable for the content they do not originate, you'll create an enormous bottleneck and stifle the Internet. If there is any liability, it should be with the person who puts the content on the Net."

Despite Berman's obvious romance with cyberspace, he is a practical man. "In my job you have to work within the political process," he said. "You can't just go to court. You have to deal with the congressional process, and sometimes that requires compromise and negotiation. It should never require compromising your fundamental principles, but we want to be a part of the policy negotiations, and we are. I fully believe in the policy process and working with Congress, the administration, the private sector, and consumer groups to find ways to advance civil liberties in the digital age. I've been associated with the writing of a lot of legislation. In 1978 I worked on the Foreign Intelligence Surveillance Act, which established warrant requirements for national security wiretapping."

Berman was in the forefront of opposition to the notorious Communications Decency Act (CDA), passed by Congress in 1996 and struck down by the Supreme Court in 1997 as an unconstitutional restraint on Internet communication.

"We put together the legislative coalition that worked against the CDA," said Berman. "We worked with Congress and did everything we could to narrow that bill, to make it the least restrictive bill possible. We supported Senator [Patrick] Leahy's [D-Vt.] call for a study, rather than a rash and ill-informed action to regulate the Internet. We initiated a petition and got thousands of Net users to support that approach. When we lost the legislative fight, we went to court. As you know, the ACLU filed one lawsuit, and we filed a second lawsuit with the American Library Association as our lead plaintiff, along with Microsoft, America Online, CompuServe, Prodigy, the newspaper publishers, People for the American Way, and a whole business and industry coalition. Our legal focus was not primarily on the traditional 'vagueness' grounds, which was the heart of the ACLU case, but on persuading the courts that the Internet was a new phenomenon that could not be treated like other media. We wired the court, brought the Internet in for those judges in Philadelphia and put on expert testimony about how the Internet works. We persuaded them that it is global, decentralized, has no gatekeepers and is not 'pervasive,' in the sense that you must pursue content rather than passively receive it, as is the case with radio or television.

"We made the argument that the imposition of an 'indecency rule' on the Internet in the name of protecting children would prevent adults from communicating with adults. We also made the argument that there were less restrictive and more effective ways for users to block out content they did not approve of. The government shouldn't be the censor. Every individual has the tools to make his own content choices."

After the Supreme Court's decision on the CDA, Berman was interviewed on the *Lehrer News Hour* with a representative of the conservative American Family Association, who claimed that the door had been left open to more carefully crafted legislation censoring the Internet. I asked Berman whether the CDA would come back to haunt us in a different form.

"In reality, the Supreme Court left very little room for a son or daughter of CDA," said Berman, "because it said that the type of indecency regime that we have placed on other media, including the print media, will not work on the Internet. Even the print media has to endure things like wrapping *Playboy* magazine in brown paper and keeping it at the front counter. This will not work on the Internet because there are no gatekeepers. Everyone is a publisher, and having the content provider 'wrap' their communication to keep it away from children will, in effect, keep it from adults as well. That's unconstitutional. The Court pointed in the direction of empowering users with technology, education, and tools to protect their children in any way they wished, and on this issue the Court was unanimous.

"We also lobbied and were instrumental in getting the White House to refocus its strategy. Rather than pursue a 'Son of CDA,' the president and vice president announced on July 16 [1997] that they would now pursue the development of tools to help parents make content choices on the Internet. The industry is working to bring these tools to the market. Given the ruling of the Court and the position of the administration, the support for screening software rather than censorship is becoming the prevailing view. [Senator] Dan Coats [R-Ind.] may try to introduce new Internet legislation, but it's going to be a very different process for them this time. There will be hearings, and there's going to be a lot of scrutiny."

Berman gave the impression that Congress has been doing its homework and will not be so easily stampeded this time around.

"We have spent a lot of time educating the Congress about this new medium," he said. "Now there is an Internet Caucus of about 80 or 90 members of Congress who teach each other about the Internet, and we chair its Advisory Committee. They are pursuing this decentralized strategy that I've described, and the administration is supporting that approach. There never was a hearing on the CDA. Ironically, some of the conservative groups are now calling for a scholarly study of the Internet, because they realize that Congress legislated without making a factual finding of how the medium worked.

"We've been very active in explaining the uniqueness of the Internet to Congress. It is a different medium with different characteristics, and the traditional reasons for regulating electronic media do not apply here. It has to be approached in a different way. We believe the Internet deserves the widest possible protection under the First Amendment. It is the first electronic medium to have the characteristics of print. Everyone is trying to figure out the proper place of the Internet among the media, and our job is to establish the constitution and bill of rights for this new global communications medium. We are dedicated to ensuring that it is consistent with the existing Bill of Rights and with the free flow of information and privacy."

I asked Berman whether the Internet could ever be fully insulated from would-be censors.

"There will always be censorship," he said. "That's part of the fabric of a free society where there are pressures for people to impose their views on others. That conflict is eternal. With respect to the Internet, Congress will now be more sophisticated in trying to find an approach that meets constitutional muster. The importance of the Supreme Court's decision on the CDA is that it lays out new law for this new medium. All the prior precedents that applied to radio and television don't apply. So Congress must begin anew with a constitutional skepticism about vague or overbroad indecency rules that are intended to protect children."

Though screening software and associated Internet ratings are certainly preferable to government regulation, I asked Berman whether they might have a chilling effect on the Internet.

"I don't think so," he said. "First, we're talking about multiple software products and many different rating systems. It's not monolithic, it's not mandatory, and the government is not imposing it. There is no imposition of ratings on web pages. Congress has not acted in that way, and it would be unconstitutional if it did. But if you or I wish to buy software which chooses content for us, that is all right. That's consistent with the First Amendment.''

In 1979, when Berman worked for the ACLU's National Security Project, he was involved in the suit that challenged the government's prior restraint of an article about the H-bomb in *Progressive* magazine (see Chapter 2), and he has some concern about national security censorship on the Internet.

''Many civil liberties have floundered in the national security context,'' said Berman. ''National security seems to swallow the Constitution. One of the important challenges of our time is to keep the national security metaphor from becoming a driving force on the Internet. We're currently facing such a battle in the effort to allow strong encryption to protect the privacy of communications on the Internet. The government is arguing that national security will not allow the private sector to use any encryption that our government cannot easily crack. Otherwise, criminals and terrorists might use it. We think that privacy and security and protected commerce on the Internet require effective protection. If you think about the Internet as a future mass medium which is a marketplace of commerce and ideas, you're talking about an open, free flow of information and goods. America's business community is completely behind us on the need for effective encryption on the Internet.''

Berman has a confident view of the Internet's future. ''We hope that it is the medium that becomes the paradigm for all future multimedia communications,'' he said. ''We anticipate that TV, cable and the Internet will all merge into a multimedia infrastructure that has no gatekeepers and which is distributed and decentralized. As web TV develops, as cable connects modems to the Internet, as bandwidth increases on the Internet to allow video transmission, it will be possible to have a many-to-many distribution system where anyone can be a content provider. We think that is the right model.''

NOTES

1. Paul Jarrico died in a traffic accident on October 28, 1997, just five months after I interviewed him for this book.

2. ''The Schorr Thing,'' *Washington Post*, October 4, 1991, B1.

3. Ibid.

4. Ibid.

5. Valerie Takahama, "Walter Cronkite Reflects on His Life in Broadcasting and Current State of TV News," *Knight-Ridder/Tribune News Service*, February 26, 1997, 226K8888.

6. Gail Shister, "The Way It Is with Walter Cronkite," *Knight-Ridder/Tribune News Service*, May 22, 1996, 522K5809.

7. Walter Cronkite, *A Reporter's Life* (New York: Knopf, 1996), 224.

Appendix A

The Student Press after Hazelwood: Censorship and Response in the 1990s

The landmark 1988 Supreme Court decision in *Hazelwood School District v. Kuhlmeier* seemed to give virtually unlimited authority to school officials to control curricular expression (see Chapter 3). In particular, *Hazelwood* affirmed the right of a Missouri school principal to censor articles on pregnancy and divorce in a school newspaper that was produced as part of a journalism class. Despite the suggestion in *Hazelwood*, reinforced by a subsequent district court opinion, that school officials may not exercise arbitrary editorial control over school newspapers produced *outside* the curriculum, the chilling effect on student journalism has been evident in the 1990s.

In 1989 the Student Press Law Center (SPLC), a nonprofit organization that provides free legal assistance to student newspapers, administered a survey of 531 student newspaper advisors and an equal number of principals. The results were reported in the *SPLC Report*, which said that censorship of student newspapers "has to be an accepted fact of life at high schools across the United States." One Minnesota school principal interviewed in the survey said, "Censorship and control are part of the educational experience." The *SPLC Report* concluded, "The *Hazelwood* decision has certainly had an effect on freedom of the student press, both in reinforcing those who were already censoring and in providing a note of caution to others that maybe they should leave controversy alone. . . . Now, maybe, with the threat of censorship both subtle and overt so strong . . . student newspapers may become less the vehicles for free student expression than for reporting bulletin board information."[1]

A 1994 study by the Freedom Forum, a nonpartisan organization dedicated to freedom of the press, confirmed the conclusions of the SPLC survey. The study, *Death by Cheeseburger: High School Journalism in the 1990s and Beyond*, was based in part upon hundreds of interviews and a statistical study of high school journalism at 234 schools. It concluded that editorial and financial restrictions on high school newspapers were worse than they were twenty years ago. Judith Hines, who helped to organize the report, said the increasingly restrictive policies of school administrators was discouraging young people from becoming journalists. "High school newspapers are dying a slow death," she said.[2]

Indeed, nearly three of every four high school newspapers were found to be "average" or "boring" because school administrators used heavy-handed tactics to squelch and censor student expression on even trivial issues. The study explained, "Many school administrators do not trust teenagers to publish a newspaper that follows traditional journalistic standards, even when adults are overseeing the newspaper's publication."[3]

John Siegenthaler, chairman of the Freedom Forum, was similarly pessimistic. "There are large pockets across the nation—and they are becoming larger—where student journalists are not allowed to exercise responsible free expression." he said.[4]

Because the *Hazelwood* decision addressed only censorship of public school newspapers, this appendix does not examine its implications for a free press in colleges and universities. However, there are ominous signs that post-secondary education will also be subject to the *Hazelwood* guidelines. "Although *Hazelwood* did not include post-secondary institutions in its decision, it is clear that many cases involving colleges are relying upon it," wrote Andrew Luna, assistant director for Research and Public Relations at the University of Alabama. "Through these decisions, an ideology emerges which supports the inculcation of society's values on college students and affirms administrative controls over student expression as a means of articulating those values."

Luna concludes, "While it seems that *Hazelwood* affects the First Amendment rights of students and faculty both directly and indirectly, none of these . . . college and university cases was decided by the Supreme Court. It seems apparent, therefore, that the high court will eventually have to decide whether to expand its *Hazelwood* doctrine to these settings."[5]

A SURVEY OF STUDENT PRESS CENSORSHIP

Within hours of the January 1988 Supreme Court decision in *Hazelwood v. Kuhlmeier*, the principal at Homestead High School in California pulled a planned story on AIDS from the student newspaper. He said he had no objection to the content of the story, but ordered it held until he could determine whether his oversight obligations had been increased by the *Hazelwood* decision. School officials throughout the nation were similarly intimidated, and a survey of student press censorship during the 1990s shows the strong influence of the *Hazelwood* decision. In January 1990, the principal at St. Charles High School in St. Louis, Missouri, prevented a survey on teenage sex from being published in the student newspaper. Missouri, of course, was the state in which the earlier Hazelwood controversy had occurred over a very similar story. In the 1990 incident, journalism teacher and advisor Sharon DePuy, who had approved the censored survey, complained of being "taken out of my classroom in front of the kids and marched to the office like a disobedient kid." The principal told her that he might replace her as newspaper advisor and suggested that she consider retiring.[6]

A similar controversy just one month later in Fort Worth, Texas, had a more encouraging result. When the Arlington Heights High School newspaper attempted to publish a survey on homosexuality, the principal refused to allow it. After a month-long battle, the editors and staff of the newspaper agreed to a compromise, whereby the principal would not exercise editorial control over the newspaper but would review all surveys distributed in classrooms. As suggested in the *Hazelwood* decision, surveys circulated after school or at lunch would not require prior review by the principal. "This means that we won," said editor Sarah Dalton. "We stood up for our rights and won."[7]

A middle school student in Pittsburgh, Kansas, considered legal action after he was removed as coeditor of the student newspaper in April 1990. Principal Robert Heck said he acted because Jason Bailey's editorial was "extremely critical" of the previous school paper. Bailey said he had followed school policy in acquiring the approval of his advisor two weeks before the editorial appeared. Principal Heck said he would probably not allow any more student publications at the school for a few years. "We probably won't have one for a while," he said. "It has turned out to be a negative-type thing."[8]

In May 1990, in Passaic, New Jersey, student editor Sabrina Tavi was told that the school superintendent objected to her review of the television cartoon program *The Simpsons*. Superintendent Louis Centolanza had earlier instituted prior review of the school newspaper after being displeased by a story about a teachers' strike. The Garden State School Press Association complained, "There are principals who, because of *Hazelwood*, are saying they now have the right to censor publications. . . . I believe it's happening more and more."[9]

Censorship of the *Valhalla*, the newspaper at California's Northview High School, led to the creation of an underground paper, the *Hammer*. The last straw came in 1990 when a letter to the editor in the *Valhalla* was censored because it described Principal Roy Moore's refusal to allow students to start a social science club. All writers for the *Hammer* used pseudonyms to protect their grades from teachers who disagreed with the underground paper. Sheryl Bremmer, adviser to the *Hammer*, said, "Initially, the faculty was very supportive" of an alternative newspaper, but their feelings soon changed. "In April, several teachers began to confiscate the paper and became increasingly hostile," said Bremmer.[10]

The growing practice of prior review of school newspapers was challenged in April 1991 when Brian Glassberg and Howard Megler, coeditors of a New Jersey high school "alternative" newspaper, asked the Metuchen Board of Education to prevent the principal and superintendent from censoring it. Glassberg said he didn't mind them checking their paper for things like profanity, but "the problem comes when they try to censor it." Edward Martone, executive director of the New Jersey American Civil Liberties Union (ACLU), said prior review should be exercised only under established criteria on matters such as libel or obscenity. About 300 students and twenty-five teachers signed a petition saying the newspaper should be distributed without prior censorship, but the principal threatened to suspend the students if they published an issue without his permission.[11]

During that same month, the prestigious Horace Mann private school in the exclusive Riverdale section of New York censored its student newspaper twice, first holding up an article on drugs and then hiding all 1,000 copies of the issue containing a substitute article on censorship. The initial article was withheld to avoid giving "the wrong impression" to prospective students. When student editor Emily Strauss questioned the principal's decision, she was threatened with suspension. "It was scary," she said. "First we're getting censored. Then there was a personal threat against me and I wasn't allowed to defend myself." The incident created a stir among the school's alumni, which included *New York Times* columnist Anthony Lewis and Pulitzer Prize–winning author Robert Caro. A letter from twenty-seven alumni declared that the administration's action "radically endangers the kind of education the students receive."[12]

When principal Jim Law at DuPont High School in Charleston, West Virginia, objected to an editorial in the school newspaper, he instituted prior review of all material submitted to the paper. The editorial in question, published in May 1991, questioned the school policy of preventing cheerleaders who quit the team from reapplying, while allowing those who were expelled for drinking to rejoin it. Faculty adviser Amy Jean said the student editors were "merely focusing on an important issue" and should not be censored. "They went against peer pressure to talk about drinking," said Jean. "What they did was right. . . . I've always told my students to stand by their values." Principal Law responded, "Ultimately, I'm the chief editor of the paper. . . . We're not against freedom of the press. You can have that, but only when there is responsibility."[13]

School administrators at Missouri's Kirkwood High School showed that even in the state that spawned the *Hazelwood* case, professional courage can resist the temptation to censor. In late 1990, when the school newspaper, *The Call*, accepted advertising from the abortion-rights group Planned Parenthood, an antiabortion group submitted a petition with more than 1,000 signatures to the school board, demanding that the ad be withdrawn. The board left the decision to the school, where Principal Franklin McCallie backed the newspaper's decision. In a speech given before a communications group, McCallie said that although the *Hazelwood* decision may have given him the right to control the student press, he made a conscious decision not to. He said that despite the petition against the Planned Parenthood ad, only 45 of 295 calls he had received opposed the board's decision.[14]

The following year, *The Call* received the 1991 Scholastic Press Freedom Award for support of the free press right of the students. Student editor Mike Griffin was singled out for his columns explaining the staff's position and for his direction of the news coverage of the controversy. The award also praised Principal McCallie, sponsor Homer

Hall and the administrators and board members who had backed the students.[15]

In Corpus Christi, Texas, the school district trustees gave preliminary approval in October 1991 for new restrictions on school-sponsored publications. The new guidelines were designed to update district policy to take advantage of the Supreme Court's 1988 *Hazelwood* decision giving school administrators broader control over student publications. The new rules allowed school officials at Corpus Christi to bar anything which:

1. Might reasonably be perceived to advocate drug or alcohol use, irresponsible sex or conduct otherwise inconsistent with the shared values of a civilized social order

2. Is inappropriate for the level of maturity of the readers

3. Does not meet the standards of those supervising the publication

4. Associates the school with any position other than neutrality on matters of political controversy.

Local journalism teachers were outraged. "We get to the point where we ban everything because we don't like it," said Diana Ausbie, Carol High School newspaper adviser. "We need to allow the kids to experiment."[16]

At California High School in San Ramon, students took advantage of a California law guaranteeing student journalists greater freedom of expression than the Supreme Court's *Hazelwood* decision allows. The principal had planned to ban a cartoon from the school newspaper because it depicted Michael Jackson grabbing his crotch with a censor bar over it. In December 1991 the students challenged the ban and won. "You just can't come in here and say the community's not going to agree with it and pull it," explained Mike Nelson, the sports editor who designed the cartoon. "I mean, we have rights." Principal Joe Rancatore initially considered the cartoon obscene, but withdrew his ban after school attorneys told him he was not authorized to censor it under California law.[17]

In December 1991, the editors of the student newspaper at Meridian High School in Idaho were told by the principal that they could not print a story covering a student protest over a ban on classroom discussion of AIDS. "He's denying us our First Amendment rights," said student editor Tina Gregory. "We were going to have a straight news story on why the rally took place, and why teachers couldn't talk about

AIDS." In place of the story, the students displayed a blank space on a portion of the front page of the next issue, with the message: "This space was reserved for the story everyone expected to see in our school newspaper but that we were not allowed to print."[18]

The problem of AIDS was also the focus of censorship in early 1992 when the principal of Fletcher High School in Jacksonville, Florida, prevented the school newspaper from publishing a story about the use of condoms as protection against AIDS. The ban was justified on the basis of the existing sex education curriculum for seventh-graders, which recommends abstinence rather than birth control. Amy Colella, editor of the school paper, said a seventh-grade program had no bearing on the need of seventeen-and eighteen-year olds to learn about condoms. "It is very irresponsible of adults to say that we cannot learn about it," she said. "Either we learn about it in school or we learn about it in the street. I have a real big problem that I can't print the word 'condom' when teenage students bring their babies to school."[19]

On January 31, 1992, the ACLU filed suit on behalf of seven students at Tigard High School in Oregon against school administrators and board members, alleging that censorship of student writing violated their constitutional rights. The suit sought to prevent future censorship and to revoke disciplinary action against students involved in two particular publications. "We have filed this suit because the students respectfully believe that their censored publications, which are not obscene, libelous or disruptive, are entitled to constitutional protection," said ACLU attorney Jonathan Hoffman. In response to the suit, the school board adopted a policy providing for administrative review of student publications. "This has been the district's position all along, in response to *Hazelwood* and the Oregon attorney general's opinion giving us the right to govern district-sponsored publications," said Russ Joki, school superintendent. But student editor Shannon Kasten said, "I think this new policy is really restrictive and unconstitutional. I hope it doesn't last long."[20]

An unusual application of the *Hazelwood* guidelines occurred in December 1992, when Ken Cantrell, principal of Coquille High School in Oregon, ordered prior review of an ongoing series of student articles submitted to the town newspaper, the *Coquille Valley Sentinel*. Cantrell acknowledged that the articles in question were not part of a school publication, to which the *Hazelwood* guidelines were intended to apply, but he claimed that they were produced in a creative writing class and were therefore part of the school's curriculum. "In that context," he insisted, "the district does not offend the First Amendment by exercising editorial control over the style and content of student speech in school-sponsored activities so long as our actions are reasonably related to legitimate educational concerns." Teacher Elaine DeBoard abandoned the creative writing project rather than comply with the new policy.[21]

In January 1993, the superintendent in a Pennsylvania school district censored an editorial in the newspaper at Emmaus High School, triggering another test of the *Hazelwood* decision. The banned editorial accused a school board member of cursing at a student reporter. "I was really angry," said Eric Doviak, the paper's opinion page editor. "My gut reaction was to run it anyway, despite the censorship." Instead, the editors left a space in the editorial's place and ran a note explaining the superintendent's action. The editors then asked the school board to officially declare the newspaper a "public forum." The *Hazelwood* opinion had stated that a public forum is created when school officials open a publication for the use of all students. "In a public forum," editor Lisa Steele argued before the board, "school papers cannot be censored unless substantial distraction of the community or school occurs."[22]

In May 1993, the principal of Georgetown High School in Texas suspended six students who began publishing an underground newsletter. In response, the students began distributing the newsletter outside school grounds, hoping to circumvent the censorship allowed under the *Hazelwood* guidelines. The size and circulation of the publication grew rapidly, but Principal Garry Crowell was not impressed. "I am obligated to enforce the rules of this district as well as create a positive environment for learning and teaching," he said. When Crowell threatened to suspend anyone caught reading the publication, five students issued a formal statement of complaint: "The publication was not published at the school, nor did we use the [school] computer system. . . . We see this punishment as blatantly unconstitutional and a violation of our rights given to us under the First Amendment."[23]

In August 1993, the school board in Westbranch, Iowa, proposed a rule that would prevent the local high school newspaper from publishing material considered "contrary to community standards." The proposal surfaced after a family planning ad ran in the school paper. Students and parents complained about the new rule, and local politicians supported them, noting that Iowa law had restored some of the rights stripped from the student press by *Hazelwood*. "We've tried to reverse what's happening nationally in Iowa," said state Senator Richard Varn, who wrote the state's Student Freedom of Expression Law. "We made students liable for their actions, so they would have freedom to do what they wanted. I think the school board would lose if they went to court. We have a history of tolerance in Iowa and of encouraging student activity."[24]

School officials in Madeira, Ohio, removed a local school board candidate's ad from the Madeira High School newspaper shortly before the November 1993 elections. Editor Amy Harrod said that School Superintendent Dennis Hockney had a history of censoring the paper, including killing an editorial Harrod wrote about First Amendment rights. Her editorial began, "Last week I learned that as a student at Madeira High School, the rights guaranteed to Americans under the Constitution do not apply to me." Harrod complained, "I'm the editor, yet I can't write an editorial or better the paper." Mark Goodman, executive director of the Student Press Law Center, said that the *Hazelwood* guidelines allow censorship of school publications only if there is reasonable educational justification. "What it boils down to is, legally, the school doesn't have a justification for censoring that publication," said Goodman. "It's educationally unsound and morally offensive to let this be the lesson the school is teaching about democracy." Hockney responded, "Obviously, we disagree with that, as does our legal counsel." He said the *Hazelwood* ruling supported his right to censor.[25]

An article about the effects of religion on society, printed in the January 1994 issue of the Lake Mary High School newspaper in Florida, caused Principal Ray Gaines to remove the paper's faculty adviser, Dianne Burd, and threaten to impose prior review on all student articles. Because Gaines, like previous Lake Mary principals, had followed a hands-off approach to student publications, students and advisers mistook that as evidence that they had broad editorial freedom. School Superintendent Paul Hagerty notified them that all school publications in the county were subject to the *Hazelwood* guidelines. "Most students that I have talked to don't agree that a principal should be allowed to censor," said student editor Elaine Heinzman. Senior Mary Huysman agreed, saying student reporters were disappointed. "I suspect that when most of them decided to go into journalism they were under the impression they could print what they wanted and speak their minds. That doesn't appear to be the case."[26]

In August 1994, the Wake school board in Raleigh, North Carolina, agreed to eliminate a requirement that student journalists submit their publications to the principal before they could be distributed. The agreement was reached as part of an out-of-court settlement after students, who had been producing an underground literary magazine, sued the board in federal court, claiming that their First Amendment rights were being violated. "We shouldn't have to lose our rights when we enter school," said one of the students. "We should be given as much responsibility as we can. How otherwise can we be expected to become good citizens?" Under the agreement, student publications cannot be blocked or censored beforehand, though they are subject to standards concerning libel, illegality, or disruption. Student publications produced outside of school are not subject to scrutiny.[27]

One 1994 censorship incident produced a state law designed to extend protection for student journalists beyond the *Hazelwood* guidelines. A controversy at Little Rock Central High School in Arkansas arose when editors of the school's newspaper were threatened with suspension if they printed stories about gang fights and vandalism. When the editors responded by producing their own underground newspaper, they were warned that disciplinary action would be taken if they distributed the paper near the high school. The embarrassing controversy was widely covered in the press, leading local politicians to seek a legislative solution. The result was Act 1109 of 1995, which provided protection for high school journalists and their advisers. William Downs, Jr., executive secretary of the Arkansas High School Press Association, said, "The problem has been that advisers weren't sure where they stood. We wanted to establish guidelines and a better line of communication between advisers and principals."[28]

Also in 1994, Sharon Wright, editor of the student newspaper at Elkins High School in Texas, was prevented from running a story about a group of male students harassing female students as part of a game. Principal James Patterson "shot it down," said Wright, because he thought it reflected negatively on the school. "Our principal wants only positive images projected," said Wright. "He gets angry when you show teen-agers dropping out and having babies. . . . Ultimately, they just don't trust your judgement. . . . I wish we'd do a lot more topical things. But there are subjects we're told to stay off of." Patterson explained, "It is the responsibility of a newspaper to be overwhelmingly positive, because in most schools . . . 98 percent of the kids are great kids."[29]

Censorship at Charles Henderson High School in Troy, Alabama, put the school newspaper out of business for most of 1994. The paper, which for several years had won state awards, was unable to get an issue past a publication review committee. The student editors said the committee was violating its own standards by deleting stories simply because they didn't agree with them. Even when the editors agreed to remove the offending passages and resubmit the issues, the review committee failed to respond and refused to meet with the students. The students tried to take the paper directly to the printer, but were told that the principal had ordered them to be turned away. When a television crew from the free press organization Freedom Forum tried to interview the students, police told them that they were trespassing. Principal Lavon Cain issued the following statement: "I can assure you that the school administration is doing what it's supposed to do in that we're following the student publication procedures approved by our school board and we will continue to do so. On the advice of our school board attorney, it would be inappropriate for me to make further statement at this time."[30]

Administrators at Pike High School in Indianapolis, Indiana, confiscated 1,700 copies of the school newspaper in April 1995, claiming that a student article would create racial tension. The article, written by an eighteen-year-old black student, criticized African American students for boisterous and rowdy behavior. Dennis Cripe, executive director of the Indiana High School Press Association, reviewed the article and found it harmless. Cripe said, "The U.S. Supreme Court made a decision [*Hazelwood*] in 1988 that pretty much gives a principal the right to censor if he feels a story would be disruptive to the educational process." Noting that even grammatical errors are being used to justify censorship under existing legal precedents, Cripe concluded that First Amendment rights were virtually dead in high schools.[31]

In Burlington, Iowa, high school principal Barry Christ censored a drawing of the sign-language symbol for "I love you" in the April issue of the school newspaper, claiming that it was commonly used as a gang symbol. Christ had earlier banned two other drawings he said contained gang symbols, as well as several editorials. Former school board member and teacher Harry Linde said the censorship did not follow Burlington district policy, which is based on Iowa law. Under that law, school officials may censor student publications when the material is obscene or libelous or could encourage students to violate the law or school regulations. "In this situation, there was no conflict, no violation of these things," said Linde. "Why should our administrators do these things? It doesn't make sense."[32]

In January 1996, Pat Lee, a sophomore at McQueen High School in Reno, Nevada, was transferred to another school as punishment for publishing three issues of an underground newspaper that voiced "anti–school spirit" and used expletives. "The punishment is just too harsh," said Lee's stepfather. "He is familiar with the school, and he doesn't want to leave his friends and start over." Lee, who had never been in trouble before, was accused of libel, using profanity, and spreading false or misleading information about a person. The ACLU and the Student Press Law Center said the First Amendment protected Lee's published opinions. They noted that the Supreme Court's *Hazelwood* decision exempted so-called underground publications, those produced privately and outside of formal school activities, from the censorship authority of school officials.[33]

In February 1996, six students at Nicolet High School in Glendale, Wisconsin, were suspended for distributing an underground newspaper. The school's top administrator said, "It's not censorship. It's a matter of following the rules." The rules in question required students to distribute nonschool materials only after school hours. In this case, the students distributed the paper *before* school began. Kevin Clancy, one of the suspended students, said the administration's rules seriously hindered the distribution of the underground paper. Given the *Hazelwood* exemption for such publications, the ACLU threatened to represent the students in court, but there has been no litigation to date.[34]

Another contest between the restrictive *Hazelwood* standards and more liberal state laws occurred in Topeka, Kansas, where school officials pulled an ad for a gay and lesbian hotline from the school paper. The ad had already run in the two February 1996 issues after being approved by the administration, which could find nothing in school policy to justify censoring it. A flurry of complaints led the school board to consider a new policy which would prohibit a wide range of subjects from being printed in the newspaper. Student journalists questioned whether school officials could legally kill the ad just because it generated complaints. They noted that the Kansas Student Publications Act protects the freedom of the student press. The act allows officials to negotiate the number, length, frequency, distribution and format of student publications, but specifies that "material shall not be suppressed solely because it involves political or controversial subject matter."[35]

In June 1996, school administrators at Hall High School in West Hartford, Connecticut, censored a story on improper College Aptitude (CAPT) exam coaching in the year-end issue of *Highlights*, the student newspaper. In place of the censored story, students ran a front-page editorial that read: "The board of education, through its lawyer, has invoked the gag rule to forbid reporting of an investigation concerning irregularities in the CAPT. . . . *Highlights* is a newspaper devoted to informing students and faculty about issues and events in the Hall community. However, we are funded by the board, which has the power to restrict what we publish." Joe Grabarz of the Connecticut Civil Liberties Union said the action was "censorship, pure and simple," but, in the context of *Hazelwood*, he concluded, "They are within their legal rights. It is an official school publication, so they have the law on their side. But certainly it's unfair and it's a bad lesson."[36]

The November 1996 issue of the student newspaper at Chugiak High School in Eagle River, Alaska, appeared with batches of question marks scattered throughout the stories. The marks were inserted by student editors to indicate sections censored by school administrators. "We couldn't say we were censored by the administration," said student editor Lorraine Henry. "They told us it wasn't appropriate." So the students simply inserted question marks. Every issue of the paper during 1996 had been censored in one way or another. "We try to make sure there is nothing that would offend anyone," said Principal Jan Christenson.[37]

After a 1996 story about gay youth appeared in the high school newspaper in Colorado Springs, Colorado, the school board introduced a proposal in 1997 to tighten restrictions on student publications. The proposed guidelines included a list of inappropriate topics for discussion and a requirement that the student newspaper not express an opinion on controversial topics. However, the school board soon discovered that their proposal could be in violation of a 1990 state law giving student editors of school-sponsored newspapers the ability to determine the news, opinion and advertising content of their publications.

In Otsego, Michigan, a student reporter for the Otsego Middle School newspaper wrote a story in early 1997 about a student shoplifter. Though the identity of the shoplifter was withheld, school administrators censored the story. "We're writing a real newspaper," said reporter Haley Pierson. "Just because the girl is a minor doesn't mean it shouldn't be reported." Superintendent Jim Leyndyke said the content of the story was inappropriate because it did not portray the school in a positive light. The school board sided with the administration and asked them to draft new rules regulating the content of the newspaper. "We have the ultimate responsibility for everything that goes out of this district," said board president Larry Collier. "We're not talking about the Associated Press, the *Grand Rapids Press*, the *Kalamazoo Gazette*. This is a middle school paper."[38] The principal and superintendent then met with student adviser Diana Stampfler to announce the new policy. Stampfler declared, "Students will still learn how to write, they'll still do their interviews—they'll just do it in a positive way."[39]

In March 1997, student journalists in Missouri testified before the state legislature in favor of a Student Freedom of the Press bill, designed to improve on the *Hazelwood* guidelines. One of the students, Jeremy Gates, testified that a story he helped write for Blue Springs South High School was "spiked" by the school administration. The story, which concerned the sale of cigarettes to minors by local merchants, was censored by the principal after a local merchant called to complain about the students' investigation. "We were aware our rights were trampled on," said Gates, who decided to run the piece with nothing but a headline, "Two Area Businesses Sell Cigarettes to Minors," followed by a block of white space where the story would have been.[40]

We conclude our brief survey with a strange incident in which a student editor in Lexington, Massachusetts, joined forces with the school administration to use the *Hazelwood* guidelines as a rationale for censoring an ad favoring sexual abstinence. In 1994 the editor of the Lexington High School newspaper and yearbook rejected an advertisement that read: "We know you can do it! ABSTINENCE: The Healthy Choice." The disputed ad came on the heels of a town referendum which approved the school's policy of distributing condoms, a policy supported by the school newspaper. The parents' group that sponsored the ad sued, saying that banning the ad was censorship.

In court, school administrators argued that, under the *Hazelwood* guidelines, advertising space in the school newspaper and yearbook did not constitute a "public forum" and banning an ad should not therefore be subject to strict scrutiny by the court. A 1997 appeals court disagreed, saying that by backing the student decision to ban the ad, the administration had violated the First Amendment. The court accepted the *Hazelwood* notion of a "public forum," but said the danger of censorship "is too great where officials have unbridled discretion over a forum's use." Judge Norman D. Stahl said that when a school provides a communications forum generally open to the public, it may not "pick and choose" what content is allowed without specific standards and guidelines. As a final irony, even the dissenting judge spoke in favor of editorial freedom, saying the court should not "interfere with the editorial judgements" of the student paper.[41]

CONCLUSION: STATE ALTERNATIVES TO *HAZELWOOD* RESTRAINTS

One of the ironic consequences of the 1988 *Hazelwood* decision was that it led states to conclude that, since the First Amendment was no longer adequate to protect student journalists, they would have to do it themselves. There are two ways in which individual states have attempted to surmount the Supreme Court's *Hazelwood* guidelines: one judicial, the other legislative. The judicial solution has come through narrow interpretations of the censorship authority granted to school officials by *Hazelwood* and through the recognition that state constitutions often provide greater protection for student journalists than does the post-*Hazelwood* federal Constitution.

The first lower court rebuke to a broad reading of *Hazelwood* came in *Romano v. Harrington* (1989), in which the U.S. District Court for the Eastern District of New York refused to give school officials carte blanche in controlling student newspapers. The case arose after Michael Romano, a tenured English teacher at Port Richmond High School, was fired from his position as faculty adviser to the school's extracurricular newspaper after the publication of a student-written article opposing a federal holiday in honor of Martin Luther King, Jr. The teacher brought a civil rights action against the principal and the board of education, claiming that his First Amendment rights had been violated.

The school district asked the court for summary judgement dismissing the complaint, arguing that *Hazelwood* gave them virtually unlimited control over the content of student newspapers. They argued that the newspaper was part of the curriculum in the broadest sense of the word, and that firing the paper's faculty adviser was reasonably related to the legitimate pedagogical goal of minimizing racial tensions at the school.

District Court Judge Raymond Dearie refused to dismiss the case in favor of the school district, holding that *Hazelwood* does not give school officials editorial control over a school newspaper that is produced as an extracurricular activity for which students do not receive course credit. The newspaper in *Hazelwood* was both school sponsored and a part of the course curriculum. The court therefore distinguished *Hazelwood* from *Romano* and relied heavily on the earlier Supreme Court decision in *Island Trees v. Pico* (1982). In *Pico*, the Court had addressed the action of a Long Island school board which removed nine books from a school library after the titles appeared on a conservative group's list of "objectionable books." By a vote of five to four, the Court ruled that the removal of the books denied the students their First Amendment rights.

In equating the school newspaper in *Romano* with the school library in *Pico*, the court held that "inroads on the First Amendment in the name of education are less warranted outside the confines of the classroom and its assignments." Judge Dearie emphasized that "because *Hazelwood* opens the door to significant curtailment of cherished First Amendment rights" and "[b]ecause educators may limit student expression in the name of pedagogy, courts must avoid enlarging the venues within which that rationale may legitimately obtain without a clear and precise directive."[42] In short, extending the *Hazelwood* guidelines to extracurricular student activities was an unwarranted expansion of school authority over student expression.

Though the district court ruling in favor of Romano was encouraging, he agreed to settle out of court rather than continue litigation. Romano's lawyer said, "It's probably better that it ended this way. With a case like this, [the outcome] depends on the judge, and [Judge Arthur] Spatt would have relied on *Hazelwood* to make his judgement."[43]

Another prominent victory over *Hazelwood*-inspired censorship occurred at Clearview Regional High School in New Jersey, where school officials censored two movie reviews that a student, Brien Desilets, had written for the school newspaper. School administrators claimed that because the movies in question were R-rated, they were inappropriate for students. When Desilets sued the school for banning the reviews, school officials asserted that they withheld the reviews under the authority granted in the *Hazelwood* decision, but they suggested ominously that if they should lose in court, they might simply abolish the school newspaper rather than be forced to publish material they considered unfit. William Buckman, an ACLU attorney hired to represent Desilets, called the threat "the ultimate censorship and a sad commentary on schools in a free society."[44]

The trial court ruled that the school's censorship of the reviews did *not* violate Desilets's First Amendment rights under the federal Constitution, because the action met the *Hazelwood* requirement that it be reasonably related to "legitimate pedagogical concerns." Nevertheless, the court found that the student's rights *had* been violated under the state constitution, which the court said provided broader protection for free expression.

In his ruling, Judge Robert E. Francis said, "Censorship of school newspapers can only be justified if the proffered speech substantially interferes with the class work, the order in school and affects the rights of others. Neither of the reviews contained any vulgar or profane language. . . . In fact, both were innocuous and inoffensive." Francis predicted that if the New Jersey Supreme Court considered the case, "it will adopt a test more expansive [of student rights] than the test enumerated by the Supreme Court."[45]

Proponents of free expression were overjoyed, perhaps precipitously. "This is a very dramatic step," said Mark Goodman of the SPLC. "It's the first decision of its kind anywhere in the country, and it will prompt other cases in other states where students claim their rights under their state constitutions."[46]

Clearview then appealed to the New Jersey Appelate Division, which affirmed the trial court's decision, but on different grounds. It ruled that the school had indeed violated the student's First Amendment rights, because, even under the *Hazelwood* standards, school officials had not shown that their censorship was "reasonably related to legitimate pedagogical concerns." Thus, said the court, there was no need to consider the state constitution.[47]

"When censorship of a school-sponsored publication has no valid educational purpose, the First Amendment is directly implicated and requires judicial intervention," said the appeals court.

> Substantial deference to educational decisions does not require a wholesale abandonment of First Amendment principles simply because the medium for the student's expression is funded by a school board. . . . The significant distinction between *Hazelwood* and this case is that the matter in *Hazelwood* was censored because of its con-

tent and journalistic style. In [this] matter, it is conceded that the censorship had nothing to do with the style of the review. Nor was the content of the review a basis for the censorship, only its subject matter.[48]

When Clearview appealed once more, the stage was set for a final determination before the New Jersey Supreme Court. In arguing before that court, the school board's attorney, Robert Muccilli, urged the justices to grant wide discretion to school officials in meeting the *Hazelwood* standards. Allowing school newspapers to publish reviews of R-rated movies, he said, would interfere with parental decision making. The justices were not convinced.

"I would hope parents are made of sterner stuff than that," said Justice Stewart Pollock.

"If the assumption should be that many R-rated movies have educational value and others go too far, what is wrong with permitting a student who has seen a good R-rated movie from communicating that fact?" asked Justice Alan Handler.

Muccilli said the school needed to be able to disassociate itself from a review that might encourage children to see movies that their parents might disapprove of, but Justice Gary Stern said, "The substantive speech regulated in *Hazelwood* was much more provocative" than De-silets's reviews. He said Muccilli was asking the court to grant "extraordinary discretion to school officials," and, indeed, if Desilets's reviews met the *Hazelwood* test, "then there isn't much speech that couldn't be regulated."[49]

When the New Jersey Supreme Court issued its opinion, it affirmed the appeals court ruling that the school had violated the student's First Amendment rights, but it left the limits of school authority over the student press unclear. The court began by noting that the power of schools to limit expression within a "public forum," as defined by *Hazelwood*, was severely limited, but it said the Clearview High School newspaper was *not* a public forum. Nonetheless, the court said that the school had failed to establish a legitimate educational policy governing the publication of film reviews, and it found that the school's educational policy in general was equivocal and inconsistent at best. It said Desilets's reviews did not present the kinds of pedagogical problems specified in *Hazelwood*, namely, articles that were poorly written, ungrammatical, inadequately researched, biased, prejudiced, vulgar, profane or unsuitable for immature readers.

The court ruled that the school board had not met the *Hazelwood* test of demonstrating a legitimate pedagogical concern, and had, therefore, violated Desilets's First Amendment rights. Because the case could be decided on federal constitutional grounds, the court did not consider the state constitutional claims. Nor did the court rule out the school's use of a more clearly defined and narrowly applied school policy against publication of R-rated film reviews. It simply said no such policy existed at Clearview. Thus the divided decision did little to clarify the limits of the *Hazelwood* guidelines.

Other lower court cases have suggested that, in dealing with particular acts of school censorship, states may be able to provide greater freedom to the student press than was anticipated after *Hazelwood*. However, the most reliable method of protecting student journalists has been new state legislation. At the time of *Hazelwood*, only one state, California, had a student press statute. Within a few years of *Hazelwood*, twenty-eight state legislatures had proposed such laws. Massachusetts became the first state to respond to the *Hazelwood* decision when Governor Michael Dukakis signed legislation in August 1988 protecting student editors' rights. The law states: "The rights of students to freedom of expression in the public schools of the commonwealth shall not be abridged, provided that such rights shall not cause any disruption or disorder within the school."[50]

Despite this law, school officials in Massachusetts later went to court to test their power to censor "vulgar" speech in underground school newspapers. An appeals court upheld the student press statute by declaring, "Where the 1st U.S. Circuit Court of Appeals has certified to us the question: 'Do high school students in public schools have the freedom . . . to engage in non-school-sponsored expression that may reasonably be considered vulgar, but causes no disruption or disorder?,' we answer the question in the affirmative."[51]

The court concluded,

The statute is unambiguous and must be construed as written. . . . The students' rights include expression of views through speech and symbols, "without limitation." There is no room in the statute to construe an exception for arguably vulgar, lewd, or offensive language absent a showing of disruption within the school. The parties agree that the authors of the bill intended to codify the First Amendment protection discussed in *Tinker v. Des Moines Independent School District* [1969]. The defendants, however, argue that more recent

> Supreme Court decisions in the area of students' First Amendment
> rights . . . have narrowed and redefined the holding of *Tinker* to al-
> low school administrators to regulate vulgar or indecent speech in
> school-sponsored expressive activities. This may be true, but there is
> no reason to believe that these cases, decided more than ten years
> after the original enactment of [the state statute] in any way limit
> the protection granted under the statute. Our legislature is free to
> grant greater rights to the citizens of this commonwealth than would
> otherwise be protected under the United States Constitution. The
> decision to do so rests squarely with the Legislature and we are not
> free judicially to create new restrictions.[52]

In July 1989, Iowa became the second state to improve on *Hazelwood*
when it passed a law allowing school officials to censor the content of
student newspapers only if stories raise legal concerns, such as libel or
violation of privacy. The law states that "students of public schools have
the right to exercise freedom of speech, including the right of expression in official school publications," provided the articles are not
"obscene, libelous or slanderous" and do not "incite students to commit unlawful acts on school property or break school rules." Under
the Iowa law, the articles censored by the Hazelwood principal would,
in all likelihood, have been protected. School officials in Iowa were
less than overjoyed with the new legislation. "We don't think it was
needed," said Wayne Beal, associate executive director of the Iowa
Association of School Boards, "but in its current form I guess we can
live with it."[53]

Colorado quickly followed with its own student-freedom-of-
expression law. Fran Henry and Marta Hedde, Colorado high school
journalism teachers and publication advisers, began a campaign in October 1989 to curb the censorship opportunities allowed by the *Hazelwood* decision. Toward that end, they secured the support of state
Senator Pat Pascoe and Representative Jeanne Adkins to sponsor state
legislation. The new law, signed by the governor on June 7, 1990, protects student expression unless it is considered libelous, obscene, in-
cites students to break the law or creates a substantial threat of
disruption to the educational process.

Proponents of the bill, including the Colorado Language Arts Society and the Colorado High School Press Association, along with such
national groups as the Journalism Education Association and the Student Press Law Center, were essential in its passage. "In those districts

where administrators want to control their student newspapers or use them as public relations vehicles, the new law will make a big difference," said Fran Henry. "Under *Hazelwood*, students and advisers often had to guess about what a particular administrator might find objectionable. Under Colorado law, now the rules are clear."[54]

On February 21, 1992, Kansas Governor Joan Finney signed into law a bill that capped four years of effort by high school journalists to prevent censorship of school publications. Under the Kansas law, school officials may not censor stories simply because they are controversial. The fight for the new legislation began immediately after the Supreme Court's 1988 *Hazelwood* decision, and the bill eventually won bipartisan support in the Kansas legislature. Governor Finney said she signed it because Kansas did not want student journalists to shy away from controversy, but to deal with it responsibly.

In 1995, in response to a censorship controversy at Little Rock Central High School (see page 212), Arkansas became the sixth state in the nation—and the only state in the South—to mandate press freedom in high schools. The new law provides qualified protection to high school journalists and their advisers with respect to all school publications, including newspapers and yearbooks.

"Arkansas will carve a unique niche for itself in this area," said Bruce Plopper, a journalism instructor at the University of Arkansas. "This law allows each individual school district to create a policy that fits its needs."[55]

Under the new law, district policies must "recognize that truth, fairness, accuracy and responsibility are essential to the practice of journalism." The law also specifies the types of publications that students are not authorized to distribute, including those judged to be obscene, libelous or slanderous, those which constitute invasion of privacy, and those which incite students "to create a clear and present danger of the commission of unlawful acts."[56]

Of all the states with laws protecting the student press, only Arkansas allows administrators and student advisers in each school district to develop their own written policies. "Twenty-eight states have tried to pass student publication acts since 1988," said Plopper. "I think what makes the Arkansas act such a plausible model is that it recognizes the need for flexibility in individual school districts."[57]

The most recent state attempt to improve upon First Amendment protection for student journalists was the Illinois Student Publications Act. The 1997 Illinois law provides safeguards against arbitrary censorship of students working on school-sponsored publications, the very kind of publication that lost full constitutional protection in the *Hazelwood* decision. The act declares that high school students have freedom of the press, and it makes student editors, under faculty supervision, responsible for the news, opinion and advertising content of their publications. The act does, however, specify that libel, obscenity and speech harmful to minors are outside of its protections.

Even Missouri, the home of the *Hazelwood* case, has attempted to surmount that decision through state legislation. In 1993 Joe Jolly and Amy Zeman, two teenagers from tiny Brentwood High School, went to the state capital to argue for legislation protecting student journalists. The proposed bill would not protect libel, slander, obscenity or advocacy of the violation of school regulations or disruption of school operations. "This bill would not set students loose to attack the world but rather set the same guidelines as professional journalists," said Zeman. "It would grant students freedom, not license without limits."

Zeman told the legislators that the *Hazelwood* decision "was a mighty blow to the Bill of Rights." She asked, "If the state is allowed to restrict our freedoms, how will we ever come to know what freedom is, what our rights truly are, or when they finally are granted? Denying rights in the classroom begins the process of denying the rights of every American citizen."[58]

In supporting the Missouri bill, Mark Goodman, executive director of the Student Press Law Center, said, "There is definitely a growing sense among journalism educators that teaching school journalism has been made more difficult by *Hazelwood*. And this legislation can remedy that without causing any difficulties for the school environment."[59]

Almost 100 students and teachers from Brentwood jammed the committee room to hear the testimony. "It didn't quite sink in until we got there that I represent all the students of Missouri," said the fifteen-year-old Zeman. "And then it hit me. This is big."[60]

Also testifying in support of the legislation was Mary Beth Tinker, who had earned celebrity status in the landmark 1969 Supreme Court Case, *Tinker v. Des Moines Independent Community School District*, which upheld a student's right to wear a black armband to protest the Vietnam War. In support of the Missouri bill, Mary Beth Tinker said, "For 19 years, high schools across the country operated very effectively under the *Tinker* standard. All we are asking is to go back to that standard." But school officials defended their right to control any student expression associated with the curriculum. Francis Huss, Hazelwood's superintendent when the Supreme Court ruled in 1988, said, "The real issue is whether school districts can establish standards. The final authority for any curriculum decision rests with the boards, be it journalism or English." Huss issued a threat to the legislators, that if they passed the bill, Hazelwood would stop financing school newspapers. "We can teach journalism," he said, "but we don't have to publish a newspaper."[61]

The Missouri bill's supporters knew that its chances were uncertain, and, indeed, it has failed to gain the necessary votes each year that it has been proposed. In 1997, when the bill was again presented before the Missouri legislature, Kirkwood High School Principal Franklin McCallie testified, "I don't want my students to write only what I want them to write. We gain nothing by muzzling the student press.[62]

As of July 1997, seven states—Arkansas, California, Colorado, Illinois, Iowa, Kansas and Massachusetts—have student publications laws, and many others are pending. For the foreseeable future, they are the only hope that the student press may regain its pre-*Hazelwood* vitality.

NOTES

1. "First National Survey Since *Hazelwood* Says Censorship Now a 'Fact of Life,' " *SPLC Report*, Fall 1990, 2, 23.

2. "Censored Newspapers Can't Shine, Study Says," *USA Today*, March 10, 1994, 4D.

3. Ibid.

4. "Student Press Is Hamstrung, Report Says," *New York Times*, May 1, 1994, 35.

5. Andrew Luna, "*Hazelwood v. Kuhlmeier.* Supreme Court Decision Does Affect College and University First Amendment Rights," *NASPA Journal* 33, no. 4 (Summer 1996): 314–15.

6. "Vetoed Principal Nixes High School's Teen Sex Poll," *St. Louis Post-Dispatch*, January 14, 1990, C1.

7. "Cancelling Homosexual Survey Leads to Student Complaints," United Press International, February 10, 1990; printed in *Fort Worth Star-Telegram*, February 17, 1990, B1.

8. "Middle School Editor Fights Removal," *SPLC Report*, Fall 1990, 26.

9. "The Chill Is On in Many School Newsrooms," *Hackensack Record*, August 14, 1990, B1.

10. "*Hammer* Makes Waves, Keeps On Publishing," *SPLC Report*, Fall 1990, 14–15.

11. "Student Press," *Newsletter on Intellectual Freedom*, July 1991, 110.

12. Andrea Peyser, "Censored: Drug Article Yanked from Bronx Prep School Paper," *New York Post*, May 2, 1991, 2.

13. "Student Press," *Newsletter on Intellectual Freedom*, September 1991, 158.

14. "Parents Give Board Petition Against Planned Parenthood Ad," *St. Louis Post-Dispatch*, February 21, 1991, 1.

15. "Kirkwood High Newspaper Wins Student Press Award," *St. Louis Post-Dispatch*, November 16, 1991, 5A.

16. "CCISD Endorses Power to Censor Publications," *Corpus Christi Caller Times*, October 29, 1991, B1.

17. "Student Press," *Newsletter on Intellectual Freedom*, March 1992, 65.

18. Ibid., May 1992, 85.

19. "Fletcher Newspaper Barred from Printing Condom Story," *Florida Times Union*, February 7, 1992, B1.

20. "Tigard High Editors Sue over Issue of Censorship," *Portland Oregonian*, February 1, 1992, D1.

21. "Student Press," *Newsletter on Intellectual Freedom*, March 1993, 45–46.

22. Ibid., May 1993, 75.

23. Ibid., September 1993, 150.

24. "School Board's Idea Smacks of Censorship, Many Believe," *Des Moines Register*, August 27, 1993, 5M.

25. "High School Newspaper Editor Is Challenging Officials' Censorship," *Louisville Courier-Journal*, November 15, 1993, 3B.

26. "Student Press: Responsibility vs. Restraint," *Orlando Sentinel*, June 2, 1994, I1.

27. "Publication Rule Killed; Students at Enloe Prevail," *Raleigh News and Observer*, August 30, 1994, B1.

28. "Bill Gives High School Journalists Limited Protection," *Arkansas Democrat-Gazette*, April 23, 1995, 5B.

29. "Freedom of Press at School Too?" *Houston Post*, June 2, 1994, A25.

30. "Student Press," *Newsletter on Intellectual Freedom*, March 1995, 46–47.

31. "Pike Paper Kept from Distribution," *Indianapolis News*, April 24, 1995, B1.

32. "Burlington's Teens Cry 'Censorship,' " *Des Moines Register*, April 20, 1995, 6M.

33. "McQueen Student to Appeal Transfer," *Reno Gazette-Journal*, January 18, 1996, A1.

34. "6 Nicolet Students Suspended," *Milwaukee Journal Sentinel*, February 27, 1996, B1.

35. " 'Expression' vs. 'Mission'," *Topeka Capital-Journal*, March 19, 1996, B1.

36. "Student's Story on Hall High Incident Banned," *Hartford Courant*, June 8, 1996, B1.

37. "Court Says Schools Can Stop the Press," *Alaska Star*, November 21, 1996, E7.

38. "School Paper Has the Scoop, Gets Censored," *Los Angeles Times*, March 23, 1997, A3.

39. "Student Editor Protests," *Chicago Tribune*, February 10, 1997, 3.

40. "Principal Backs Student Press Bill," *St. Louis Post-Dispatch*, March 26, 1997, B2.

41. "U.S. Court: Yearbook Erred in Rejecting Ads," *Boston Globe*, May 21, 1997, B5.

42. *Romano v. Harrington*, 725 F.Supp 687 (E.D. N.Y. 1989).

43. "Six-Year Court Case Ends," *SPLC Report*, Fall 1990, 37.

44. "N.J. Court Backs Student Writer in Censorship Case," *Philadelphia Inquirer*, May 8, 1991, 3B.

45. Ibid.

46. Ibid.

47. Ibid.

48. Ibid.

49. *Desilets v. Clearview Regional Board of Education*, 266 N.J. Super. 531 (App. Div. 1993).

50. "Student Press Freedom Debated Before Court," *New Jersey Law Journal*, May 9, 1994, 4.

51. Ibid.

52. Ibid.

53. "Public High School Students—Vulgarity—State Law," *Massachusetts Lawyers Weekly*, August 5, 1996, 9.

54. "Colorado Passes Free Press Law," *SPLC Report*, Fall 1990, 4.

55. "Bill Gives High School Journalists Limited Protection," *Arkansas Democrat-Gazette*, April 23, 1995, 5B.

56. Ibid.

57. Ibid.

58. "Students Seek Control over School Papers," *St. Louis Post-Dispatch*, February 14, 1993, 1C.

59. Ibid.

60. Ibid.

61. Ibid.

62. "Principal Backs Student Press Bill," *St. Louis Post-Dispatch*, March 26, 1997, B2.

Appendix B

A Selective List of Media Advocacy and Censorship Organizations

Accuracy in Media (AIM). 1275 K Street, NW, Suite 1150, Washington, DC 20005. Accuracy in Media is a conservative organization that functions as a news-media watchdog against "liberal bias." Founded in 1969 by Reed Irvine, its executive director, it airs a daily radio show, *Media Monitor*, and publishes the *AIM Report.*

Action for Children's Television (ACT). 20 University Road, Cambridge, MA 02138. Action for Children's Television works to encourage and support quality television programming for children and to eliminate commercialism. Founded in 1968, the organization conducts national symposia on children and the media and lobbies networks, Congress and the Federal Communications Commission (FCC). In 1987 it challenged the FCC's indecency policy in court, forcing the FCC to back down. Peggy Charen is the president of ACT. Its publications include books and films about children's television.

Adult Video Association. 270 North Canon Drive, Suite 1370, Beverly Hills, CA 90210. The Adult Video Association was founded in 1987 as the Adult Film Association of America, a trade organization for the producers of adult films and videos. The organization defends the public's right to view adult films in the privacy of one's home and fights against laws that would make the production, sale or possession of such films illegal. Legal services are provided to members charged with possession of obscene materials. Cochaired by Ron Sullivan, it publishes the monthly *Newsletter of the Adult Video Association.*

American Civil Liberties Union (ACLU). National Office: 132 West 43rd Street, New York, NY 10036. The ACLU is a nonprofit, nonpartisan public interest organization devoted to protecting the civil rights of all Americans. It defends the right of the people to express their views, not the views expressed. The ACLU was founded by Roger Baldwin in 1920, when American citizens were being jailed for expressing antiwar views, and its modern focus includes free expression in the media. One of its most prominent recent cases, *ACLU v. Reno* (1997), successfully challenged the Communications Decency Act, which sought to censor the Internet. In 1991 Nadine Strossen became the ACLU's first female president.

American Family Association (AFA). P. O. Drawer 2440, Tupelo, MS 38803. The American Family Association, formerly the National Federation of Decency, was founded in 1977 to foster a biblical sense of decency in America by influencing the content of television and radio. Directed by Reverend Donald E. Wildmon, the AFA protests sex, violence and profanity in broadcast programming. The AFA publishes the *AFA Journal.*

American Newspaper Publishers Association Foundation. The Newspaper Center, Box 17407, Dulles Airport, Washington, DC 20041. The foundation works to inform and educate the public on the First Amendment rights, with emphasis on freedom of the press. Founded in 1961 as the educational arm of the American Newspaper Publisher's Association, it is a nonmembership organization supported by newspaper publishers. It sponsors projects related to the Bill of Rights and is affiliated with the First Amendment Congress. Its publications include *Press to Read* and *Update.* The foundation's president and director is Rosalind G. Stark.

Americans for Constitutional Freedom. 900 Third Avenue, Suite 1600, New York, NY 10022. Americans for Constitutional Freedom was founded in 1990 after a merger with the Media Coalition (founded in 1973). This organization of individuals, trade associations and businesses from the periodical publishing and distribution industries works to combat censorship and lobbies for the First Amendment rights of its members. It also conducts opinion polls on censorship and the First Amendment. Its executive director is Christopher M. Finan.

Americans for Decency. P. O. Box 218, Staten Island, NY 10302. Americans for Decency, a group of individuals and organizations, works to combat pornography, sexual education, vulgar music and other social problems. It was founded in 1975 by Paul J. Gangemi to promote decency in the United States.

Authors League of America. 234 West 44th Street, New York, NY 10036. The Authors League, the professional association of authors of books, plays and magazine articles, deals with professional issues and enters into litigation when authors are censored. The league's administrator is Peggy Randall. Its publications include the *Authors Guild Bulletin* and the *Dramatists Guild Bulletin.*

Center for Democracy and Technology (CDT). 1634 Eye Street, NW, Suite 100, Washington, DC 20006. The Center for Democracy and Technology is a nonprofit, public interest policy organization whose mission is to develop and implement public policies to protect and advance individual liberty and democratic values in the new digital media. It marshals legal, technical and public policy expertise on behalf of civil liberties goals, including the protection of free speech in on-line media, communications privacy in a global network environment, public access to electronic government information and universal access to the Internet. The CDT, whose executive director is Jerry Berman, has played a major role in opposing congressional attempts to censor the Internet.

Children's Legal Foundation (CLF). 2845 East Camelback Road, Suite 740, Phoenix, AZ 85016. The Children's Legal Foundation, originally called Citizens for Decent Literature, was founded in 1957 by Charles Keating. Its current title was adopted in 1989, and its current president is Robert J. Hubbard, Jr. The CLF is dedicated to keeping obscenity, pornography and other communications regarded as harmful to children out of publication, broadcasting and motion pictures. It publishes the *CLF Reporter.*

Concerned Women for America (CWA). 370 L'Enfant Promenade, SW, Suite 800, Washington, DC 20024. Concerned Women for America was established in 1979 by wives of evangelical Christian ministers. It opposes feminism, liberal policies in education and "un-Christian" curricular or library materials. It has also formed a network of legal offices, called the American Justice League, to counteract the American Civil Liberties Union.

Eagle Forum. Box 618, Alton, IL 62002. Founded in 1975 by Phyllis Schlafly, the Eagle Forum is a conservative organization that claims to stand for God, Country and Family. It works to remove immoral content from textbooks and other publications and frequently involves itself in censorship disputes.

Electronic Frontier Foundation. 1667 K Street, NW, Suite 801, Washington, DC 20006–1605. The Electronic Frontier Foundation is a nonprofit civil liberties organization working in the public interest to protect privacy, free expression, and access to public resources and information on-line, as well as to promote responsibility in news media. It is a major Internet advocacy group. Contact: Darby Kay Costello.

Fairness and Accuracy in Reporting (FAIR). 130 West 25th Street, New York, NY 10001. FAIR was founded in 1986 as an interest group to encourage pluralism in the media. It reports on the performance of the news media and promotes freedom of the press and free speech through publications, presentations and media programs. Its executive director is Jeff Cohen, and its principal journal is *Extra!*

First Amendment Congress. 1250 14th Street, Suite 840, Denver, CO 80202. The First Amendment Congress is an organization of journalism and communications-related associations founded in 1979 to increase public awareness of the First Amendment. It conducts local, state and national First Amendment congresses to provide public discussion of media-related issues and produces educational materials on the First Amendment. Directed by Claudia Haskel, it publishes the quarterly *First Amendment Congress–Newsletter.*

Free Press Association. P. O. Box 15548, Columbus, OH 43215. The Free Press Association was begun in 1981 as an international network of freelance writers whose primary purpose is to protect individual rights and defend the First Amendment. The organization opposes all government censorship of the press and reports on intellectual freedom court cases. Its Mencken Award is conferred annually for the best news story. Its executive director is Michael Grossberg, and its bimonthly newsletter, *Free Press Network,* reports on press issues such as pornography and censorship.

Freedom of Information Center. University of Missouri, 20 Walter Williams Hall, Columbia, MO 65211. The center is a research service of the Journalism Library at the University of Missouri-Columbia. Established in 1958, it maintains a clearinghouse for materials on the flow of information, serving legal professionals, reporters, scholars and students on censorship, First Amendment issues, libel, pornography, shield laws and minorities in the media. The center publishes the *Freedom of Information Files Index,* and its manager is Kathleen Edwards.

Freedom to Read Foundation. 50 East Huron Street, Chicago, IL 60611. The Freedom to Read Foundation was created in 1969 to protect the freedoms of speech and press, with emphasis on First Amendment protection for libraries and library materials. The foundation provides legal counsel and support to libraries whose collections are challenged. It publishes *News,* a quarterly newsletter documenting its activities and First Amendment issues. The foundation's executive director is Judith Krug.

Fund for Free Expression. 485 5th Avenue, New York, NY 10017. The Fund for Free Expression was founded in 1975 as a society of journalists, writers, editors and publishers to support freedom of expression throughout the world. The fund sponsors *Article 19: Index on Censorship*, a report on worldwide censorship, as well as other international publications on freedom of expression. Its chairman is Roland Algrant.

Liberty Federation. P. O. Box 190, Forest, VA 24551. The Liberty Federation founded as the Moral Majority by the Reverend Jerry Falwell in 1979, assumed its current title in 1986. Its primary purpose is to organize political conservatives and religious fundamentalists to oppose pornography, abortion, homosexual rights and "liberal" political views. The federation has organizations in every state and a membership of over four million.

Media Alliance. Fort Mason Center, Building D, San Francisco, CA 94123. The Media Alliance is a support group for journalists, photographers, and broadcast and public relations personnel. It works to maintain a free press by encouraging cooperation within the profession and by publishing progressive positions on free press issues. Its publications include *Media File*, a bimonthly review of press issues, and *Propaganda Review*. The executive director is Micha Peled.

Morality in Media. 475 Riverside Drive, New York, NY 10115. Morality in Media is an organization of citizens opposed to the spread of pornography. Founded in 1962 as Operation Yorkville by Father Charles Coughlin, the organization is supported by the Catholic Church. It publishes the bimonthly *Morality in Media Newsletter*. The organization also operates the National Obscenity Law Center, a clearinghouse of legal information on obscenity for use by prosecutors. Its bimonthly *Obscenity Law Bulletin* examines obscenity prosecutions.

National Center for Freedom in Information Studies. Loyola University of Chicago, 820 North Michigan Avenue, Chicago, IL 60611. The center, a professional service of the University of Chicago, provides research and resources on the Freedom of Information Act. It sponsors research on such issues as the First Amendment, information access for journalists, libel, privacy and trial coverage. The director is Edmund Rooney.

National Coalition Against Censorship (NCAC). 2 West 64th Street, New York, NY 10023. The National Coalition Against Censorship is an alliance of forty-five religious, artistic, educational and civil liberties groups, including the Association of American Publishers, the American Library Association and the American Civil Liberties Union, that promotes freedom of expression and opposes censorship. NCAC publishes *Censorship News*, which examines censorship cases and current issues. Its long-time executive director, Leanne Katz, died in 1997 and was succeeded by Joan Bertin.

National Coalition Against Pornography. 800 Compton Road, Suite 9248, Cincinnati, OH 45231. The coalition was founded by Dr. Jerry Kirk, a Presbyterian minister who serves as its current president. Kirk formed the organization as a protest to the report of the 1970 President's Commission on Pornography and Obscenity, which he felt was soft on porn. The coalition has organized Christian groups to protest pornography in communities througout the country.

Office for Intellectual Freedom (OIF). 50 East Huron Street, Chicago, IL 60611. The Office for Intellectual Freedom, a service of the American Library Association, provides assistance to libraries in defense of intellectual freedom. Under the direction of Judith Krug, it documents examples of censorship nationwide, compiling statistics and maintaining a database on censorship incidents. The OIF's *Newsletter on Intellectual Freedom* is an important source of information on censorship of all forms of media, art, drama and speech.

People for the American Way (PAW). 2000 M Street, NW, Suite 400, Washington, DC 20036. People for the American Way is a public interest organization that promotes freedom of expression and religious diversity. It was formed in 1980 by the prominent television producer Norman Lear to counter the growing political influence of the Moral Majority. PAW provides support to groups facing challenges to their First Amendment rights. It publishes the annual *Attacks on the Freedom to Learn*, which analyzes censorship incidents nationwide. Its current president, former Representative Thomas H. Andrews (D-Maine), succeeded Arthur J. Kropp, who worked successfully to defeat Supreme Court nominee Robert H. Bork.

Project Censored. Sonoma State University, Department of Communications Studies, Rohnert Park, CA 94928. Project Censored was founded in 1976 by Professor Carl Jensen, who directed the organization for two decades until his colleague Peter Phillips took over in 1996. The project functions as a media industry ombudsman, alerting the public to important sociopolitical issues that are not well covered by the mainstream press. The project annually selects and publishes the most important under-covered news stories in *Censored: The News That Didn't Make the News—The Year's Top 25 Censored News Stories.*

Reporters Committee for Freedom of the Press. 1735 I Street, NW, Suite 504, Washington, DC 20006. The Reporters Committee for Freedom of the Press was founded in 1970 to protect the First Amendment rights of journalists in all media, and it has gone to court as either the plaintiff or friend of the court in every major case affecting the rights of reporters and editors since 1972. It provides free legal advice to members of the press and publishes the quarterly *News Media and the*

Law, which reports on cases and legislation affecting the rights of reporters, editors and broadcasters. The committee's executive director is Jane E. Kirtley.

Student Press Law Center. 1735 I Street, NW, Suite 504, Washington, DC 20006. The center is the nation's support group for high school and college journalists. Established in 1974, it is supported by educators and student journalists. Its purpose is to protect the First Amendment rights of student journalists through free legal advice, amicus curiae briefs in major cases and research on student journalism and free press issues. It presents the annual Scholastic Press Freedom Award to student journalists or publications. Publications include the quarterly *Student Press Law Center-Report* and the monograph *Law of the Student Press.* Its executive director is Mark Goodman.

Women Against Pornography (WAP). P. O. Box 845, Times Square Station, New York, NY 10108–0845. Women Against Pornography was founded in 1979 by a group of antipornography feminists, including Susan Brownmiller, author of *Against Our Will.* It provides programs and materials showing the dangers of pornography and publishes *Women Against Pornography-News Report,* which analyzes current trends and legislation related to pornography and sexual violence. Dorchen Leidholdt is the organization's contact person.

Selected Bibliography

BOOKS

Dick, Bernard F. *Radical Innocence: A Critical Study of the Hollywood Ten.* Lexington: University Press of Kentucky, 1989.

Dovey, Jon, ed. *Fractal Dreams: New Media in Social Context.* London: Lawrence and Wishart, 1996.

Foerstel, Herbert N. *Banned in the U.S.A.: A Reference Guide to Book Censorship in Schools and Public Libraries.* Westport, CT: Greenwood Press, 1994.

Gardner, Gerald. *The Censorship Papers: Movie Censorship Letters from the Hays Office, 1934 to 1968.* New York: Dodd, Mead and Company, 1987.

Haney, Robert W. *Comstockery in America: Patterns of Censorship and Control.* Boston: Beacon Press, 1960.

Heins, Marjorie. *Sex, Sin and Blasphemy: A Guide to America's Censorship Wars.* New York: New Press, 1993.

Institute on Computer Law. *17th Annual Institute on Computer Law: The Evolving Law of the Internet—Commerce, Free Speech, Security, Obscenity and Entertainment.* New York: Practicing Law Institute, 1997.

Lippman, Walter. *Public Opinion.* New York: Macmillan Company, 1950.

Marnell, William H. *The Right to Know: Media and the Common Good.* New York: Seabury Press, 1973.

Martin, Shannon E. *Bits, Bytes, and Big Brother: Federal Information Control in the Technological Age.* Westport, Conn.: Praeger, 1995.

Pell, Eve. *The Big Chill.* Boston: Beacon Press, 1984.

Powe, Lucas A. *American Broadcasting and the First Amendment.* Berkeley: University of California Press, 1987.

Rose, Lance. *Netlaw: Your Rights in the Online World.* New York: McGraw Hill, 1995.

Rudenstine, David. *The Day the Presses Stopped: A History of the Pentagon Papers.* Berkeley: University of California Press, 1996.

Smolla, Rodney A. *Jerry Falwell v. Larry Flynt: The First Amendment on Trial.* Urbana: University of Illinois Press, 1990.

Spitzer, Matthew L. *Seven Dirty Words and Six Other Stories: Controlling the Content of Print and Broadcast.* New Haven, Conn.: Yale University Press, 1986.

Steinberg, Charles S. *The Information Establishment: Our Government and the Media.* New York: Hastings House, 1980.

Vizzard, Jack. *See No Evil: Life Inside a Hollywood Censor.* New York: Simon and Schuster, 1970.

Wallace, Jonathan D. *Sex, Laws, and Cyberspace: Freedom and Censorship on the Frontiers of the Online Revolution.* New York: Henry Holt and Company, 1997.

Williams, Francis. *The Right to Know: The Rise of the World Press.* London: Longmans, Green and Company, 1969.

WEB SITES

American Civil Liberties Union.
URL: http://www.aclu.org

American Communication Association.
URL: http://www.uark.edu/depts/comminfo/www/ACA.html

Censorship and Intellectual Freedom Page.
URL: http://ezinfo.ucs.indiana.edu/^quinnjf/censorok.tl

Center for Democracy and Technology.
URL: http://www.cdt.org

Citizens Internet Empowerment Coalition.
URL: http://www.ciec.org/about

The Communications Decency Act of 1996 (an index to comments, cases and material).
URL: http://www.decez.com/^alewine/cda96/cdaindex.html

Computer Professionals for Social Responsibility.
URL: http://www.cpsr.org/dox/home.html

Electronic Frontier Foundation.
URL: http://www.eff.org

EPIC: Free Speech on the Internet.
URL: http://epic.org/freespeech

First Amendment Cyber-Tribune.
    URL: http://w3.trib.com/FACT
Free Expression Clearinghouse.
    URL: http://www.Free Expression.org
Free Speech TV.
    URL: http//www.freespeech.org
Media Access Project.
    URL: http://www.mediaaccss.org
National Coalition Against Censorship.
    URL: http://www.ncac.org
People for the American Way.
    URL: http://www.pfam.org
Progress and Freedom Foundation.
    URL: http://www.pff.org
Project Censored.
    URL: http://censored, sonoma.edu/ProjectCensord
Society for Electronic Access.
    URL: http://www.sea.org

Index

About the Author

HERBERT N. FOERSTEL is author of *Surveillance in the Stacks* (Greenwood, 1991), *Secret Science* (Praeger, 1993), *Banned in the U.S.A.: A Reference Guide to Book Censorship in Schools and Public Libraries* (Greenwood, 1994), *Climbing the Hill* (Praeger, 1996), and *Free Expression and Censorship in America* (Greenwood, 1997). He recently retired as Head of Branch Libraries at the University of Maryland, College Park and serves on the board of directors of the National Security Archive.